Johannes Scherr

A History of English Literature

Johannes Scherr

A History of English Literature

ISBN/EAN: 9783337205522

Printed in Europe, USA, Canada, Australia, Japan

Cover: Foto ©Thomas Meinert / pixelio.de

More available books at **www.hansebooks.com**

A HISTORY

OF

ENGLISH LITERATURE.

BY

Professor Dr. J. Scherr.

TRANSLATED FROM THE GERMAN
BY M. V.

London:
SAMPSON LOW, MARSTON, SEARLE, & RIVINGTON,
CROWN BUILDINGS, 188, FLEET STREET.
1882.
[*All rights reserved.*]

LONDON:
PRINTED BY GILBERT AND RIVINGTON, LIMITED,
ST. JOHN'S SQUARE.

THE AUTHOR'S PREFACE.

THE task I proposed to myself was the following: to present within a moderate compass a picture of the literature of Great Britain, including the Anglo-American. The term "picture" may appear rather pretentious, and I should say "sketch" instead, but that the word would have a flavour of false modesty, which I dislike. For I have indeed attempted to execute a picture, i. e. to bring groups of persons into their proper historical light, to distribute light and shade according to the demands of truth, and to throw the colour of life into it everywhere.

However industriously Englishmen may have studied their own literary history, they do not possess a comprehensive and complete history of their national literature. Warton's "History of English poetry" (3 vols. 1775-81) extends only to the sixteenth century, and has never been continued; since his time no similar attempt has been made by an Englishman. National Literature as a whole has been made the subject of compendious or anthologic-biographical works, and praiseworthy efforts have been made to throw light upon some single periods or problems of literary history, as for instance by Mr. Payne Collier, in his "History of English Dramatic Poetry" (1831). The investigation of English literature as a whole, from its beginnings to the present time—an investigation by which the subject is placed on a level with historical, scientific, and philosophical criticism in this age, and the vast material is represented with corresponding breadth and method—has been accomplished by a foreigner, M. Taine.

The first edition of my work appeared nine years before the publication of M. Taine's work, I need not therefore assert my complete independence of the latter. Though differing from him on many points, I frankly acknowledge that as a literary historian M. Taine has done more than any of his contemporaries up to the present time. For he is the first Frenchman who has so penetrated into the very genius of a foreign nation as to form a completely impartial judgment of its productions both in prose and poetry.

J. SCHERR.

ZURICH, *Spring*, 1874.

TRANSLATOR'S NOTE.—The third edition of Professor Scherr's "History of English Literature" is in the press; the chief emendations and additions will be found in this translation of the work.

M. V.

ZURICH, *September*, 1882.

CONTENTS.

CHAPTER I.

INTRODUCTION 1

CHAPTER II.

BRITISH BARDS—LITERATURE OF THE ANGLO-SAXONS 7

CHAPTER III.

THE BEGINNINGS OF ENGLISH LITERATURE—MINSTRELSY—CHAUCER AND HIS TIME 18

CHAPTER IV.

THE AGE OF QUEEN ELIZABETH—BACON—NOVELS AND EPICS—LILY—SIDNEY—SPENSER—LYRICS AND SATIRE—THE DRAMA—MIRACLE PLAYS AND MORAL PLAYS—INTERLUDES—HEYWOOD—"THE GORBODUC"—TECHNICALITIES OF THE STAGE—PEELE—GREENE—MARLOWE 35

CHAPTER V.

SHAKESPEARE 61

CHAPTER VI.

BEN JONSON AND HIS SCHOOL 85

CHAPTER VII.

ABSOLUTISM AND PURITANISM—HOBBES—MILTON—BUTLER—WALLER—COWLEY—DENHAM . . . 93

CHAPTER VIII.

THE RESTORATION—SOCIETY AND LITERATURE—THE STAGE: DRYDEN — TRAGEDY: OTWAY — COMEDY: WYCHERLEY, CONGREVE, VANBRUGH, FARQUHAR—SATIRE: ROCHESTER—NOVELISTS: BOYLE, HARRINGTON, APHRA BEHN, MRS. HEYWOOD, MISS MANLEY, BUNYAN—ORATORICAL, POLITICAL, AND HISTORICAL PROSE: TAYLOR, BARROW, BARNET, TILLOTSON, SIDNEY, WHITELOKE, CLARENDON, TEMPLE 116

CHAPTER IX.

THE AGE OF WILLIAM III. AND MARY; QUEEN ANNE; GEORGE I. AND II.—GENERAL CHARACTER OF THE LITERATURE OF THIS PERIOD. REALISTIC PHILOSOPHY: LOCKE — FREETHINKERS: TOLAND AND OTHERS—WITS IN HIGH LIFE: SHAFTESBURY AND BOLINGBROKE — NATURAL SCIENCE: NEWTON — HISTORIANS: HUME, ROBERTSON, MITFORD, FERGUSON, GIBBON, ROSCOE—MEMOIRS: WALPOLE—POETS: POPE, GAY, PRIOR, YOUNG—ESSAYISTS: STEELE AND ADDISON, SWIFT AND JOHNSON—LETTERS AND EPISTLES ON THE SUBJECTS OF WORLDLY WISDOM AND POLITICS: CHESTERFIELD AND JUNIUS—NOVEL WRITERS: NOVELS OF IDEAL AND REALISTIC VIEWS: RICHARDSON, FIELDING, MISS BURNEY—HUMOROUS NOVELS: GOLDSMITH—NOVELS WRITTEN FOR SPECIAL PURPOSES: GODWIN, MISS EDGEWORTH — SENSATIONAL NOVELS: WALPOLE, MRS. RADCLIFFE — MATTHEW GREGORY LEWIS 129

CHAPTER X.

A NEW LIFE—ITS FORERUNNERS: THOMSON, GLOVER, GRAY, CHATTERTON, COWPER — MACPHERSON'S

"OSSIAN"—PERCY'S "RELIQUES"—REVIVAL OF SHAKESPEARE'S PLAYS: GARRICK, KEMBLE, MRS. SIDDONS—THE THEATRE: LILLO, FOOTE, SHERIDAN—THE MOST BRILLIANT PERIOD OF PARLIAMENTARY ELOQUENCE: PITT, BURKE, SHERIDAN, FOX, THE YOUNGER PITT, GRATTAN—SCOTCH POPULAR POETRY: BURNS, AND HIS SUCCESSORS—THE TRANSITION FROM THE EIGHTEENTH TO THE NINETEENTH CENTURY: FROM THE POETRY OF REASON TO THAT OF ROMANTIC SENTIMENT—CRABBE, MONTGOMERY, ROGERS, CAMPBELL 159

CHAPTER XI.

SCOTT AND MOORE. . . . .

CHAPTER XII.

THE LAKE SCHOOL: WORDSWORTH, COLERIDGE, SOUTHEY, (WILSON) 208

CHAPTER XIII.

BYRON 219

CHAPTER XIV.

SHELLEY 244

CHAPTER XV.

MODERN AND CONTEMPORARY POETS AND AUTHORS: LEYDEN, WHITE, KEATS, ELLIOTT, HUNT, LANDOR, WOLFE, PROCTER, BARTON, HOOD, MILNES, AIRD, AYTOUN, MACKAY, TENNYSON, SWINBURNE, ROSSETTI; FELICIA HEMANS, LETITIA LANDON, CAROLINE NORTON, ELIZABETH B. BROWNING—DRAMA: MATURIN, MILMAN, SHEIL, TALFOURD, KNOWLES, TAYLOR, BROWNING, MARY MITFORD — NOVEL WRITERS:

HANNAH MORE, JANE AUSTEN, HOPE, MORIER, TRELAWNEY, ROWCROFT, LOVER, LEVER, CROKER, CARLETON, GRIFFIN, MRS. S. C. HALL, WILSON, MARRYAT, CHAMIER, GLASCOCK; HOOK, WARREN, D'ISRAELI, HARRIET MARTINEAU, BULWER, DICKENS, THACKERAY, TROLLOPE, RUFFINI, KINGSLEY, CHARLES READE, COLLINS, CURRER BELL (CHARLOTTE BRONTË), MISS CRAIK, MISS KAVANAGH, MISS YONGE, MISS BRADDON, GEORGE ELIOT (M. EVANS)—WRITERS ON HISTORY: MALCOLM, NAPIER, ALISON, TYTLER, TURNER, LINGARD, HALLAM, MACKINTOSH, MISS MARTINEAU, MACAULAY, FROUDE, KEMBLE, WRIGHT, GROTE, BUCKLE—PARLIAMENTARY ORATORY: CANNING, O'CONNELL, PEEL, BROUGHAM—REVIEWS AND REVIEWERS, HISTORY OF LITERATURE, AND ESSAYS: JEFFREY, GIFFORD, HAZLITT, LAMB, MRS. JAMESON, COLLIER, ISAAC D'ISRAELI, SHAW, DUNLOP, CARLYLE, DIXON, GRANT 255

CHAPTER XVI.

SKETCH OF THE ANGLO-AMERICAN LITERATURE—ITS RISE AND CHARACTER. POETS AND POETESSES: HOPKINSON, BARLOW, DWIGHT, PIERPOINT, SPRAGUE, BRAINARD, STREET, PERCIVAL, DANA, WHITTIER, HALLECK, HOLMES, BRYANT, POE, LONGFELLOW, MARY BROOKS, LYDIA SIGOURNEY — NOVELISTS: IRVING, COOPER, BROWN, PAULDING, FAY, AND OTHERS; CATHERINE SEDGWICK, HARRIET BEECHER-STOWE—ORATORS, POLITICAL WRITERS, ESSAYISTS, AND HISTORIOGRAPHERS: HENRY, ADAMS, CLAY, WEBSTER, CALHOUN, AND OTHERS; FRANKLIN, JEFFERSON, AUDUBON, CATLIN, CHANNING, EVERETT, HUDSON, TUCKERMANN, EMERSON, PRESCOTT, SPARKS, BANCROFT 293

A

HISTORY OF ENGLISH LITERATURE.

CHAPTER I.

Introduction.

BRITAIN was for centuries regarded with curiosity and awe by the ancients ; in their ignorance of geography they related many strange and horrible things of it, which were only contradicted fifty years B.C. when Julius Cæsar invaded the country. That great general, who began the conquest of the island (which was completed A.D. 84 by Agricola), told his countrymen that the inhabitants of the British Isles belonged to that race which we know by the name of " Celts," whose fate it was to be driven to the West of Europe by the Germanic tribes. We have to imagine the culture of the British Celts similar to that of the Gauls as Cæsar describes it in his " Commentaries." Between these two tribes of the same nation Druidism was the connecting link. The language of the Britons was a Celtic dialect, analogous with those still spoken in the Scottish Highlands and Islands, in Ireland, in the

Isle of Man, and in Wales, and which may also be traced in the speech of the Bretons and Biscayans.

The Romans colonized Britain as they did all countries they conquered. They constructed walls and forts to keep in check the savage tribes of the north, the Picts and Scots; they built towns and made roads; and the country must have looked like a Roman province, to judge by the innumerable Roman antiquities which are found dispersed all over England, and by the remains of Roman roads, bridges, aqueducts, temples, and tombs. But though the Romans succeeded in settling quietly on the distant island—though a Roman poet[1] boasted that his verses were sung in Britain, and a chronicle-writer of the sixth century[2] that England had become a Roman island, the influence of the Romans in Britain was but superficial, and Latin, as far as it had been the popular tongue, was almost entirely displaced by the language of the Saxon conquerors, while it was engrafted for all time on the other western countries of Europe conquered by the Romans—in France, Spain, and Portugal.[3]

[1] "Dicitur et nostros cantare Britannia versus."—MARTIAL.

[2] "Ita, ut non Britannia, sed Romana insula diceretur."—GILDAS.

[3] In the English of the present day only the words *chester*, *street*, and *coln* (e. g. in Lincoln) may be traced without dispute to the time of the Roman supremacy in Britain. The primitive words are *castrum, strata* (via), *colonia.*

The Saxon conquest of Britain was very gradual. The Germanic tribes inhabiting Denmark down to the Dutch marshes—Jutes, Angles, and Saxons— had often come to Britain for plunder; and their bravery was so well known that the Britons sent to them for help against the surrounding tribes, when the Romans had left them, in the beginning of the fifth century. The Germans not only fought the enemies of the Britons, but the Britons themselves, and went on settling in the island, until the beginning of the sixth century; while the Britons took refuge in the mountainous districts of Wales, Cornwall, Scotland, and in Ireland.[1] The Angles seem to have been the chief among the invaders, for Britain was called Anglia, Engla-land, after them. But in later times the Saxons were the prevailing tribe, so that the Celts, who had been driven to the west and north of the island, gave to all their conquerors the name of " Saxons." In spite of this, the language of all the German tribes was called " English," and they called themselves " Englishmen." Christianity, introduced among the Saxons in 597, was as it were a powerful cement to make one nation of the different tribes.

The inroads of the Danes, which began in the ninth century, and lasted for six generations, did not much hinder or influence the development of the nation, the Danes being a Germanic tribe, similar to the Saxons in customs and language.

[1] Turner, " History of the Anglo-Saxons," Lond. 1799— 1805.

A very different nation were the Normans, to whose power and lust of conquest the Saxons were to fall a prey. They also were a Teutonic tribe; they had been Scandinavian sea-robbers, but from the time they settled in the valley of the Seine they became the first nation of Christendom. Their wild, powerful character was softened by the Frankish culture and manners, which they adopted. Their enjoyment of life was refined; chivalry flourished among them. For their language they adopted a dialect of the northern French, which, by means of the poetry composed in it, soon became a written language, whose productions greatly influenced European literature in the middle ages.

The conquest of England had been long prepared by the Normans. The court of Rouen had practised the arts of diplomacy before it seized the sword. When, after fifty years of Danish supremacy, the Saxon dynasty was restored in the person of Edward the Confessor, it was not difficult to see that the young king had been brought up at the Norman court. Norman-French became the court language in the palace of Westminster; Norman bishops and Norman knights were settled in England; and at last Edward formally left the throne to the Duke of Normandy. The Anglo-Saxons made one last effort to maintain their independence, but in the battle of Hastings, Harold, the last of the Saxon kings, lost his life, and William the Conqueror won the crown of England. Now a time of fearful oppression began for the Saxon and Danish inhabitants of England. Each Norman baron from his fortified castle acted the part of tyrant towards a people whose rights were trampled upon, and whose customs and language were scorned. And yet the influence of the conquerors was beneficial in the end; and when we consider the fearful sufferings by which three Germanic tribes were amalgamated into the one English nation, we are reminded of the noble Damascene blade, formed by heavy blows out of different pieces of metal.

For a century and a half the Saxons were oppressed by the Normans; in the beginning of the thirteenth century a decided change took place. Normandy was lost to the English crown by King John, and the proud Norman barons began to consider England their home. They obliged King John to sign Magna Charta, the foundation of the English constitution and liberty. The Saxons in their turn were strong enough under King Stephen to prevent Roman jurisprudence from being forced upon them instead of their old national right. Marriages took place between Saxons and Normans. The German principle of liberty, kept up by illustrious town-guilds, counterbalanced Norman feudalism. The Saxon tongue, enriched by Norman-French, continued to develop with the nation. It became the language of instruction when the Universities of Oxford and Cambridge were founded (the chief colleges of both rose 1250—1350). In 1363 Edward III. ordered that lawsuits in all royal courts of law should be conducted in English. The first parliamentary paper in English, a petition of the tradesmen of London, dates from the year 1388. The government of Edward III. was inimical to France and thus emancipated England from French influence. From his reign dates the English nation.

CHAPTER II.

British Bards—Literature of the Anglo-Saxons.

JULIUS CÆSAR in his account of the war in Gaul speaks of the Druids (vi. 13, 14), and mentions that they are considered to be of British origin, and to have been transplanted into Gaul; he adds, that those young Gauls who were anxious to penetrate more deeply into the wisdom of the Druids went to Britain to be instructed therein. By these observations he favours the conclusion that Celtic culture was of earlier date in Britain than in Gaul?[1] It is certain, at all events, that the priestly order of Druids not only occupied the first social rank among the Celtic tribes of Britain and Gaul, but that the life of those tribes was entirely regulated and governed by the Druids, just as the old Egyptians were governed by their priestly caste. We have only suppositions as to the mysteries of Druidical lore, as our earliest information on the subject is tinged with Christian doctrines. The number three plays an important part in the views and maxims

---

[1] Interesting studies on the earliest state of England are: "The Celt, the Roman, and the Saxon, a History of the early Inhabitants of Britain," by Th. Wright, Lond. 1852; and "The Saxons in England," by J. M. Kemble, 1848.

of the Druids.[2] Several of their teachings give proofs of a diligent study of nature and of humane views, with which, however, their human sacrifices form a strong contrast. The Druids increased their influence by exercising the functions of judges; they transmitted their teachings to their numerous disciples by word of mouth only; they were intimately connected with the Bards (beirdd), who put Druidical wisdom into verse, sang epic and lyrical poems to the sound of the chratta, and were exceedingly popular.

The Celtic nationality clung with extraordinary fondness to its own poetry. The Irish still had their bards when William III. had subjected them; the Welsh long after their subjugation by Edward I., even to the time of Queen Elizabeth; the Highlanders, when the Hanoverian Georges had dissolved their clans, though the Scottish bards were degraded to minstrels of the ale-house and the fair.

The inhabitants of Cornwall and Wales were converted to Christianity before the rest of England, and in their poetry they began to mix their old national traditions with the new faith. The most important compositions of this kind are the legends of "King Arthur and the Knights of the Round Table," and, closely connected with these, the myth of "The Holy Graal."

[2] Davies, "Celtic Researches," p. 182, mentions the following triad :—"Three first principles of wisdom : obedience to the laws of God : concern for the good of mankind : and bravely sustaining all the accidents of life."

The French and German poets of the middle ages made great use of these legends. The finest poems on the subject are "Parcival," by the German Wolfram von Eschenbach, and "Tristan and Isolt," by the former's rival Gottfried von Strassburg.

The position of the British bards has been likened to that of the Hebrew prophets. Like them they were the organs of public opinion; they accompanied the warriors to the battle, encouraged them by their war-songs, and sang the deeds of their ancestors at festive gatherings. The courage and perseverance which the Britons opposed to their Saxon and Norman invaders was owing in a great measure to the stimulating zeal of their bards. Their songs had long been forgotten, but were collected in the beginning of this century by the editors of the "Myrvyrian Archaiology," and by others.[3] The oldest of these date from the sixth century. The oldest Irish songs celebrate chiefly

---

[3] The "Myrvyrian Archaiology of Wales," collected by O. Jones, E. Williams, and W. Owen, Lond. 1801-7. "Specimens of the ancient Welsh poetry by E Evans," Lond. 1764. Miss Brooke: "Reliques of Irish Poetry." Walker: "Historical Memoirs of the Irish Bards." Lady Guest: "Mabinogion" ("Stories for the Young"), and "Hênn Chroedlan" ("Old Tales"); both of these collections contain Celtic novels in prose. "The Literature of the Kymry, being a critical Essay on the History of the Language and Literature of Wales," by Th. Stephens, 1849 (chapter ii. being the most important for our subject). "Ancient Wales," by F. Walter, 1859 (especially chapter xii., on the Bards).

the deeds of the hero Finn, whose son Oisin (Ossian) is said to have composed many of them. Their great age is proved by their mythical allusions; they make us look into a strange world, in which witchcraft, wizards, and witches play a great part. In the second half of the eighteenth century, a clever Scotchman, Macpherson, published a volume of "Ossian's Poems," which excited the interest of all cultivated minds. These poems are however only very clever and beautiful imitations.

Among the Kymry in Wales the institution of the bards maintained its political and social position down to Queen Elizabeth's time, in spite of the persecution under the Plantagenets. Arthur and Cadwallan are the national heroes, and the chief subjects of the Welsh bards, the long series of which begins in the sixth century with Myrrdin Wyllt and Taliesin, and goes down to Dafydd ab Gwilym, who lived after his race had lost its independence. In their endeavours to enhance the glory of the British nationality, in opposition to the Saxons and Normans, these poets and story-tellers mixed the historical persons and events so arbitrarily with those of their imagination that it is impossible for us to separate the one from the other. Such an intermingling is found in the "Triads of Britain" ("Trioedd ynys Prydain"), so called from the peculiarity of the Druidical bards in forming groups of three, out of events, ideas, persons, and maxims: this peculiarity has made the stanza of three lines with end-rhymes prevalent in Kymrian poetry.⁴ The compositions consist chiefly of what would be called "political lyrics" in the present day. Burning complaints of the loss of freedom, and patriotic wrath against the foreign masters, are grandly expressed in them. Their melancholy and patriotism remind us of the effusions of the Hebrew psalmists and prophets. But the love-songs of one of the later bards, Dafydd ab Gwilym, are also of exceeding sweetness. In their last struggles against the English, the songs of the bards once more rose to their full power, and Gruffud ab yr Enad Coch accompanied the loss of national existence with wild and touching complaints.⁵

Anglo-Saxon Literature.

The Anglo-Saxons brought their fondness for song and heroic tales with them from their German homes to England. The Saxon singers (scópas) occupied as honourable a position as the Celtic bards, but did not, like them, form a caste. The art of song, chiefly of the epic kind, was free; and though there were singers by profession, there were also some who first performed the deeds of which they sang. Even kings knew how to sing and strike the harp, like the old king in "Beowulf," and in later times King Alfred. The form of the Anglo-Saxon

⁴ "The Triads of Britain," contain the legendary history of Britain from the earliest times to the beginning of the seventeenth century.
⁵ See his "Ode on the Death of Llywelyn," the last prince of Wales, who died 1282 the death of a hero.

poems was of course very simple and primitive; there was neither metre nor rhyme in them; alliteration alone rounded off the verse. These poems, which were only handed down by word of mouth, must have experienced many changes before they were committed to writing in the tenth, eleventh, and twelfth centuries.[6]

There was, however, a written literature long before this time, during the Anglo-Saxon period of English history. This was a clerical Latin literature, which began shortly after the introduction of Christianity. Latin, which in ancient times had so long been the ruling language of the world, again became the language of civilization in western Europe in the middle ages. Celtic monks first practised their awkward Latin pens in England in composing legends, theological treatises, and fabulous chronicles, until their Anglo-Saxon brethren outstripped them.

The Anglo-Saxons were very ardent in their endeavours to appropriate to themselves the new Christian-clerical culture; and when the last heathen tribe, the South-Saxons, had been converted, in 681, English missionaries went abroad to convert their brother tribes in Germany; such were Wilbrod, and after him Winfred, surnamed Bonifacius. The German convent schools also, the first seminaries of Christian culture in the Carlovingian age, were established on the pattern of the English ones. The

---

[6] The most famous collection of old Saxon poems is the "Codex Exoniensis," printed in London, 1842.

learned Alcuin, the friend and tutor of Charlemagne, was educated at the convent school of York.

The most famous clerical author was Beda (673—735), called the Venerable Bede. He spent his life as a simple monk in the convent of Wearmouth, the chief seat of Anglo-Saxon learning. Bede's acquirements in the different branches of knowledge were astonishing. He was a most industrious writer on theology, grammar, and science, but his fame is chiefly founded on his excellent "Church History of the Anglo-Saxons."[7]

The Anglo-Saxon scópas and gleemen (poets and harp-players) kept up in England the popular myths and legends of their old home. It was probably in this manner that the most important poetical monument of Anglo-Saxon literature was produced in the eighth century, and perhaps even earlier, the mythical heroic "Song of Beowulf," put in writing in the tenth century. This is the oldest epos of Germanic origin (the Nibelungen were written down in the thirteenth century).[8]

[7] "Venerabilis Bedæ Historia Ecclesiastica Gentis Anglorum," Lond. 1838.

[8] The Anglo-Saxon poem of "Beowulf," ed. by J. M. Kemble, Lond. 1833. The chief story of the poem, into which eight episodes are introduced, is as follows : Hrothgar the Danish king, after many successes in warfare, has built a splendid hall to feast in with his men. But the noisy merriment is disagreeable to a cruel monster called Grendel, who lives in a neighbouring marsh. Grendel goes into the hall at night while the athelings are sleeping, seizes thirty of them, drags them to its watery house, and devours them.

It is not only venerable from its great age, and important on account of the sketches it gives us of the life of our ancestors in the time of their

This visit being repeated, everybody flees from the dangerous place, and the hall remains deserted for twelve years. Beowulf, a chief of the Geats (Goths in the Swedish province Götaland), hears this tale, and at once starts for Denmark with fourteen companions to fight Grendel. Hrothgar receives them kindly, and gives the deserted hall into his keeping. The Geats prepare to spend the night in it, and Beowulf, before going to sleep, vows to fight the unarmed Grendel with his fists only. Grendel, who gets scent of the prey, comes, seizes one of the sleepers, tears him to pieces, and devours him. He then takes hold of Beowulf; but he defends himself manfully, and tears one of the enemy's arms out, whereupon the mutilated creature escapes. Beowulf's victory is celebrated the following day. But in the succeeding night Grendel's mother, a fearful giantess, appears on the spot to revenge her son's misfortune, and Hrothgar's dearest friend becomes her victim. Now Beowulf determines to look for the giantess, and to fight her in her own habitation, at the bottom of the morass. He throws himself into the waves. Grendel's mother appears at once and drags him to her den. But the close links of his armour resist her deadly clutches; and while wrestling with her Beowulf sees an old stone sword lying on the ground; he seizes it, and with it kills the giantess. He also sees Grendel lying dead on his couch, whereupon he cuts off the monster's head with his stone sword. He returns with this trophy to Hrothgar's castle, who gives him many rich presents and much praise. Beowulf then goes home to Gautland, and after King Hygelak, Beowulf's cousin, and the king's sons, have been killed, Beowulf is called to the throne. He reigns gloriously for fifty years and dies as gloriously from the wounds received in the struggle with a horrible dragon who desolated the country. Beowulf's solemn funeral brings the poem to its close.

heathenism, but it is also not without poetical merit in its rude power.

Besides "Beowulf," the so-called "Traveller Song" ("Scópes Widsith") ought to be mentioned among the productions of Anglo-Saxon literature. In it the minstrel describes his travels through the countries of men, and praises the princes from whom he has received presents. The poem has come down to us with numerous interpolations, and therefore in an imperfect and indistinct form.

The Anglo-Saxon clergy, in their zeal to spread Christianity, attempted very early to compose poetry in the popular tongue; they wrote biblical histories and legends, and some of these compositions contain passages of real poetical beauty. They are not all epic, there are also songs of victory, hymns, and didactic poems:

The first document of Anglo-Saxon prose dates from the seventh century, and consists of eighty-nine paragraphs of law by Ethelbert, king of Kent. Alfred the Great has left a more famous collection of laws. Kanute the Great also issued an Anglo-Saxon code of laws, remarkable for their humanity.

Alfred the Great (848—901), who raised the Anglo-Saxons to the height of their power and civilization, did more towards the formation of Anglo-Saxon prose than issue laws in that tongue. This monarch had an ardent desire to promote the culture of his people, and amidst the noise of arms and the cares of government he succeeded in finding leisure to work for his own improvement and that of others. In order to spread useful books he encouraged translations into the Anglo-Saxon, and was himself active in the same work. His most important translation is that of Bede's "Church History," written in the West-Saxon dialect.

The most important Anglo-Saxon prose work is the Saxon Chronicle,[9] probably begun in Alfred's time, and continued to the year 1154. Besides Bede this is the chief source of the older history of England.

Other monuments of Anglo-Saxon prose are transcriptions of some parts of the Bible, and a translation of the well-known novel "Apollonius of Tyre."[1]

In consequence of the Norman ascendency over the Saxons, Anglo-Saxon culture declined fast. Norman-French became the language of the state, court, and society; all bishoprics were filled by Normans; the language of the conquered race was degraded to a dialect, and lost all literary importance.

The oldest literary productions of the Norman-French language date from the beginning of the twelfth century. The conquerors had their own

---

[9] The "Saxon Chronicle," ed. by T. Ingram, Lond. 1823.

[1] More detailed accounts of the Anglo-Saxon literature are to be found in Warton (i., 53 and succ.), and in Taine (i., 48 and succ.). The decided predilection of Taine for the Normans prevents him from being just to the Anglo-Saxons.

jongleurs, trouvères, and menestriers (menestriers= menestrels=minstrels, from the Latin *ministerialis*). One of these, Taillefer, had sung the song of Roland at the battle of Hastings, and given the first blow on the Saxon line of battle.

The courtly epos, which occupied the first place in the literature of the middle ages both in Germany and northern France, was also cultivated by the Norman trouvères in England. About 1155 Master Richard Wace, from Jersey, wrote his heroic poem " Li Romans de Brut," or " Le Brut d'Angleterre," consisting of 18,000 verses. It was translated into the popular tongue by an Anglo-Saxon priest Layamon ; and this translation shows that an assimilation of the two languages had begun.

. Richard Wace, who also wrote the "Romance of Rollo " (" Roman de Rou,") and others, took his materials for the " Brut d'Angleterre " from the " Britannic Chronicle " of Geoffrey of Monmouth, a Latin work full of fables, enumerating a long series of fictitious kings of Britain, beginning with Brutus, a pretended great grandson of the Trojan Æneas. Wace was undoubtedly the most remarkable of the Norman trouvères.

CHAPTER III.

The beginnings of English Literature—Minstrelsy—Chaucer and his time.

THE distinction between Anglo-Saxon and Norman literature ceased with the distinction between the conquered and conquering race ; and the year 1300 may be looked upon as a milestone, on our side of which English literature begins. Towards the end of the thirteenth century Robert of Gloucester composed a " Chronicle " in rhymes, taken from Geoffrey of Monmouth, where the Norman principle of the end-rhyme was adopted for the first time.[1] Similar Chronicles followed. The battles of King Edward III. were sung by Lawrence Minot, whose songs of victory may be looked upon as the first independent English poems, for up to his time there were only translations and imitations.[2]

[1] Rob. of Gloucester's "Chronicle," ed. by Hearne, Oxf. 1742.

[2] "Minot's Poems," ed by Ritson, Lond. 1825. The following is the first stanza of one of these war-songs :—

>   Edward owre comely cing
>   In Braband has his woning
>   With many comely cnight ;
>   And in that land, truely to tell,
>   Ordains he still for to dwell
>   To time he think to fight.

Towards the middle of the fourteenth century was written, "The Visions of Piers Plowman," by Robert or William Langland, a very important work in old English literature.[3] It is a satirical poem, showing its German tendency by adopting the alliteration-rhyme, and making opposition especially to the corruptions of the clergy and to the Roman superstitions. The poem also contains the first traces of English humour, and of those endeavours after reform in Church and Science which characterize England in the fourteenth century, and of which Wicklif and Roger Bacon are the chief representatives.

When the tumult of the Norman conquest had abated, English love of learning revived to activity. Cathedral cities, abbeys, and the newly founded universities of Oxford and Cambridge, became centres of this learned emulation. Theology was the science of that time, and Scholastic Philosophy was her handmaid. The mental horizon was narrowed on all sides by clerical dogmas, and to explain the mysteries of these dogmas was the chief work of the learned. One such master in subtleties was John Duns, surnamed Scotus, who was sent to Paris in 1304 to take part in a solemn

[3] Ed. by Th. Wright, Lond. 1842. Copious extracts in Warton (new edit. Lond. 1842, ii. 102—121). The Early English Text Society, under the direction of F. T. Furnivall, is most assiduous in disinterring and publishing the ancient literature of England, from the time of the Norman conquest to the seventeenth century. In 1873 seventy-four volumes had been published by this society.

disputation about the immaculate conception of the Virgin Mary.

Scholastic Philosophy, however, met with early opposition in England. A century before Langland wrote his satire, Robert Greathead, Bishop of Lincoln, spoke most energetically against the abuses of the Roman Church. A pupil of Duns, William Occam, boldly attacked the worldly ambition of Pope John XXII., and cleared the way for the famous Wicklif, who must be accounted one of the great reformers. For he attacked the ruling system of the church at its very root, and by translating the New Testament into English he furnished everybody with the means of judging of it for themselves.[4]

---

[4] Wicklif's translation of the New Testament is a work of the greatest importance, not only in the history of the English Reformation, but also in the history of English literature, it being the first English prose work of any consequence. The following example of its style contains the first seven verses of the 24th chapter of St. Luke's Gospel :—

"But in a day of the woke ful eerli thei camen to the grave, and broughten swete smelling spices that thei hadden arayed. And thei founden the stoon turnyd away fro the grave. And thei geden in and foundun not the bodi of de Lord Ihesus. And it was don, the while thei weren astonyed in tought of this thing. So twey men stodun bisidis hem in schynyng cloth. And whanne thei dredden and bowiden her semblannt into erthe, thei seiden to hem, what seeken ye him that lyueth with deede men? He is not here: but he is risun: have ye minde how he spak to you whanne he was yit in Golilee, and seide, for it behoueth mannes sone to be bitakun into the hondis of synful men: and to be crucifyed: and the thridde day to rise agen?"

The traditions of Science also met with early opposition, and Roger Bacon (1214—1292), a Franciscan friar, is the representative of this reform. Highborn patrons enabled him to make his experiments, their donations amounting to 30,000*l.* sterling. He invented and constructed physical and astronomical instruments. He collected his studies on mathematics and natural science in a Latin work, "Opus Majus," in the form of an Encyclopedia; and his knowledge was altogether so wonderful that he was said to be in league with the devil. Bacon may be considered as the founder of the Exact Sciences in England.

A short time after him, Sir John de Mandeville published his travelling adventures—a manifestation of the English love of travelling, but also, by its monstrous inventions and exaggerations, a contribution to the geographical fables of the middle ages.

To return to old English poetry. It had been a poetry of different races; it now became national, and at the same time adopted the characteristic feature of all the literature of the middle ages: it became romantic.

The meaning of the term "romantic" has met with various explanations;[5] in summing them up we feel inclined to find its chief element in the accent which the romantic ideal lays on the individuality of man. The Spirit of Christianity was the soul of

[5] Dunlop, in his "History of Fiction" (Edinb. 1814, iii. 8), chap. iii., makes a full exposition of the question.

the poetry of the middle ages ; endeavours after individual perfection, attachment to the native country, love of nature, the glorification of woman, and other romantic characteristics, are the various rays beaming from that one unity. The literary history of the middle ages begins with the troubadours in the south, and the trouvères in the north of France. The former cultivated romantic lyrics ; the latter, romantic epics. Their influence and style spread over Germany, Spain, Italy, and England. Here, as we have seen, the Norman menestriers became English minstrels, who occupied the place of the British bards and Saxon scópas, though in a subordinate position. At first they sang only in the great Norman baronial houses ; but by degrees they became poets of the people, and drew English traditions, beside the French ones, within the circle of their poetical activity. From the productiveness of these wandering minstrels, who stood in close relation to the people, sprang English minstrelsy.[6] English Minstrelsy, by which we understand the poetry of popular Ballads and Romances, flourished from the fourteenth to the sixteenth and seventeenth centuries ; the fifteenth century has produced the most powerful of these. Only a few have been handed down to us in their original form. The oldest ballads sing of the heroes and exploits of the Anglo-Saxon and

---

[6] The reasons for this hypothesis may be found in Warton, whose " History of English Poetry " opens with a Dissertation of the Origin of Romantic Fiction in Europe.

Danish warfare in England (romances of Havelock, King Horn, Guy of Warwick, &c.), of the English-Scotch border wars (ballads of the Chevy Chase, of the battle of Otterbourne, &c.), adventures of the knights of King Arthur ; then there are the thoroughly English stories of Robin Hood, the famous outlaw, and his companions ; and lastly, creations of the imagination, such as the romances of King Estmer, of Fair Rosamond, of the Jew's Daughter of Milan, of the Nut-Brown Maid, of Master Waters, and numerous others. The most popular of all were, and still are, the ballads of Robin Hood ; they are full of that humour and fantastical imagination which are characteristic features of all these popular poems, the heroic ones excepted.

Scottish Minstrelsy is of a darker, bolder, and more passionate character. A boundless love of revenge is one of its chief elements. Humour appears but on the sly in this turmoil of fierce passions, which the raid (outlaw) Ballads of the Border exhibit. On this much and fiercely disputed Border, Scotch minstrelsy displayed most of its wild beauty. But there is no lack of strong and tender feeling,[7] especially where the Scotchman is inspired by his attachment to his home. The wandering Scotch minstrels were still highly

[7] In the literature of the world there is hardly an expression of womanly love and faithfulness which can be compared to the ballad in which the Border widow mourns the death of her husband, the freebooter Kockburne of Henderland, whom King James V. caused to be hanged. It is overwhelmingly touching in its simplicity.

revered in the middle of the seventeenth century, when the English minstrel had already become despicable. English and Scotch minstrelsy has exercised an important influence on English literature, by keeping alive the national traditions.

At the time when minstrelsy began to flourish, in the second half of the fourteenth century, artistic poetry also found a cultivator; and one of such importance, that two centuries were marked by his style of writing, and that he has been called the father of English poetry. His name is Geoffrey Chaucer.

He was not without precursors; one of them, John Gower (who died 1408), even survived him. Gower's long moral-allegorical poem, "Concessio Amantis," of 30,000 verses, was not calculated to make the upper classes lose their taste for French romances and fabliaux. It remained for a man of a larger mind and greater talent, a real poet, to show that there existed a national English literature.

Geoffrey Chaucer was born in London, probably in the year 1328. He studied law, and then entered the diplomatic service, Edward III. entrusting him with several foreign messages. In 1372, he was sent to the Duke of Genoa, and in travelling through Upper Italy he is said to have made the acquaintance of Petrarch. Chaucer rose to still greater favour at court after Edward's death, for he was a connexion by marriage of John of Gaunt, Duke of Lancaster, who became regent during the minority of Edward's grandson, Richard II.

Chaucer fell into disgrace with John of Gaunt when Richard II. ascended the throne. He was entangled in the party struggles that made Richard's reign so turbulent, was obliged to flee, and was thrown into the Tower on his return. He was only set at liberty on showing his contrition, and led an uneasy life until Henry Bolingbroke, son of John of Gaunt, ascended the throne. Through the king's favour, Chaucer was allowed to pass the evening of his life in quiet retirement. He died the 25th of October, 1400, and was buried in Westminster Abbey, the first poet of the " poets' corner."

Chaucer was a man highly cultivated, both by life and study. He took a lively part in the political and religious struggles of his time (he was an adherent of Wicklif's reformatory views), and he knew men and the world intimately, as is proved by his writings. He formed his taste by the great Italian poets, Dante, Petrarch, and Boccacio, whose noble diction began to throw the French trouvères into the shade all over Europe.

Chaucer's writings are numerous, some of them are translations, or foreign tales worked out in English ; such as his " Tale of Troilus and Cressida," taken from Boccaccio, and his " Romance of the Rose," a translation of the famous " Roman de la Rose," an allegorical satirical poem by Guillaume de Lorris and Jean de Meung. Besides a good many short poems, he wrote the longer ones of " The Book of the Duchess,"" The House of Fame," " Chaucer's Dream," " The Assembly of Fowls," " The Flower and the Leaf."[8] But his most famous compositions are the "Canterbury Tales." In these he is altogether a national poet. His manner of thinking, and his language, have exercised a lasting influence, and have shed such splendour on the beginnings of English literature that Chaucer has been called by later generations "the Morning Star."

The plan of the "Canterbury Tales," is as follows: A party of twenty-nine persons meet at the Tabard Inn, in Southwark, to go on a pilgrimage to the shrine of Thomas à Becket, at Canterbury. In order to shorten the way, they agree that each member of the party shall tell two stories in going and two in returning. Twenty-four of these tales have come down to us, some serious, others humorous; two of them are prose compositions; others are incomplete.

The most important part of Chaucer's work is the Prologue, in which the old poet gives a graphic description of his pilgrims, full of good-natured satire; an instructive and amusing characterisation of the different classes of society of his time. There is plastic power in Chaucer's pen; his figures live, they move before our eyes. We see the pious cavalcade in the yard of the Tabard Inn, preparing to start. There is the stately knight who has travelled far and wide in Christian and heathen lands in search of adventures; by his side is his son, the young squire, a graceful rider, dancer,

[8] For a more detailed account of these works see Warton's "History of English Poetry," ii., 176 and succ.

flute-player, and rhymer, with curly locks and richly embroidered surcoat; they are attended by a yeoman carrying the huge old English bow, and a bundle of arrows in his belt. Here we see the prioress, Madame Eglantine, half nun, half lady of the world, dainty in appearance and manners, showing off her French, wearing a costly trinket engraven with an amorous device.[9] There is the fat monk,

---

[9] The portrait of the nun is one of the most successful. It is given as an example of Chaucer's style:—

"There was also a Nonne, a Prioresse,
That of hire smiling was full simple and coy;
Hire gretest othe n'as but by Seint Eloy;
And she was cleped Madame Eglantine.
Ful wel she sang the service devine,
Entoned in hire nose ful swetely;
And Frenche she spak ful fayre and fetisly
After the scole of Stratford atte Bowe,
For French of Paris was to hire unknowe.
At metè was she wel ytaughte withalle;
She lette no morsel from her lippès fall,
Ne wette hire fingres in hire saucè depe.
Wel coude she carie a morsel, and wel kepe,
That no drope ere fell upon hire brest.
In curtesie was sette ful moche hire lest.
Hire over lippè wiped she so clene,
That in her cuppè was no ferthing sene
Of gresè, whan she dronken hadde hire draught.
Ful semèly aftèr her mete she raught,
And sikerly she was of grete disport,
And ful plesànt, and admirable of port,
And peined hire to contrefeten chere
Of court, and ben estatelich of manère,
And to ben holden digne of reverence.
But for to speken of hire conscience,
She was so charitable and so pitoùs

boldly proclaiming his worldliness by the true-lover's knot fastened to his cap; and in contrast to him the thin pedantic student of Oxford, on his half-starved mare. Further on the bailiff, with his bloated, pimpled face, and nose covered with carbuncles, the terror of the children; then the widow of Bath, who has buried five husbands; and beside her the Franciscan begging-friar, with cunning blinking eyes and lisping tongue, "a wanton and a merry." There is the stout red-haired miller, who precedes the cavalcade blowing the bagpipe; the well-to-do merchant, with his forked beard and Flemish felt-hat, stately and solemn in his speech; then a doctor, a peasant, a cook, a boatman, and a pardoner, or seller of indulgences, who

> She woldè wepe if that she saw a mous
> Caughte in a trappe, if it were ded or bledde.
> Of smalè houndès hadde she, that she fedde
> With rosted flesh and milk and wastel bred.
> But sore wept she if an of heim were ded,
> Or if men smote it with a yerde smert,
> And all was conscience and tendre herte.
> Ful semely hire wimple ypinched was;
> Hire nose tretis; hire eyen grey as glas;
> Hire mouth ful smal, and thereto soft and red;
> But sikerly she hadde a fayre forehèd.
> It was almost a spannè brode I trowe;
> For hardily she was not undergrowe.
> Ful fetise was her cloke, as I was war.
> Of smale coràll aboute hire arm she bar
> A pair of bedès, gauded all with grene;
> And thereon hung a broche of gold ful shene,
> On whiche was first ywritten a crouned A,
> And after: " Amor vincit omnia."

traffics with a shred of the veil of the Virgin, a piece from St. Peter's sail, and similar sacred curiosities, and upon whom Chaucer throws a strong ray of Wickliffian irony.[1]

The stories which the pilgrims tell are as different in kind as the pilgrims themselves. They move amongst scenes of the most charming fairy-fantasy, of heroism and pathos, down to the coarsest burlesques. Decorum in sentiment and expression was unknown at that time (in what fearful indecencies did the great Rabelais indulge !) ; and Chaucer wrote in the spirit of his time, and therefore very coarsely indeed. But that does not prevent an unprejudiced critic from acknowledging that his humorous tales, though they abound in obscenities, are his best ; they are the true offspring of English humour, brimming over with comic power. Among the stories of this

[1] Warton, excusing Chaucer's obscenity, which he attributes to the spirit of the times in which the poet lives, makes the following appropriate remark (ii. 266) :—" We are apt to form romantic and exaggerated notions about the moral innocence of our ancestors. Ages of ignorance and simplicity are taught to be ages of purity. The direct contrary, I believe, is the case. Rude periods have that grossness of manners which is not less friendly to virtue than luxury itself. In the middle ages, not only the most flagrant violations of modesty were frequently practised and permitted, but the most infamous vices. Men are less ashamed as they are less polished. Great refinement multiplies criminal pleasures, but at the same time prevents the actual commission of many enormities : at least it preserves public decency, and suppresses public licentiousness."

kind the prize must be awarded to The Miller's Tale, The Tale of the Norman Priest, and that of January and May; among the serious tales, to those told by the knight, the squire, and the Oxford clerk: the latter introduced into England the famous legend of Griselda. There was no want of materials for both kinds of tales, Italian novelists and French fabliaux-writers having collected masses of them. The beginnings of the novelistic and humorous poetry of the middle ages point to the East, to the old Indian fable-book Hitopadesa, and to the tale of the Seven Wise Masters. Added to these were the didactic anecdotes of Vetrus Alfonsus, a Spanish Jew, who took them from Spanish-Arabian sources; and the collection of old fairy tales, traits of customs and manners, legends, humorous stories, and historical recollections, known by the title of "Gesta Romanorum."[2] Chaucer knew how to choose his materials, and he told his stories extremely well; but he is most charming where he shows himself the enlightened and patriotic Englishman that he was, and where he gives full play to his genial humour.[3]

[2] Compare, on the novelistic sources of the middle ages, Dunlop's "History of Fiction," chap. viii.
[3] The following are some of the works written on Chaucer, his writings, and his time: Godwin, "History of the Life and Age of Geoffrey Chaucer" (1803). ·Nicolas, "Life of Chaucer" (introduction to the beautiful edition of Chaucer's Works, in 6 vols., 1845). Tyrwhitt, "Essay on the Language and Versification of Chaucer" (introduction to the edition of the "Canterbury Tales," in 4 vols., 1775).

Whenever an eminent mind opens new paths, a swarm of imitators rushes in upon his wake. And so it was with Chaucer: many imitated, none equalled him. Between his poetry and that of Queen Elizabeth's time there is a long blank. English historians of literature fill it up with about seventy poets, but we may let their names sleep, for even the compositions of the better ones, of a John Lydgate (about 1430) and a Stephen Hawes (about 1500) cannot interest any but students of the history of the English tongue. It would be more to our purpose here to follow up the traces of the English drama, which date back as far as Henry II.'s reign, but we prefer treating this subject, in connexion with its later development, in the succeeding chapter.

In Scotland, at which we can only glance, the romance of minstrelsy vied with that of England, as we have seen. The formation of the language followed much the same course as it did in the south of the island. Norman-French became at first the court language in Scotland as well as England. Then the reaction of the national element took place; the Gaelic retired to the Scottish highlands, and the English of the lowlands, which had become the common tongue in the thirteenth century, retained more Germanic words than it did in England. A lasting difference between the English and Scottish dialects is to be found in the broad Scottish pronunciation of the vowels and in the hardness of the Scottish guttural sound *ch.* Nevertheless, only the national enmity between England and Scotland could justify the Scots in speaking of their own as of a separate Scottish language; the English took their revenge by calling it a dialect, "broad Scotch." Among a people which possesses a popular poetry like the Scots, the heroic age of a Wallace and a Bruce would also stimulate artistic poetry, and therefore from the middle of the fourteenth century we find in Scotland a number of poets whose special aim was the glorification of their national independence. First among them is John Barbour (died 1396), who wrote an epic, or rather a heroic chronicle in four-feet iambics, the hero of which is Robert Bruce, and which is not only of poetical but also of historical importance. The other national hero, Wallace, found his poetical chronicler in the blind minstrel Henry, generally called "Blind Harry," who is said to have died about 1446.[4] Besides these rhymed chronicles, translations of French romances of chivalry were made in Scotland as in England. At the time of the early Henrys and Edwards the original romances of Arthur and his Knights of the round table formed one of the chief entertainments of the aristocracy.[5] They soon became popular, and in the time of Edward II. an English compilation of these knightly stories appeared.

[4] "The Bruce and the Wallace," ed. by T. Jamieson (Edinb. 1820).
[5] Compare Dunlop, chap. xiv.

Then William Caxton[6] printed a number of similar books, the materials for which he had chosen from among the legendary world of the Middle Ages and of antiquity. In Scotland also this novelistic literature found a favourable soil ; and not less did the admiration and imitation of Chaucer, whose acquaintance the Scots probably first made through their king James I. James was a poet, and celebrated his lady-love and future queen, the Lady Jane Beaufort, in an allegorical poem, written in Chaucer's style, "King's Quhair" (*cahier*)="King's Book"). The king's life was a romance in itself. Imprisoned at the court of England when he was a young man, he sees from the window of his tower at Windsor—so he tells us in his graceful poem—the beautiful Lady Jane, walking in the garden with other ladies. Her golden hair gathered into a net of pearls, a chain encircling her slender throat, her bosom on which a locket of rubies threw sparks of fire, her white robe caught up for walking, her noble mien and gait, in short her whole appearance charms him, and after her disappearance he remains by the window of his prison, lost in longing dreams, until "Phœbus has bid farewell to leaf and flower." James regained his liberty and his throne, the Lady Jane became his queen, and her faithfulness was proved in the fearful catastrophe in

[6] Caxton put up the first English printing-press (1477) in the Almonry, not far from Westminster Abbey. Its first production was "The Game and Playe of the Chesse," translated by Caxton from the French.

which the life of the poet-king came to such a tragic conclusion in 1437. James being surprised by his rebellious barons, the queen threw herself between her husband and his murderers, received several stabs, and had to be torn by brute force from his arms before they were able to kill him. But the most excellent of all the Scottish imitators of Chaucer was William Dunbar (died about 1520), who was no unsuccessful rival of his model in the comic tale and in the moral allegory. First among his allegorical poems is "The Daunce," a description of the seven deadly sins celebrating their orgies in hell.[7]

[7] "The Poems of William Dunbar," ed. by D. Laing, 1834, 2 vols.

CHAPTER IV.

The age of Queen Elizabeth—Bacon—Novels and epics—Lily—Sidney—Spenser—Lyrics and satire—The drama—Miracle-plays and moral plays—Interludes—Heywood—" The Gorboduc "—Technicalities of the theatre—Peele—Greene—Marlowe.

ENGLISHMEN look back with pride and pleasure on Elizabeth's reign, when old England shone once more in all the romantic brilliancy of the middle ages, while the great future of the country was shadowed forth in its relation to the European continent and to the New World beyond the Atlantic. The popularity of " Queen Bess " is easy to understand : she had inherited from her father, Henry VIII., a strong tendency to absolutism, but she possessed also the wisdom which is taught in the school of misfortune, and a profound knowledge of the character of the nation which she was called to govern. It is especially owing to the latter quality that the queen reined in her very high-flown notions of royal power. She knew that the English nation would not submit quietly to a government such as was imposed upon the nations beyond the Channel, a government whose chief elements were the despotism of Spanish bigotry and the falsehood and deceit of Italian Macchiavellism. Elizabeth always knew how to yield to the English sense of liberty whenever her inborn rashness had caused her to offend. In all important questions she went hand in hand with the nation and therefore her government was successful and happy both at home and abroad, and her memory has been blessed among succeeding generations.

It was a great, a wonderful time this century and a half, from 1440 to 1600; one of those grand phases of universal development in which everything that is noble in man rises against conventional illusion, falsehood, and oppression; in which every nerve is strained to satisfy his endless longing after enlightenment, liberty, beauty, and happiness. At that time, the literature of antiquity having been revived, rose like a shining cloud on the horizon of a world dark with monkish superstition and narrow-mindedness; at that time the invention of printing furnished thought with never-resting wings; at that time Columbus added a new hemisphere to our earth; at that time Protestantism was born, opening to man the world of free thought and free will; at that time modern art began to flourish, for Leonardo da Vinci, Michael Angelo, Raphael, Titian, Correggio, Dürer, Palestrina, built, painted, and composed; at that time Rabelais and Cervantes hid great thoughts under the garb of satire and humour; at that time Copernicus, Kepler, Galileo, Bruno, and Bacon, thought and studied; at that time wrote Ariosto, Tasso, Lope, and Shakespeare.

England had its full share of the triumphs which the progress of mankind achieved in that age. In the sixteenth century she regained the influence over the fate of Europe which she had wielded under some of the Plantagenets; but that influence was now of a much nobler kind: it was based on the resistance which the principle of Germanic liberty opposed to the principle of Roman absolutism embodied in the Spanish power. In the Tudor dynasty the royal authority triumphed over baronial feudalism, and gave its support to the middle classes. The Reformation was effected apparently by the caprice of Henry VIII.; but even that despotic king would not have dared to annul the supremacy of the pope over the people had not their minds had been so well prepared by Wicklif for the great change. The far-reaching effects of Protestantism were also felt in England; free inquiry arose, unbiassed by prejudice or authority; Puritanism silently began to muster its powers, awaiting the hour which was to call it on to the stage of universal history. But that hour had not yet come, and Mary's reaction against English Protestantism tended only to make the vast majority of the nation rally the more firmly around the throne of Elizabeth. Great dangers threatened England at that time, but she overcame them victoriously. Her power increased in Ireland; her influence on Scotland became more decided; great tracts in America were subdued, and the name Virginia bestowed npon them; settlements were made in the West Indies; the Protestants were protected in France and in the Netherlands; and the glorious defeat of Philip II.'s Armada delivered Europe of its terror of the Spanish power. This great victory gave a strong impulse to public life; it filled all hearts with confidence, and stimulated all minds to activity and great achievements. The nation being satisfied with its foreign relations, and justified in proud hopes of the future, turned its attention and energy to its home concerns. Agriculture received a new impulse from the appropriation of the lands which had been in the possession of the clergy. Commerce, protected in its rapid progress and grand undertakings by the Orlog vessels which had done such good service against Philip's enormous fleet, gave a powerful impulse to manufacture. Prosperity, comfort, and enjoyment of life entered the English towns; and foreigners who lived in England at that time tell us expressly that the lower class of the people also lived well and comfortably. About the year 1600, London had already 300,000 inhabitants, and the town was filled with rich storehouses. The Court festivities were frequent and splendid; and the great lords vied with their queen in arranging gorgeous processions, masques, tournaments, and other shows; neither were the citizens and countrypeople wanting in amusements, to which the gravity of the Puritans formed a strange contrast. Serious moralists might probably have found plenty of opportunity for fault-finding, for the morality of the Court was by no means lofty or ascetic (though it was higher than in the preceding and succeeding periods), and its influence spread in wide circles. An adored queen, vain of her personal attractions, and unwilling to be without an admirer, introduced a tone of gallantry which could not be refined, at a time when delicate Court ladies breakfasted on a good piece of roast beef and a pot of ale, and listened with satisfaction to the most wanton comedies, though hiding their smiling or blushing faces by masks. Still there was in the Elizabethan era one thing which stamped an ideal impress upon life; an intense and universal desire for knowledge and enlightenment.

The queen, who knew the ancient languages, and who was well informed in music and poetry, set the example. She appreciated learning, and knew how to introduce an improving element even into the courtly festivities. It became the fashion for young ladies to understand Greek and Latin; and the unlearned public were so anxious to become acquainted with the classics, that translations of ancient authors were the books most eagerly sought for. Long before the close of the sixteenth century there existed English translations of Homer, Virgil, Horace, Musæus, Ovid, Martial, Euripides, Seneca, Plutarch; and the English authors of that time, even those who wrote for the theatre and for the public at large, dealt so bountifully in classical allusions that they must have taken for granted a knowledge of the classics even in the unlearned. This acquaintance with the culture of the ancients lay like a poetical haze on the life of English society at that time; it did not prevent the development of the national literature, but it favoured the taste for graceful forms, it enlarged the boundaries of the world of imagination, and it maintained an ideal of humanity independent of the theological squabbles of the time.

These theological disputes, however, though they turned upon very immaterial questions, had the beneficial effect of encouraging serious thought, of developing the art of debating, and of sharpening the critical judgment; and there were men clever and bold enough to make use of such qualities.

First among these ranks Francis Bacon, born in London, January 22nd, 1561; made Attorney-General in 1613, and Lord Chancellor of England in 1618; created a peer soon afterwards, first by the title of Lord Verulam, and later by that of Viscount St. Albans; accused in the spring of 1621, by the House of Commons, of bribery and abuse of his office, condemned to pay a large fine, to lose his office, and to be banished from court; died in his retirement, and amidst learned and scientific occupations, April 9th, 1626. Bacon offers one of the most famous instances of the contradictions existing in human nature—a mind of depth and acuteness, and a soul full of meanness and vulgarity. He affords a startling proof of the fact that learning alone does not form character; for outside his study he was an ungrateful friend, a fawning courtier, an unscrupulous intriguer, a corrupt and partial judge. On the other hand, Bacon was a most industrious worker, and it is astonishing how he managed to compose his works amid his many official duties. He is one of the first of a long series of English statesman, who, even to the present day, combine their public duties with literary taste, a combination which has greatly contributed to give a practical character to English literature, and to bring about the fertile influence which the political and social life exercise upon one another.[1]

Bacon wrote partly in English, partly in Latin. The noble and powerful language of his Essays became a pattern for English prose; but his most important philosophical works he published in Latin, so as to be understood by all the learned men of Europe—" Instauratio Magna," divided into " De Augmentis Scientiarum " and " Novum Organum." As a philosophical author, Bacon shows that he possessed a thorough knowledge of all the learning

[1] We may recall on this occasion another lord chancellor, one of Bacon's predecessors, Thomas More (Morus, 1480—1538), who preferred being beheaded to taking the oath of supremacy to Henry VIII. He was a noble character, and one of the most famous scholars of his time; his literary reputation is chiefly owing to his work, " De optimo reipublicæ statu deque nova insula Utopia libellus vere aureus" (1517). The book, like Campanella's " Civitas Solis," is based upon Plato's " Book of the State," and is a remarkable anticipation of the socialistic studies and movements of our time. A hundred years later the communistic dreams of More were taken up by James Harrington (1611—1677), who laid them down in his book " Oceana."

of his time. But he did more: for the sterile Scholastic Philosophy he substituted an entirely new method, founded on the principle of thoughtful investigation of nature—a method which is capable of development and which is directed to practical ends. He proved that the Scholastic Philosophy had arrived at nothing but idle disputes about words, because it had separated itself from nature and from experience, and that if philosophy was to do any good to mankind,[2] all learning ought again to be based on nature and experience. This he considered the condition of scientific reform, for the reception of which man had to prepare himself by clearing his mind and his senses from all traditional prejudices and from all abstract theories.

The powerful and lasting influence which this philosophical realism exercised on the civilization of England may be traced down to the present day.[3] The principles of English freethinkers or Deists have their root in Bacon's realism. Their activity did not arise only in the eighteenth century. Even during Bacon's lifetime Edward Herbert,

---

[2] "To better the state of human society, to enrich human life with new inventions and new blessings;" these and similar words he repeats continually. He also expresses the most benevolent opinions as to the essence of legislation: he says, the aim and purpose of the laws are nothing else but the happiness of the citizens.

[3] "The Works of Francis Bacon," 10 vols., Lond. 1819. They are preceded by the "Life of Francis Bacon," by Mallet. Perhaps the best thing that has been written on Bacon is a masterly essay by Macaulay.

Earl of Cherbury (1581—1648), began his literary activity, which cannot but be called freethinking.[4]

Warton has characterized by a fine simile the long period of sterility which set in for English poetry after Chaucer's time: he compares the poet of the Canterbury Tales to a lovely day in spring on which the warm rays of the sun called forth buds and flowers, which however were quickly destroyed by the returning winter's frost.

Proceeding with this image, the age of Queen Elizabeth may be said to be the month of May in English literature, checked by no return of winter, and in whose genial atmosphere the earth was clad with grass and flowers. It has been called the golden age of English literature, and so far as dramatic poetry is concerned it well deserves the epithet; but many branches of literature were much more highly developed in after-times.

The art of printing, which had been introduced into England in 1471, had a great share in the literary movement of that time, for it fixed the construction and the orthography of the language. Among the first productions of the printing-press were translations of chivalrous romances, the liking for which outlasted the sixteenth century. In Elizabeth's time the famous romances of "Amadis"[5]

---

[4] "De Veritate," 1624; "De Religione Gentilium," 1645.

[5] This most famous of all chivalrous tales was most probably of Portuguese origin, composed by Vasco de Labeira, who is said to have died in 1325 or 1403. The oldest existing form

and "Valmorin" were translated, and Emanuel Ford and Henry Roberts wrote original ones of the same kind. By degrees the inventions of the Italian novelists gained the preference of the public, and found English imitators, as, e.g., Paynter's " Palace of Pleasure," Whetstone's " Heptameron," and Grimstone's " Admirable Histories."

A strange style of speaking was the fashion at Elizabeth's court. The queen's learning made the courtiers vie with each other in turning pretty and learned compliments. Foreign literatures were ransacked for poetical similes and mythological images, for witty remarks and puns. This stilted language was adopted by the novel-writers, and even the best poets of the time could not altogether emancipate themselves from it.

A characteristic instance of this style is the novel of "Eupheus," by John Lily (1556—1600); its hero is a young Athenian who visits England on his travels. The novel became fashionable at court, gentlemen and ladies talked in " euphuisms," and Lily found many imitators. The most noteworthy are Lodge and Greene. The former is the author of "Rosalynd, or Euphues' Golden Legacy" (1590), a novel which furnished Shakespeare with the materials for his comedy, " As You

was given to the book by the Spaniard Garcia Ordoñez de Montalvo, who lived in the reign of Ferdinand and Isabella. A French translation (containing the first book of the novel) appeared in Paris in 1540, an Italian one at Venice in 1618, a German one in Frankfort in 1583. Compare Dunlop, " History of Fiction," chap. v.

Like It." Greene's "Pleasant History of Danastius and Favonia" has probably been put to a similar use in "A Winter's Tale."

The favour of people of fashion then turned to the Pastoral Romance. About the year 400 A.D. a Greek work of this kind, "Daphnis and Chloë," was composed, and attributed to a certain Longos; it was printed in Florence in 1598. Before that it had been translated into Latin, and had excited the attention of the classic scholars of Italy. Possibly Virgil's Bucolics exercised a still greater influence on the pastoral romances of modern times. The great master of novel-writing, Boccaccio, also composed a prose work of the pastoral kind, "Arneto," interspersed with numerous stanzas. This mixed form became the standard for the Pastoral Romance, which acquired a very influential position in literature, as it responded to the sentimental idealism, and to that silent longing which calls man from the artificial habits of society to the joys of nature. Spain and France produced the most famous romances of this kind. They found a very polished imitator in Sir Philip Sidney (died 1586). His novel "Arcadia," which introduces heroic knights as well as shepherds, is rather tedious to our taste. His language, however, is always graceful, though not quite free from euphuism.

Sir Philip Sidney, who was considered the pattern of an English gentleman, showed great appreciation of poetical talent in others. Among his protégés was one who has been called the

Ariosto of England, a true poet, and deservedly famous, Edmund Spenser.

Edmund Spenser was born in London, in 1510, or more probably twenty years later. His patron made him enter the diplomatic service, and then gave him an office in Ireland; but Spenser was obliged to leave that country on account of the rebellion, in 1592. He spent the rest of his days in need and distress, and died in London, 1596 or 1598. According to his wish he was buried in Westminster Abbey, by the side of Chaucer.

Spenser first tried his talent in composing pastoral romances, which were then the fashion. His "Shepherd's Calendar" consists of twelve eclogues; his verses in praise of Rosalinde show great depth and nobility of feeling; this is a characteristic feature of all Spenser's poetry. Spenser then began the execution of a design which he had conceived very early, that of giving an epos to his country. He was as well acquainted with the Italian poets as Chaucer had been, and seems to have admired Ariosto very much. His chief work reminds us of this fact, but can in no sense be called an imitation. The three first books of the "Faëry Queene" appeared in 1590. Sir Philip Sidney's delight with the poem [6] made

---

[6] A pretty anecdote has been handed down to us on this subject: Spenser was showing extracts from the "Fairy Queen," to Sir Philip; the latter had hardly read a few stanzas when he told his steward to give 50*l.* to the young poet. As he went on reading he ordered the sum to be

Spenser continue his work, so that gradually twelve books were composed. Only six have come down to us; the rest were lost during the poet's lifetime, through the negligence of a servant. The form of his stanzas, which consist of nine iambic lines, has been called, after him, the " Spenserian stanza." The poem is an allegory, solemn and serious in tone. It is founded on the legends of King Arthur. The Fairy Queen, Gloriana (an allegorical impersonation of true glory, but at the same time intended to represent Queen Elizabeth), holds a solemn court ; complaints of twelve great evils are made to her, and she sends out twelve knights to fight them ; these knights are the allegorical representatives of twelve virtues—Justice, Temperance, &c. The adventures of each of the twelve are told in twelve legends, and these make up one book. Now and then King Arthur appears, and casts all others into the shade by his deeds ; he is the impersonation of all manly virtues, and is finally to win Gloriana. Spenser develops in these legends a wonderful fertility of imagination, and a happy gift of description ; he is in many places a true poet. But as a whole his epos is rather tedious ; its symbolical character does not admit of real life, and cannot exclude monotony.

It may be noticed that during this period—that

doubled ; and the steward delaying to fulfil at once this generous order, Sir Philip called after him to bring 200*l.*, and immediately, for if the servant left him time to go on reading he might be tempted to give his whole fortune for such a poem.

is, the passage from the Middle Ages to modern times—the South, and especially Italy, exercised a great influence on English literature, in contradistinction to the popular minstrelsy which retained its national character. Lyrical poetry also experienced this influence and adopted the Italian form of the sonnet. One of the first who distinguished himself as a sonnet-writer was Henry Howard, Earl of Surrey, one of the victims of Henry VIII., who caused him to be beheaded in 1547. Surrey was a thorough gentleman in mind and manners, and was much admired at the Court of the Medici in Florence. His songs and sonnets in praise of the "fair-haired and blue-eyed Geraldine" are very tender and sweet.[7]

In imitation of him English courtiers vied with each other in giving a metrical form to their gallantries, but few knew how to put such true feeling into them as Surrey and Sir Walter Ralegh. The latter, equally famous as a warrior, navigator, and statesman, rendered great services to his country in Elizabeth's reign, and also composed some meritorious songs.[8]

[7] Surrey also attempted a metrical translation of some passages of the Æneid, for which he made use of five-footed rhymeless iambics; this metre gained a very prominent position in English poetry, under the name of "blank-verse."

[8] Ralegh, in consequence of a most trivial accusation, was imprisoned in the Tower under James I., and having passed many years there, he at last died on the scaffold (1618). Besides his poems, he left a "History of the World," a work of great merit for his time.

The other kinds of poetry also were successfully, cultivated. Thomas Sackville, Earl of Dorset, composed allegories referring to tragic incidents of English history, which he called "A Mirrour for Magistrates;" Joseph Hall, Thomas Nash, and John Donne were clever satirists; and Michael Drayton showed a fine lyrical talent in his idyls, odes, and sonnets; he rivalled Spenser by his allegorical poem of "Nymphidia, or the Court of the Fairies," and wrote a poetical topography of England.[9]

It will be seen that novels, epics, lyrics, and satires were actively cultivated in this age, but its chief glory consists in the rise of dramatic poetry, and we shall therefore give a short account of the development of the English stage down to the first appearance of Shakespeare.

The Drama.

The modern, as well as the ancient drama, is a product of the religious service with which its first beginnings are connected. The fathers of the Christian church rightly held the heathen plays of their time in abhorrence, for the chief elements of their drama. as well as of their social life, were cruelty and voluptuousness. But they did not succeed in destroying the liking of the people

---

[9] Many other names of poets might be mentioned here, but it is our intention to pass by the "Dii minorum gentium," as we aim rather at a clear historic development of our subject than at the dry succinctness of a catalogue.

for theatrical shows; they therefore did what they had done with other pagan customs: they made the theatre serve religious purposes. The liturgy, especially that of the Mass, developed into a liturgical drama. In process of time the theatrical element in the Church assumed larger dimensions, owing to the principle that the mind should be worked upon through the medium of the senses. On the great Church festivals, especially on Christmas Day, the Epiphany, Palm Sunday, and during Passion Week until Easter Sunday, scenes in commemoration of the day were represented in the churches, at first only pantomimically, then accompanied by dialogue. These representations developed into the so-called "Mysteries," that is dramas which have for subjects the Mysteries of Religion. The churches soon became too small for the throng of spectators, the sacred stage was therefore erected in churchyards or other spacious places, and decorations, costumes, and appliances for disappearing underground and for flying, were added. Before long the clergy alone could no longer sustain all the parts, and travelling players and buffoons were engaged to assist: this was the first step towards the emancipation of the theatre from the church. The Mysteries were at first acted in Latin; by degrees speeches in the popular tongue were introduced, and at last the entire plays were composed in it. The subjects were taken from Biblical history, and later on legends of saints and martyrs were added. The scenes were joined together without any plan, sometimes beginning at the Creation and ending with the destruction of the world. The representation of such a Mystery sometimes took a whole week. The Mysteries did not long remain the only kind of drama; the so-called "Moralities," or "Morals," took their place beside them. The actors in these were personifications of Virtues and Vices, and aimed at the demonstration of some truth. Both Mysteries and Moralities were for a long time ecclesiastical performances, and were even recommended by the clergy as a means of obtaining indulgences.[1]

The growing popularity of theatrical representations induced professional poets to write the text for them, and lay companies to represent them; thus by degrees they assumed a secular character.

In England the representation of Mysteries (miracle-plays)[2] may be traced back as far as the reign of Henry I., in the twelfth century. About 1110 a miracle-play on the life of St. Catherine was enacted at Dunstable, under the management of a Frenchman who had been called to the

---

[1] In Henry IV.'s reign a miracle-play on the creation and destruction of the world was acted at Chester; it lasted more than a week, and an indulgence of a thousand years was granted to the spectators who should attend the whole representation. Collier, ii. 173.

[2] The following are collections of miracle-plays: "The Towneley-Mysteries," ed. by Hunter, 1836. "The Chester Plays," ed. by Wright, 1843. "Ludus Coventriæ," ed. by Halliwell, 1841. "English Miracle-Plays," ed. by Marriott, 1838. These plays are sometimes called "pageants."

convent-school of St. Albans. This was probably the first miracle-play acted in England.³ In the city of Chester miracle-plays were enacted at Whitsuntide, with few interruptions, for three centuries, beginning in the year 1258. The scene was outside the church; in the beginning the clergy took some of the parts, but soon the "trading companies" acted alone. A little later, Wildkirk Abbey and the city of Coventry followed the example of Chester. The miracle-plays were at first performed in Latin and French, but in the beginning of the fourteenth century English was used, and they assumed more and more a secular and popular character. The introduction of moral-plays in the fifteenth century was an important step towards the development of the drama; by them action, including the moral agency of man, was added to the plays, which had previously been rather of an epic and dogmatic character.

Meanwhile the secular amusement of "Shows" was also developing itself. In the middle ages "Mummeries" were a favourite amusement in the houses of princes and nobles, they gradually changed into pantomimes with tableaux vivants.

³ Collier, ii. 3. This literary historian believes that the beginnings of the modern drama were introduced into Western Europe by pilgrims from the East. But German and French investigations of later date—the results of which we have given above in the text—leave no doubt that the origin of our drama is to be found in the Church, and that it sprang from the Roman Catholic liturgy much about the same time in all the countrie of wes.ern Europe.

"Dumb-shows" and "Interludes" were introduced from the French court and soon became a necessary appendage to courtly festivities. People then began to make a profession of such representations, and for that purpose went from castle to castle. There were "strolling players" in the reign of Henry VI., but soon the princes and nobles added a company of players to their households. Edward IV.'s brother, Richard of Gloucester, kept one and among his household we find the " garçons du capell," afterwards called "gentlemen of the chapel," who had charge of the music in the royal chapel, but who were also employed in scenic representations. Henry VII. had his "players of interludes," who wore the royal livery. This was the time when the moral-plays attained to their highest development. There were generally four parts in them, the "Devil" and "Vice" being the most important.[4] Henry VIII.'s love of display and magnificence caused him to spend a great deal in masks and costumes. In 1546 he had eight actors in his service, who were under control of the Master of the Revels.

By degrees popular scenes were also introduced into the moral-plays. John Shelton, poet laureate to Henry VIII., wrote a moral-play, entitled "Magnificence," in which allegory forms only the frame-work for popular fun and remarks on the

[4] The reader will find an excellent description of the representation of a moral-play in Victor Hugo's famous novel " Notre Dame de Paris," chaps. i.—iv.

events of the day ; and there were others like this. John Heywood, in the time of Henry VIII. and Mary, wrote a number of interludes whose subjects were drawn from the life of the people and thus paved the way for real comedy. The allegorical figure of Vice was taken up by the "Clown," the type of old English humour. Nicholas Udall gives the title of "Comedie" to his "Ralph Royster Doyster," describing the mishaps of a London dandy; his play is divided into acts and scenes and contains thirteen parts. Similar in style is "Jack Juggler," whose author is unknown, and "Gammer Gurton's Needle," by John Still who afterwards became a bishop.

In 1562, four years before the representation of "Gammer Gurton's Needle," the first regular English tragedy was produced on the stage. "The Tragedie of Gorboduc," was composed on the model of the Greek classics by Thomas Sackville and Thomas Norton. It is a learned, formal composition, which was admired and imitated by the learned, but which could not satisfy the popular instinct. "The Gorboduc," void of all dramatic life, has, however, one great merit, that of making use of blank-verse, the most appropriate metre for the drama; from this time blank-verse was used in England for all dramatic poetry.

The reigns of Edward VI. and Mary were not favourable to the stage, being too much taken up by religious struggles ; but in Elizabeth's reign the theatre began to flourish with renewed vigour.

The queen had a permanent theatre at her court, the annual salaries of the players amounting to 1230*l*., and some of the nobles also maintained companies of actors. But the people also required play-houses instead of the occasional stages erected in churches and chapels, law-courts and school-rooms, at street corners and inn yards. Lord Leicester's players turned part of the Blackfriars' Convent into a play-house, having acquired it in 1576; and after this sixteen or seventeen play-houses were established in London during the reigns of Elizabeth and James, of which the Globe, the Fortune, the Phœnix, and the Red Ox were the most important. Their decorations and machinery were very primitive at first, but soon became more complicated. Movable scenery only came into use after the Restoration; but as early as Elizabeth's time so much luxury was displayed in the costumes of the actors, that the Puritans talked wrathfully of "two hundred actors parading about London in silk and velvet." The play-houses were built at first of wood, and had no windows; in some there were representations in the daytime, in others at night. The decorations of the stage consisted at first only of a carpet, and the scene of the action was inscribed on a board facing the audience and exchanged for another as occasion required. The pit and the gallery were used by the people, while the upper classes sat in stalls, placed in immediate connexion with the stage, and whence the gentlemen would converse with the actors. In the old English theatres actors and spectators were by no means so rigorously separated as they are in our days. Poets and actors had, by the very arrangements of the play-houses, the pleasant feeling of a close connexion with the people for whose amusement and cultivation they had to work—a feeling which our poets and artists hardly know—while it only depended on them and on their talents to prevent immoderate transgressions of the necessary limits. The whole looked more like a cheerful, refreshing, and elevating play of fancy,—which the theatre is and ought to be,—while the etiquette of the present day has put it on the same footing as a social assembly of diplomatists. Actors, as a class, were not held in esteem at first, but dramatic art rose with dramatic poetry; the actors who performed Shakespearean dramas must have been real artists. The female parts were acted by youths, and in England this custom lasted a long time. The Spanish theatre was the first to introduce women on the stage (about 1534); France followed nearly a hundred years later (about 1629). In Italy and Germany the development of the opera caused the female parts to be given to women and girls. The first English woman seen on the stage was Miss Coleman, in 1656.

The authors of the "Gorboduc," and their imitators, were not the only ones who wished to form a learned drama in England on the model of the classics. Endeavours were made to create a refined

Court *Comedia*, composed according to classical theories, and containing elegant flatteries to the queen, in opposition to the rude popular plays. John Lily, the author of " Eupheus," composed some in the style of his novel, of which " Alexander and Campaspe "[5] alone rises above mediocrity. He wrote in prose, which was thus introduced into drama beside the lyrical rhythms of the old miracle-plays, morals, and interludes, and the blank verse of the "Gorboduc." Lily and the other poets of the learned style have the merit of having brought rule and measure into the enormous irregularities and improbabilities of the popular stage. But abstract theories alone could not be of real use. A poet had yet to come who should possess creative genius as well as a thorough understanding of the true nature of the drama ; this poet was Shakespeare.

He was not without forerunners on the same path. Towards the end of the sixteenth century we meet with a group of poets who had cultivated their minds and tastes by the study of classical and Italian literature, and who placed their talents at the service of the popular stage, refining its spirit and making it more acceptable to the educated classes. Their names are Thomas Kyd, Thomas Lodge, George Peele, Robert Greene, and Christopher Marlowe.

Kyd's chief work is the " Spanish Tragedie,"

[5] " The most excellent comedie of Alexander, Campaspe, and Diogenes," Lond. 1584.

printed in 1599, but performed from 1588, and with great success; it is full of bombast and improbabilities, but parts of it are most pathetic and interesting. Lodge's tragedy "The Wounds of Civil War," whose heroes are Marius and Sulla, proves that these dramatists dared boldly to attack the highest problems of the historical drama, but also what licence they took with history in order to satisfy their poetical sense. The piece is much rather an epic romance than a drama. The same may be said of Peele's historical pieces which are chronicles put on the stage with a deafening noise of arms but without any historical sense. "The Arraygnment of Paris," by this poet, is remarkable only as an illustration of the flatteries offered to Queen Bess in these courtly comedies;[6] but his comedy, "The Old Wife's Tale," is composed in a style appropriate to the subject, and the drama "King David and Fair Bathsabe," abounds in passages of true love-poetry, and the characters are drawn firmly. Greene, a man of great talents, lived the dissipated life of many literary men of that time, wavering between

---

[6] The piece starts with the well-known story of Paris, the three goddesses, and the apple. Juno and Minerva protest against the judgment of Paris before the assembled gods, whereupon his verdict is annulled, and Diana is summoned to decide the question. She declares that the Apple of Beauty does not rightly belong to either Juno, Minerva, or Venus, but to the wise, powerful, and beautiful virgin nymph Eliza (Queen Elizabeth): with this decree the three goddesses are perfectly satisfied.

debauchery and short-lived remorse; he died in 1592 between thirty and forty years of age. He has written various things; his name has been mentioned as a novel-writer, he is also the author of the beautiful tale "Philomela." In his fits of remorse he wrote edifying things, and then again published the most reckless pamphlets. His dramas are not wanting in warmth of feeling nor in harmonious flow of language, but they are composed too carelessly. He is most successful where he chooses his subjects among the popular legends. This he did in two dramas, whose fine parts outweigh their deficiencies: "The pleasant conceited comedie of George-a-Greene, the pinner of Wakefield," in which Robin Hood plays a principal part; and "The honourable historie of Frier Bacon and Frier Bungay," in which Roger Bacon, the old man of science popularly supposed to be in league with the devil, is brought upon the stage.

Marlowe surpassed those that have been named in energy and fire of genius. His was a wild, volcanic nature, storming through life with the licence of genius: he was killed in a tavern fray in 1593, while in the prime of manhood. The glowing imagination of this poet delighted in portraying the terrific struggle between the most violent passions, but he was never able to keep within the bounds of beauty; the conciliatory and elevating element is wanting in his tragedies; his delineation of character generally degenerates into monstrosity, and his energetic diction into an inflated and bombastic style. The boldness of his genius led him to choose subjects of historical significance or such as allowed of revelling in demoniacal emotions. To the former kind belong his tragedies : "Tamburlaine the Great," probably the poet's first work, "The Massacre at Paris," "The troublesome Reign and lamentable Death of Edward II. ;" to the latter, "The famous tragedy of the Jew of Malta," and "The tragical history of the Life and Death of Doctor Faustus."[7] The latter is an old German legend with which Marlowe probably became acquainted by the German puppet-shows, which, as well as German singers and players, came to England as early as Richard III.'s reign. Marlowe's "Faust" is composed in the style of these shows. The leading idea of both—the ruin of an uncommonly gifted man by his own Titanic aspirations—loses itself in sentimentality and vulgarity. Two hundred years later the story was formed into the grandest work of the literature of Germany, by her greatest poet.

[7] "Works," ed. by Robinson, Lond. 1826, iii. Compare also Mézières, " Prédécesseurs et Contemporains de Shakespeare " (1826).

CHAPTER V.

Shakespeare.[1]

A NATION full of activity in every department, headed by a wise, energetic, and popular queen,

[1] The books written on Shakespeare and his works fill a library by themselves. The following notes are intended to mention all this more important writings on this subject :—
Editions of Shakespeare's works : Editio princeps : "Mr. William Shakespeare's Comedies, Histories, Tragedies. Published according to the True Originall Copies," Lond. 1623, fol. (On the other oldest editions in folio and quarto see "Shakespeariana," catalogue of all the books, &c., Lond. 1827.) "Shakespeare's Plays," ed. by Rowe, 1709 ; ed. by Pope, 1714 ; ed. by Warburton, 1747 ; ed. by Johnson and Steevens, 1778. "The Plays and Poems of Shakespeare," ed. by Malone, 1790. "The Works of William Shakespeare, with a Life of the Poet and a History of the Early English Stage," ed. by J. P. Collier, 8 vols. 8vo, 1842-44. "The complete Works of Shakespeare, with the author's Life," by Ch. Symmons, 1837. "The Works of William Shakespeare," ed. by Halliwell, 1853. "The Works of Shakespeare," by Clark and Wright, 1864. "The Works of Shakespeare," ed. by Dyce, 1866.
The first attempt at a connected account of Shakespeare's life was made by Rowe, in his edition of the poet's works (1709). Among Englishmen, Malone, and later on Collier and Halliwell, have done most towards producing Shakespeare's biography. Halliwell is an indefatigable Shakespearean student, and his "Life of Shakespeare" (1848) is probably the most trustworthy. Collier, who has been very often

shining in the glory of a great victory; the spirit of adventure awakened, and directed towards great aims; the religious struggles subdued; the country flourishing through agriculture and industry; commerce pouring the treasures of distant climes into the storehouses of London; the Court, the nobles, and the citizens bent on the enjoyment of life; popular superstition peopling woods and heaths with kind elves and fairies; social intercourse enhanced by the setting sun of chivalry, and adorned by the grace of antique civilization; thirst for practical knowledge awakened and ready to break the scholastic leading-strings; poetry reviving in many new forms; the nascent stage ministered to by rival dramatists;

proved mistaken, was the originator of the "Shakespearean Society," which has done so much towards spreading the knowledge of Shakespeare and of his works. A Shakespearean Society has also been formed in Germany, a country that has done as much, or more for the poet as England, perhaps indeed too much. It is well known that Lessing, Herder, Goethe, and Schiller knew how to appreciate Shakespeare at a time when his own country esteemed him but lightly.
. Amongst the contributions to the poet's biography and to the critique, apology, or even apotheosis of his works, may still be mentioned: Drake, "Shakespeare and his time," 1817. Hazlitt, "Characters of Shakespeare's Plays," 1817. Mrs. Jameson, "Shakespeare's Female Characters," 1833. Barry Cornwall, "Essay on the Genius of Shakespeare," 1846. Knight, "Studies of Shakespeare," 1849. Kenny, "Life and Genius of Shakespeare," 1864. Neil, "Shakespeare, a critical biography," 1864. Fullom, "History of Shakespeare," 1864. Cohn, "Shakespeare in Germany," 1865.

everywhere an active interchange of material and ideal powers,—such was England when Shakespeare entered the capital to begin his career.

William Shakespeare [2] was born in Stratford-on-Avon (Warwickshire), and baptized April 26th, 1564—born, probably, one or two days previously. His father, John, carried on different trades by turn, and in 1568 the dignity of bailiff was conferred upon him; he was a well-to-do citizen, and possessed the necessary means to give his eldest son a good education. William acquired his first knowledge at the Grammar-School of his birthplace. Later the circumstances of his father became less favourable, and the education of the son suffered accordingly. Tradition tells us that the boy had to leave school in order to assist his father in his profession, that of a butcher. Whether this be true or not, the fact remains that the course of the poet's education was not quite regular, and that he had to make up for deficiencies by autodidactic zeal. In later times a somewhat idle dispute arose as to the degree of Shakespeare's learning. In our days we do not ask whether his knowledge of Latin was superficial or otherwise, or whether he understood little or no Greek. His work proved that his mind was as cultivated as that of the best of his contemporaries, and that he

[2] In the official acts of the archives at Stratford the name is spelt in the following various ways: Shackespere, Shackesper, Shacksper, Shakspere, Shaksper, Shakspare, Shakspeyr, Shakyspere, Shakspire, Shaxpeare, Shaxper, Shaxpear.

had acquired the best part of classical culture, namely, an understanding of the Greek and Roman spirit. In his youth he seems to have fallen amongst loose companions and to have led a somewhat reckless life. He was not yet nineteen when he married Anne Hathaway, seven or eight years older than himself. It does not seem that Shakespeare's marriage was a happy one; in his will he speaks with coldness of his wife, and he was separated from her for a long time. While at Stratford he seems to have entered the service of a lawyer to gain a livelihood for his family. But at last his life there became unbearable, and in his twenty-second or twenty-third year, about 1686 or 1687, he left all and went to London. Possibly the decision was brought about by the celebrated incident recounted by Rowe, who was the first to write a biography of Shakespeare (1709). Poaching was a favourite pastime among the more daring youths of Warwickshire, and tradition says that Shakespeare was one of them, and was caught with his comrades on the grounds of Sir Thomas Lucy, at Charlecote. The knight had him prosecuted, and on this occasion, tradition says, Shakespeare's muse found her first expression in a satirical ballad upon Sir Thomas, on whom he bestowed no very flattering epithets, to judge by the lines that have come down to us.[3] It is supposed that in even later times Shakespeare remembered the

---

[3] "A parliament member, a justice of peace,
    At home a poor scarecrow, at London an asse," &c.

kill-joy of his deer-stealing prank, and has given us his portrait in the " Merry Wives of Windsor," in the figure of Shallow, the country Justice. Sir Thomas, tradition goes on to say, exasperated by the culprit's laugh at him, took his revenge by prosecuting him all the more severely, whereupon Shakespeare thought it advisable to leave his house, business, and family, and to go to London, where his genius found a fitting sphere for its development.

London actors during their annual wanderings through the country had played no less than twenty-four times in Stratford during the years 1569—1587. Shakespeare probably had some connexion with them, at least in 1589, he is among the actors of my lord Chamberlain and was a sharer of the business, earning about 10*l*. by each representation.[4] This troup was perhaps the best of all, Richard Burbage, the great actor of heroes, being at their head. They played at Blackfriars and at the Curtain—for those theatres Shakespeare composed his first pieces—afterwards they built the Globe at their own cost and there the poet's

[4] Payne Collier's publications concerning Shakespeare's biography seemed trustworthy; but the acute criticisms of Halliwell and Ingleby question everything. We cannot enter into the controversy, but we may call the reader's attention to the fact that everything we have to say concerning the business part of Shakespeare's life must be taken hypothetically.

Halliwell, in the Athenæum, 1872, denies Shakespeare's having been a "sharer" in the Blackfriars and Globe theatres.

F

most finished plays were acted. In 1597 Shakespeare was already well to do. He supported his father and bought a pretty house in Stratford; a little later he bought several pieces of ground there and then a house in London. Collier proves that the yearly income of the poet for many years amounted to 400*l.*, a sum equal to 2000*l.* at present.[5] But his inner life also changed for the better. He understood life and the world more and more truly; a manly seriousness, founded on true morality, took the place of the follies of his youth,[6] while glory shed her lustre around him. His person must have been attractive, and his character very much esteemed, for his contemporaries call him the "mild," "noble," "beloved," Shakespeare. Men of high birth and brilliant position strove to gain his friendship; the Earls of Southampton, Pembroke, and Montgomery rendered the homage of friends to his genius, though Shakespeare was only an actor, and as

[5] In his best time Shakespeare received from 10*l.* to 25*l.* for a new piece, or the receipts of one representation.—There already existed at this time a Censorship of the Stage, attached to the office of the Master of the Revels. He forbade various things, for instance, in "Richard II." the scene where the king abdicates the throne before his Parliament; in "Hamlet," the allusion to the monstrous drinking of the Danes, because the King of Denmark happened to be in London. When James I. came to the throne, Portia, in the "Merchant of Venice," was not allowed any longer to make fun of the "Scottish lord."

[6] This is forcibly proved by one of his sonnets, the 129th.

such occupied one of the lowest ranks of the society of his time.

To Henry Wriothesley, Earl of Southampton, Shakespeare dedicated his two first works, "Venus and Adonis," being the well-known legend of the goddess wooing the coy youth, and the "Rape of Lucrece," incorporating the narrative which Livy gives of Tarquin's outrage on the wife of Collatinus. The former of these works was not printed until 1593 and the latter a year later, but there is evidence that they are his first productions. In the dedication of "Venus and Adonis" the poet calls that work expressly "the first heir of my invention." Both poems are descriptive, not epic as they are generally called; they are imperfect youthful compositions in the Italian taste of the time, heaping image upon image, antithesis upon antithesis, and both have been surpassed by Marlowe's fragmentary tale of the legend of "Hero and Leander" written in the same style. Similar in style and subject to these two works of Shakespeare's are two shorter poems, his "Passionate Pilgrim" and "A Lover's Complaint," which were probably produced at an earlier date than the two descriptive poems.

Very different from these are his 154 sonnets. The first complete edition of them appeared in 1609, but in parts they must have been known to his friends some years before, for a contemporary speaks of them in terms of praise in

1598.[7] They were probably composed from 1592—1609, at a time when there were many sonnet-writers in England. Surrey, Wyatt, Ralegh, and Sidney were the first; then came Daniel, Constable, Spenser, Drayton, and others. It may safely be said that Shakespeare surpassed them all. His first 126 sonnets are addressed to a young friend, William Herbert, afterwards Earl of Pembroke, and are a noble monument to loving and intimate friendship; others sing his love for an exceedingly charming but not beautiful woman; others contain wise rules of life: all are precious reflections of a rich inner life, a sort of poetical diary.

Shakespeare's activity as a dramatic poet probably began soon after his arrival in the capital, about 1586-87. The state of the English Stage at that time gave plenty of scope for practice to a beginner, by allowing him to remodel the pieces of others, or to have a share in the composition of new ones. The dramatic poets of the day were not very particular about their rights as authors; they intended their works to be acted, not to be read, and they were therefore careless about the publication by printing and left it mostly to chance; they borrowed from each other, enlarged, remodelled others' pieces, made one out of two, just

---

[7] Meres in his work "Palladis Tamia," where he says: "As the soule of Euphorbus was thought to live in Pythagoras, so the sweete wittie soule of Ovid lives in mellifluous and honytongued Shakespeare, witnes his Venus and Adonis, his Lucrece, his sugred Sonnets among his private friends."

as it suited them. This explains the difficulty of fixing the authorship of a number of dramas in which there are sparks of Shakespearean genius, but whose authenticity on the whole must be denied The pieces which the most conscientious and careful critics now refuse to consider Shakespeare's are—"Sir John Oldcastle," " The Merry Devil of Edmonton," " The Fair Em," " Mucedorus," " The London Prodigal," "The Puritan Widow," and "King Stephen," There are others in whose composition Shakespeare certainly seems to have had a hand ; they are— " King Henry VI." (part first), " Locrine," " Arden of Feversham," " King Edward III.," " The Life and Death of Lord Cromwell," " A Yorkshire Tragedy," " The Birth of Merlin." If we take for granted— and we may do so—that Shakespeare had a share in these pieces, we can judge from their date that his fertility as a dramatist showed itself very early.

It has been very difficult to fix the time when the different pieces, acknowledged to be Shakespeare's, were composed, and even now we have no chronological order of his plays quite free from doubt. This could not be otherwise, for Shakespeare probably did not arrange a single one of his pieces for the press himself. They appeared first in an incomplete and non-critical folio edition in the year 1623. The year 1589 is fixed by the best authorities as the date at which Shakespeare's original productions begin. But some of his oldest pieces may belong to a still earlier date.

The following is a chronological list of the composition of Shakespeare's dramas according to the most advanced critical researches. The list is divided into four periods, the dates of which may be considered undoubtedly correct, while the dates of the single pieces are mostly only presumptive.

First Period, from 1587 *till* 1591-92.

"Pericles," 1587, "Titus Andronicus," 1587-88, "King Henry VI." (in its first form), 1589, "The Comedy of Errors," 1591.

Second Period, from 1591-92 *till* 1597-98.

"Love's Labour Lost," "Two Gentlemen of Verona," "All's Well that Ends Well"—these three comedies from 1591—1593; "Romeo and Juliet," first acted in 1592; "Henry VI.," remodelled, and "Richard III." 1593-94; "Richard II." 1594-95; "Henry IV." (first part), 1595; "Henry IV." (second part), and "The Taming of the Shrew," 1596. "The Merchant of Venice," 1597.

Third Period, from 1597—1605.

"Midsummer Night's Dream," 1597; "Hamlet," 1598 (in its first form);[8] "What You Will, or Twelfth Night," 1598; "Much Ado about No-

---

[8] The last form given to this tragedy is assigned by Collier to the year 1603. In his "Annals of the Stage," Collier's data often differ from the above; e.g. both parts of "Henry IV." he assigns to the year 1597, and the "Midsummer-Night's Dream" to 1598. But as he speaks only of the time of representation on the stage, the differences are only apparent, as the composition naturally precedes the performance of a piece.

thing," and "Henry V." 1599; "As You Like It," and "The Merry Wives of Windsor," 1600; "Measure for Measure," 1604; "King Lear," 1605.

Fourth Period, from 1605 till 1613-14.

"Julius Cæsar," 1606; "Antony and Cleopatra," 1607; "Coriolanus" (1608); "Troilus and Cressida," 1608 (in its last form);[9] "Macbeth," and "Cymbeline," 1609-10; "The Tempest," "The Winter's Tale," and "King John," 1610-11; "Othello," 1612 (last form);[1] "Henry VIII." and "Timon of Athens," 1612—1614.

It hardly ever happens that genius reveals itself at once in all its power and fulness. Its revelation is often preceded by very imperfect attempts, by hesitating imitations, and by following in the wake of the ruling taste. The history of modern literature proves this again and again. In Dante's Vita Nuova we could not forecast the author of the Divina Commedia, in the Galatea of Cervantes the author of Don Quixote, in Tasso's Rinaldo the Tasso of the Gerusalemme Liberata. Lessing wrote very ordinary comedies

[9] Printed in the first form 1609, but acted probably in 1601 or 1602.

[1] According to a manuscript discovered and published by Collier (New particulars regarding the works of Sh. 59) "Othello" was acted in 1602, by Burbage's company, before the Queen at the country residence of LordEllesmere. Shakespeare's name is not mentioned on the occasion, but his pieces were sometimes printed by unscrupulous booksellers without his knowledge or his name.

before he produced his Minna, his Emilia, his Nathan. Byron rhymed his indifferent Hours of Idleness before he composed Childe Harold. Sometimes a great poet foretells his future development by some powerful strokes in his first work. Schiller did so in his "Robbers," for all his later works are only variously phrased expressions of the one great idea of liberty which lies at the foundation of that wildly-powerful tragedy. Sometimes, however, such a first attempt entirely misleads the critic as to the future development of the poet. Who could have guessed from Goethe's comedy the "Mitschuldigen," that its author would create Götz and Egmont, Werther and Wilhelm Meister, Faust and Iphigenie, the Bride of Corinth and Hermann and Dorothea? Similar is the relation of Shakespeare's earliest to his later productions. Time was needed for his genius to become conscious of itself and of its destiny. In his two descriptive poems he followed in the wake of the Italians, like so many of his contemporaries, in his dramatic first-fruits he imitated the manner of his predecessors. When Shakespeare first appeared on the scene the playgoing public were chiefly attracted by Greene's old legends full of fanciful inventions and pompous scenes, and by Marlowe's tragical scenes of horror. In accordance with these predilections Shakespeare wrote his "Pericles" in Greene's style, taking the subject from the old novel "Apollonius of Tyre,"[2] and his

[2] Regarding the sources from which Shakespeare took

"Titus Andronicus" in Marlowe's. By showing the public that he could surpass his predecessors and contemporaries in their style, he prepared it to receive his own : that the poet first revealed in "Romeo and Juliet." With this tragedy, "written by Love itself," his rule over the English stage began.

To praise Shakespeare is unnecessary, at least in countries of Germanic language. It would be rudeness to suppose any cultivated man or woman to be ignorant of the works of the greatest poet of all times who shows the whole world and mankind as in a glass. Having given the above historical account of his person and his compositions we shall now point out the chief points which strike us while contemplating his dramas. After that the biographical sketch shall be brought to a close.

Voltaire's and his imitators' shallow view of Shakespeare, as of a wild genius of nature who was unconscious of his own mind and deeds, is now obsolete. A more thorough critique has proved that the man who was creative Nature's poetic darling, was at the same time a clear thinker and a thoughtful artist. Only as such was he capable of executing the task which fell to his share in the historical development of mankind, and to execute it both in relation to his own time and to the future. This task may be defined in the following

the materials for his plays, see Collier's "Shakespeare's Library."

manner: Christianity had given rise to the spirit of romantic and fantastic idealism which had proved a powerful factor in modern history. The Reformation, on the other hand, set up the principle of reasonable realism for the spread and realization of which society is incessantly working. Shakespeare standing on the boundary between the middle ages and modern times the task of harmonizing the principles of idealism and realism and of amalgamating the romantic with the modern spirit fell to his share, for poetry alone was able to bring about such a harmony at first. Circumstances favoured Shakespeare's mission inasmuch as the popularity of the rising stage directed his genius in the right way. For in order to exercise that influence over the world which he wielded he had to make use of an artistic form which would correspond to the spirit of modern times. This form could be no other than that of the drama. Just as the epos is appropriate to antiquity and lyrics to the middle ages, so does the drama correspond to our own time. It is the poetry of free action and demands not only a clear conception of history resulting from an extensive knowledge of the world and of men, but also grand ideal views on the government of the world. Shakespeare possessed these in more perfect proportions than any other poet. He also possessed the clearest insight as to the means by which these properties could be made fertile. No one had a higher ideal of the drama than he, and no one ever expressed it by more significant words. The drama is, or ought to be, the poetical reflection of the world's history. That is the meaning of that famous passage in "Hamlet" (act iii. sc. 2).[3] Action is the essence of the drama, but action presupposes the free-will of man. Shakespeare's men are free, their deeds are acts of free-will. But the free-will of man is only one factor in the historical process of the world; in opposition to it we have that mysterious eternal element which men agree to call fate, God, moral necessity. Unless man rules his free-will by self-command he will perish by these eternal laws. The passions war against moral necessity, nature against the spirit; and in this conflict perish not only the low and bad but also the noble and good as far they oppose themselves to the eternal laws. That is the tragic part of Shakespeare's views on the government of

[3] Hamlet says to the actors : " Suit the action to the word, the word to the action ; with this special observance, that you o'erstep not the modesty of nature ; for anything so overdone is from the purpose of playing, whose end, both at the first and now, was and is to hold as it were, the mirror up to nature ; to show virtue her own feature, scorn her own image, and the very age and body of the time his form and pressure." We do not mean to say, of course, that Shakespeare had made for himself a perfect theory of the drama at first, and had then composed according to this scheme. The tact of genius finds *à priori* what the ordinary understanding discovers by analyzation *à posteriori*; and Shakespeare, as is well-known, made his works alone speak for him, as true poetic artists do, never giving us a hint as to his ideas and plans regarding them.

the world. The comic consists in his looking on human life as on a comedy enacted by human arbitrariness which gets into conflict with its self-made and unessential laws, in the course of which its nothingness comes to light and causes the triumph of what is good and right. Shakespeare's humour, that wonderful mixture of Olympian serenity and profound seriousness, is the connecting link between the two. This humour—which is of an elevated kind in the characters of Hamlet, Talbot, the Fool in "Lear," the Bastard in "King John," Mercutio, and Prince Henry, and comic in the unique character of Falstaff—enables Shakespeare to blend into one work of art the greatest contrasts, such as the fairy world born of moonlight and the breath of flowers by the side of the broad-grinning stolid artisans Quince, Bottom, and Co. This play upon contrasts is not arbitrary, it is necessary: for Shakespeare's dramas are as realistic as history itself, they are as true as life which steps from the sublime to the ridiculous and makes us hear the laughter of scepticism while our heart is aglow with ecstasy. Shakespeare's plays are living organisms, having their roots in real life but reaching into the ethereal regions of idealism, each embodying one chief idea whose rays penetrate every part, just as the heart of man sends the blood through the most distant veins of his body. Such leading ideas are: in "Hamlet," the relations of thought to deed ; in the "Merchant of Venice," the relation of the spirit to the letter of justice ;

in "Romeo and Juliet," the conflict between the ideal rights of love and the reality of circumstances; in "Othello," the true character of married life; in "Lear," the idea of the family; in "Macbeth," the demoniacal power of evil in the form of ambition. But these leading ideas are not discussed in the plays, they are dramatized, that is to say, they live and act in the characters. And here the poet shows a knowledge of the human heart of unparalleled extent and of as much depth as lucidity. The most gentle feelings as well as the most furious passions, the most common as well as the most abnormal conditions of the human spirit, have been penetrated and laid bare by him, and he may well be called the "Master of the human heart."[4] This art of creating living, individual, complete characters has not been attained by any other poet. None but Shakespeare succeeded in producing such a number of male and female characters in equal perfection.[5]

Shakespeare's language corresponds perfectly

[4] Symmons.
[5] Mrs. Jameson in her "Essay on Shakespeare's Heroines" points out the infinite variety of woman's love he presents to us. She says: "All Shakespeare's women, being essentially women, either love or have loved, or are capable of loving; but Juliet is love itself. The love that is so chaste and dignified in Portia, so airy, delicate, and fearless in Miranda, so sweetly confiding in Perdita, so playfully fond in Rosalind. so constant in Imogen, so devoted in Desdemona, so fervent in Helen, so tender in Viola, is each and all of these in Juliet."

with the genius displayed in his compositions, with the truthfulness of his characterization, with the truly dramatic course of his plays. It fits the action as the skin fits the body; it plays gracefully round the witty sallies of the humorist, it tosses off the disconnected thoughts of the dreamer, and it soars along with the eruption of passion like a wild mountain torrent overflowing its banks. It is rough, hard, bitter, sarcastic, in the mouth of hatred, while its gentle, caressing tones fall from the lips of love like the sweet perfumed breath of a night in May.

Shakespeare's plays, independently of the chronology of their composition, may be divided into three great groups :—

Firstly, Tragedies proper: "Titus Andronicus," "Romeo and Juliet," "Othello," "King Lear," "Macbeth," "Hamlet," "Timon of Athens."

Secondly, Comedies: "As You Like It," "Twelfth Night," "Comedy of Errors," "Midsummer Night's Dream," "Tempest," "Love's Labour Lost," "Two Gentlemen of Verona," "All's Well that Ends Well," "Winter's Tale," "Much Ado about Nothing," "Taming of the Shrew," "Merchant of Venice," "Measure for Measure," "Merry Wives of Windsor," "Cymbeline," "Troilus and Cressida."

Thirdly, Historical Plays: "Coriolanus," "Julius Cæsar," "Antony and Cleopatra," "King John," "Richard II.," "Henry IV.," "Henry

V.," "Henry VI.," "Richard III.," "Henry VIII."

"Pericles" is a mixture of history, tragedy, and comedy, and recalls in its composition the old Dumb-shows. Some of the comedies, such as "The Merchant of Venice," "Measure for Measure," "The Tempest," and "Cymbeline," do not quite answer to the traditional idea of comedy. The action in them takes a tragic turn, but the dreaded catastrophe is brought to a cheerful ending ; and all the comedies, no less than the tragedies, are pervaded by the spirit of morality.

Much dispute has arisen as to which are the finest plays. If we may be allowed to express our own personal judgment, we should say that the poet seems to have reached the summit of tragedy in "King Lear," and that of comedy in the "Midsummer Night's Dream." But a repeated examination makes us confess that it is not possible to make a choice amid so much excellence.

Of the historical plays the three first are taken from Roman history, to which Shakespeare has given a new life by entering into its spirit with marvellous penetration. These three poems might be called the Bible of politicians, just as the whole of Shakespeare's works have been called a worldly Bible, out of which even an anchorite could learn to know and to appreciate the events of the world. In the Roman as well as in the English histories, historical understanding and political wisdom are blended with the creative power of the poet, in a manner which can only be called Shakespearean as there is no other word to convey comparison. These plays, which reproduce the progress and spirit of. English history from the time of the Crusades to the Reformation, form together a grand dramatic epos of which the English may be proud as of a national treasure. No other nation possesses anything to be compared to it.

The years from 1595 to 1605 may be considered as the zenith of Shakespeare's activity and glory among his contemporaries. In 1598 Meres called him the most excellent of the English poets both in tragedy and comedy. Happy in the love of his friends, elated by the applause of his country, flourishing in the full power of his genius, free from all outward care, at peace with himself, he gave a triumphant expression to his own and England's felicity by the words which he put into the mouth of John of Gaunt in "Richard II," and which we have chosen as a motto for this book. But the glory of the Elizabethan age died with the queen, and a man like Shakespeare must have been painfully touched by the symptoms of a quick decay of the State which was felt at once under her successor. The public temper took a darker colouring, and Puritanism, the enemy of art, lifted a distant but threatening hand against the stage. A change had come over the theatre also: a new dramatic school had arisen, supported by considerable talents, and animated by principles which made open and secret war against Shakespeare's dramatic style. The poet's power did not fail him ; he created at this time some of his greatest works : " Cæsar " and " Coriolanus," " Macbeth " and " The Tempest." But his frame of mind and his style became graver, sterner, more cutting ; and at that time he may have entered in his poetical diary that sonnet which depicts the state of English society under James I. with such true and sorrowful strokes.[6] The evident decay of everything great and beautiful seems to have disgusted him with the metropolis. He left London in the year 1613, or the following, and retired to his residence, New Place, in Stratford, where he spent the rest of his life in calmness and leisure, cheered by the society of his eldest daughter Susanna, who seems to have been his favourite. She married a physician named Hall ; his younger daughter, Judith, became the wife of a wine merchant in

[6] " Tired with all these, for restful death I cry :—
As, to behold desert a beggar born,
And needy nothing trimmed in jollity,
And purest faith unhappily forsworn,
And gilded honour shamefully misplaced,
And maiden virtue rudely strumpeted,
And right perfection wrongfully disgraced,
And strength by limping sway disabled,
And art made tongue-ty'd by authority,
And folly (doctor-like) controlling skill,
And simple truth miscall'd simplicity,
And captive Good attending captain Ill :
Tired with all these, from these would I be gone,
Save that, to die, I leave my love alone."
Sonnet lxvi.

G

Stratford. The son of the poet died in boyhood.[7] Neither history nor tradition can tell us anything remarkable of Shakespeare's last years. But it seems that the flame of his spirit consumed his body before the time, for he died in his 53rd year, April 23rd, 1616. If we take for granted that the 23rd of April was also his birthday, one and the same day would have given Shakespeare to, and taken him from, the world. He was buried in the chief church of his native town, a simple stone with as simple an inscription marking his resting-place at first. Seven years later a monument was erected to him, probably by his son-in-law Hall, with Latin and English inscriptions to tell what a man was buried there. But more than a century passed before England began to recognize the significance of Shakespeare's poetry, after having entirely forgotten or misjudged her greatest national genius. Then, in 1741, a national monument was erected to the poet in Westminster Abbey. It represents his full-length figure in life-size, leaning against the base of a column on which the words are engraven—written in the evening of his life, a mournful expression of the transitory nature of everything created—

> The cloud-capped towers, the gorgeous palaces,
> The solemn temples, the great globe itself,
> Yes, all which it inhabit, shall dissolve,
> And, like this insubstantial pageant faded,
> Leave not a rack behind.
> "Tempest," iv. 1.

---

[7] In 1670 Shakespeare's family died out, with his childless granddaughter Elizabeth.

But his spirit has remained with us, and will live as long as there are men on earth. If we, who believe in the perfectibility of the human race, imagine to ourselves a more ideal society of the future, it would have to be one where every member should be capable of understanding Shakespeare's works and of being influenced by them. That may be a dream, but every one who has been touched by the spirit of Shakespeare's poetry will agree that his sublime mission is not yet accomplished.

The high, lasting, and in some sense unique position Shakespeare occupies in the literature of the world has thus been acknowledged; but it would be wrong and foolish to exalt him above all other great poets; as has been done by some, in Germany especially. Shakespeare is indeed a poet " for all time ;" but every great poet is that. We cannot understand why he should have a superior privilege to Homer, Æschylus, Aristophanes, Dante, Cervantes, Molière, Goethe, Byron. Shakespeare was an Englishman of the Elizabethan era, every inch of him, sharing the prejudices and superstitions of his time and of his countrymen. As one proof of this see his coarse treatment of the Maid of Orleans in "Henry VI." That he wrote his pieces for the English public of his time, and paid due regard to their manners, views, passions, and follies, no one can deny. Besides this, everything connected with the stage was very different in his time from what it is in ours, and thus his plays cannot produce the same effect now as then. His pieces cannot be acted now without a large amount of alteration and omission. The way in which his characters express themselves at times could not possibly be admitted on the stage of the present day. Independently of this occasional coarseness Shakespeare's diction is not seldom bombastic to the last degree and at other times so replete with euphuistic artificiality and punning as to become quite distasteful. Many of the poet's comedies give us little pleasure for this reason. Falstaff and the artisans in the "Midsummer Night's Dream" may never cease to excite our hearty laughter, yet, as a writer of comedy Molière ranks above Shakespeare. The French poet has the advantages of an advanced civilization. And how palpably is this progress of civilization felt when we compare the works of the Englishman of the sixteenth and seventeenth centuries with the creations of Goethe, Schiller, and Lessing! We see that the true criterion for judging Shakespeare is his own time. Looking upon him in that light we shall be truly just to him. The form of his works, which is undoubtedly faulty at times, belongs to his time and to his country. The spirit of his poetry is and remains the precious possession of mankind, among whose teachers and prophets he will always occupy the front rank. Jonson's words will indeed remain true: "He was not of an age, but for all time!"

CHAPTER VI.

Ben Jonson and his School.

WHILE the national drama was still celebrating its most brilliant triumphs other opinions and tastes arose by its side. Shakespeare had created a national theatre in the noblest sense of the word, and the former endeavours to create a learned drama, represented by the "Gorboduc" and by Lily's Court-comedies, had been pushed into the background for a time. Queen Bess, in spite of her learned education, had taste enough to prefer Falstaff's humour to the stiff mythological compositions of courtly dramatists. But now a learned pedant sat on the throne, who, if he influenced the stage at all, would do so in favour of the learned drama. There were, however, more weighty influences at work in favour of the new opinions: the romance of the middle ages disappeared more and more, giving way before the sober reasoning of modern times. Prosaic reason became the criterion of all the romantic illusions in which society had delighted until now. No wonder, therefore, that very little remained of "merry old England." Puritanic melancholy spread over the country.

The people forsook the places of public amusements and went to religious conventicles instead. This temper especially affected the citizens of London; who made vexatious opposition to the Drama,[1] severe edicts on the censorship of the Stage were issued at their instigation, and gradually the playhouses were considered as ungodly resorts of highborn idlers. The consequence was that the dramatic poets had to look for an audience amongst the upper classes to please which more learned forms became necessary. In proportion as the courtly stage rose the popular stage sank; while the splendour of the national drama was dimmed, that of the so-called artistic drama increased.

The boundary between the national dramatic school called after Shakespeare or sometimes after Greene and Marlowe, and the learned dramatic school, taking its name from its leader Ben Jonson, can only be drawn distinctly in relation to their two respective leaders; their adherents often imitated both, so that it is difficult to say to which of the two schools some of these poets belong. Most members of both the poetic camps were un-

[1] The treatment which the Stage received in later times at the hands of the Puritans began to show itself by some premature attempts. In 1606 appeared the legal prohibition to mention the names of God, of Christ, and of the Holy Ghost on the stage. In 1617 the lord mayor and aldermen of London opposed the erection of a second theatre in Blackfriars, and on the Tuesday of Passion-week in the same year the apprentices of London tried to demolish the Phœnix theatre. In 1619 the lord mayor and aldermen attempted to close the Blackfriars theatre and were only prevented from doing so by the king's intercession.

commonly productive, and the repertory of the old English stage can only be equalled in fulness by that of the Spanish.

The taste for the popular dramatic style did not disappear all at once, as has been said before. A group of dramatists still cultivated it, copying either Greene and Marlowe, or Shakespeare, more or less successfully. Such were Shakespeare's older contemporaries—Anthony Munday,[2] Henry Chittle,[3] Thomas Heywood,[4] Thomas Dekker,[5] George Chapman,[6] and others. The younger contemporaries of the great poet, as Thomas Middleton,[7] William Rowley,[8] John Marston,[9] and John Webster [10] betray a decided inclination in the new direction.

[2] Author of "The Downfall of Robert, Earl of Huntingdon," and "The Death of Robert."
[3] Author of "The tragedy of Hoffman," a play of crime and horrors.
[4] Author of "The Four Prentises of London," "A Woman Killed with Kindness," and numerous other pieces. Heywood boasts of having written about 220 plays, alone or with others.
[5] Author of "Old Fortunatus," "Patient Grissil," "The Wonder of a Kingdom," "The Honest Whore.'
[6] "The Duke of Byron," "Bussy d'Ambois," "All Fools."
[7] "The Mayor of Gainsborough," "Women beware Women," "A Mad World."
[8] "A New Wonder," "Match at Midnight," "The Changeling."
[9] "Antonio and Mellida," "The Malcontent," "The Parasitaster."
[10] "Appius and Virginia," "The Duchess of Malfi," "The White Devil," "The Devil's Law-Case."

The leader of this new school, Ben (jamin) Jonson, was born in London in 1573. From an artisan he became a soldier, then an actor, then he gave himself up to private studies; in 1616, James I. created him poet laureate with a salary of 400 marks, and in 1637 he died in poor circumstances.[1] Ben Jonson was endowed with a superior understanding, which he cultivated to the utmost by private studies, and he became one of the most learned men of his age. He was proud of his learning, a man of intellect and reason, but quite deficient in creative imagination. It is easy to understand from this that his ideas on dramatic poetry were as reasonable and as unemotional as his views of life and history. Without being fully conscious of his lack of imagination, feeling, and plastic talent, he yet tried to make up for those defects by a strict adherence to the classical rules of dramatic composition, of which he held the Aristotelian unities of time, place, and action to be the chief. His clear, inquisitive glance did not reach as far as the ideal world; his

---

[1] In Hume's "History of England," chap. lxiii., there is a note on Ben Jonson when old, poor, and sick, asking Charles I. for some assistance. The king sent him a trifle, whereupon the poet said : "My lodging is very small, but I see that the soul of the monarch is as little." He was buried in Westminster Abbey but owed his epitaph to mere chance: one of his friends happened to arrive as the mason was resetting the stone over the grave, and he gave eighteenpence to the man if he would engrave the words, " O rare Ben Jonson ! " on the slab, which was done accordingly.

domain was the real world, prosaic reality. Truth in the shape of beauty is a stranger to him, she must wear a common working dress to be understood by him. Wherever he tries to clothe her in beauty and solemnity, as in his short melodramatic pieces (masques), she at once changes into cold and lifeless allegory under his clumsy touch. The one-sided realistic tendency of his mind proved entirely insufficient to dramatize historical subjects or to carry out tragic conceptions. Proofs of this are his "Sejanus" (1603) and his "Catiline" (1611), for they consist of nothing but pragmatic dialogues seasoned with common-place morality, without dramatic action or tragic plot. But wherever Jonson chooses a subject from the reality of common life, amongst the social follies and vices of his time, to show them by the light of his satire, there he is great. In Jonson's comedies we find neither the superior comic style nor the humour of Shakespeare; he was not a "humorous poet," though he liked to call himself so, he was only a satirical one. His art consisted in throwing the piercing lights of irony and reproach on the vices of his time, and he accomplished it with a cleverness and energy which do great honour to his polemical talents. But he was not satisfied with that. He did not aim only at the destruction of the traditions and illusions of the middle ages, he also wished reason, not imagination, to become the chief principle of poetry. And he was successful, for what he attempted fell in with the general dissolution which the romantic views of the world underwent through the modern elements of sceptical criticism.

The first piece with which Jonson created a sensation was the comedy " Every Man in his Humour," acted in 1598. In it he does not yet attack the national style of the drama openly, but he makes, as it were, silent opposition to it by attempting to keep up the three unities of time, place, and action. The following year a second comedy appeared, "Every Man out of his Humour," and in 1600 a third, "Cynthia's Revels." In Jonson's succeeding pieces his opposition to the national stage and his satirical tendency became more evident. In 1601 appeared his "Poetaster," against which Dekker wrote his "Satiromastix." His best comedies, in respect of plan and execution, are "Every Man in his Humour," "Volpone, or the Fox" (1605), and "The Alchemist" (1610). In spite of their correct method, they are wanting in artistic idea and form, but the picture they give of the manners of their time is terribiy true, and their satire is striking.[3]

Ben Jonson's relation to Shakespeare was peculiar. Personally they were on very friendly terms, and Shakespeare's genius inspired his rival with so much respect that he wrote a preface in verse to the first folio edition of Shakespeare's works, in which he speaks of the great departed poet in terms of the highest praise. On the other

---

[3] "The Works of Ben Jonson," ed. by Whalley, 1756, vii.; ed. by Gifford (with criticisms, explanations, and biography), 1816, ix.

hand Jonson looked on the author of "King Lear" with the feeling of superiority which the scholar has for mere natural genius.

The dramatic poets considered to be of Ben Jonson's school are—Francis Beaumont (1586—1615), John Fletcher (1576—1625), Philip Massinger (1584—1639), John Ford (died about 1650), and Nathaniel Field. These did not regard Jonson altogether as their master, but they adopted his principles of dramatic composition. Beaumont, Fletcher, and Massinger undoubtedly possessed poetical talents superior to Ben Jonson's, but all of them erred in aiming chiefly at producing a sensation on the stage; their works, therefore, are full of exaggeration and caricatures.

Beaumont and Fletcher are generally mentioned together because they wrote in collaboration; a manner of composing which was not unfrequently practised at that time, and which in our days has been revived in Paris amongst French dramatists and novelists. Beaumont and Fletcher began to work together in 1607; Fletcher survived his friend ten years and wrote twenty-five pieces more in that time. Among their best tragedies, are "The Maid's Tragedy," and "The Tragedy of Valentinian;" and among their most successful comedies "The Knight of the Burning Pestle," "The Wild Goose Chase," and "The Passionate Madman." Fletcher's "Spanish Curate" would be a masterpiece of comedy if its moral were not pushed so much into the foreground. The moralizing of Fletcher and of the other poets of this group is all the more disagreeable as they take pleasure in very doubtful situations, and in so great an obscenity of expression that Shakespeare's moral beauty, even in his most wanton humour, strikes us most forcibly by comparison. Massinger shares Beaumont's and Fletcher's exaggerations, but also their excellence; his diction especially is rich and vigorous both in tragic and comic compositions. Among his tragedies "The Duke of Milan" is the best; his comedy "The City Madam" is full of satirical power, and in "A New Way to Pay Old Debts," the character of the usurer, Sir Giles Overreach, is drawn in a masterly manner. That excellent tragedy "The Fatal Dowry," Massinger composed together with Field. Ford is not equal to Massinger; he heaps horrors upon horrors. The historical tragedy "Perkin Warbeck" is considered his best work.[4]

[4] "The Works of Beaumont and Fletcher," ed. by Theobald, Seward, and Sympson, 1750, x.; ed. by Dyce, 1841, xiii. "The Dramatic Works of Massinger and Ford, with an introduction by Coleridge," 1839.

CHAPTER VII.

Absolutism and Puritanism—Hobbes—Milton—Butler—
Waller—Cowley—Denham.

SHAKESPEARE has called the reign of James I. a "limping sway." But though under that king English royalty was indeed lamed, another factor was already prepared to develop a power greater than that which royalty had ever possessed. The people stepped into the king's place to carry on the development of the nation at a time when it was about to be interrupted by its monarchical rulers.

The English had always possessed and loved free institutions; but they did not rebel against the despotic government of the princes of the House of Tudor because it was exercised with a powerful hand. The power of the nobles who might have opposed it had been broken by the Civil Wars, and the middle classes were not yet strong enough to do so. This explains how the tyrannical Henry VIII. was able to put to death 72,000 people on the scaffold, and to confiscate the property of a third part of the landowners. Mary was as despotic as her father, and Elizabeth, although she chose a milder form of government and succeeded in making her people happy, was equally so. But matters changed when the Stuart dynasty came to the throne. James I. was the very man to degrade royalty in the eyes of the people,[1] and the seed which he sowed grew up and bare fruit in his son's reign. Charles I., blind to the signs of the times, was not content to rule despotically himself, but wanted to found a despotic constitution, being convinced that the king should be absolute sovereign in political and religious matters. In opposition to such views the Germanic principle of liberty arose with incredible force. We need not speak here of the great struggle which ensued, and which ended in the execution of Charles I. in the courtyard of his own palace,[2] we only wish to point out that the policy of the "Great Rebellion" had a religious colouring. Puritanism, which had been kept down, since the time of Elizabeth had gained more and more adherents. The reformation of Henry VIII., Edward VI., and Elizabeth had been sufficient for the Court, the Nobility, and higher Clergy; the real reformation of the people was only effected by Puritanism, which began a battle of life and death against absolutism in church and state, using Par-

---

[1] "It was no light thing that, on the very eve of the decisive struggle between our Kings and their Parliaments, royalty should be exhibited to the world stammering, slobbering, shedding unmanly tears, trembling at a drawn sword, and talking in the style alternately of a buffoon and of a pedagogue."—Macaulay, "History of England."

[2] On the 30th of January, 1649.

liament as its weapon. The issue was uncertain until Cromwell filled his ranks with Puritan descendants of the Saxon yeomanry, who were glad to revenge themselves for the sufferings of their forefathers upon the royalist cavaliers, offspring of the feudal Norman nobles. The people felt strong in the Puritan army, and in its head, Oliver Cromwell, the real founder of England's greatness.[3] Through him the people were victorious in their struggle against despotism; but Cromwell had not time to reconcile parties, or to give a solid basis to the commonwealth. The greater part of the English nation chafed at the military government, and at the moralizing zeal of the Puritans, and after the Protector's death they longed for the re-establishment of royalty and of their old merry life.

Charles I. in spite of the great troubles of his reign, had never lost sight of the ideal interests of life. He loved and protected art and learning. Vandyck the great painter, Inigo Jones the architect, Laws the excellent musician, were employed and favoured at court; nor was a great scholar wanting who made the king's cause his own, Thomas Hobbes (1588—1679) showing himself a sceptic in religion in his work "On Human Nature" (1650), tries in his

---

[3] "Cromwell was no more; and those who had fled before him were forced to content themselves with the miserable satisfaction of digging up, hanging, quartering, and burning the remains of *the greatest prince that has ever ruled England.*"—Macaulay.

books "De Cive" (1642) and "Leviathan" (1651) to prove the right of the monarchical principle from physico-astronomical causes. As the sun in the centre of the universe is the ruling and motive power of the worlds around it, so, he contends, must absolute royalty reign in the midst of human society, possessing in itself the conditions of existence, never receiving them from without. And further, Hobbes teaches that it belongs to the king to decide how God should be worshipped, and what the people should believe. But that was not the time nor England the country where such theories could flourish, and the Puritans' response to them was the erection of the scaffold at Whitehall. They desired also to destroy everything that could remind them of royalty, and struggled fanatically against art, poetry, and the enjoyment of life; they wanted to make a "commonwealth of saints" of the English nation, the dreariness of whose life would have ended in despair or in idiocy. This is the dark side of Puritanism; from love of liberty its adherents became insufferable tyrants. They raged against works of art;[4] everything that made life cheerful and beautiful was persecuted. Popular amusements were stopped; betting and bear-baiting were forbidden; the maypoles had to be cut down all over England; dances and masques were prohibited; poets and novel-writers were looked upon with dis-

[4] "Nymphs and Graces, the work of Ionian chisels, were delivered over to Puritan stone-masons to be made decent." —Macaulay.

trust. But the deepest hatred of the Puritans was turned against the Stage; and not quite without reason, for the writers of comedies had long considered it their chief task to ridicule the "saints of the Lord." In addition to this, in 1629, a troop of French players in London had had the women's parts acted by women for the first time on English soil, and this was considered a fearful scandal. In opposition to so horrible an innovation, and to the theatre in general, Prynne published his "Histriomastix" (1633), a huge quarto volume of 1006 pages, of which the title alone fills a whole page. The zealot was condemned to a cruel punishment by the Star Chamber because he had not even spared the Court in his book.[5] The Puritans succeeded in causing all dramatic representations to be forbidden by Act of Parliament in 1642, and still more severely in 1648 when they succeeded to the government; all actors were then characterized as "rogues" and every theatre was ordered to be destroyed.

These extreme effects of Puritanism lasted only so long as the Puritans were at the head of the government, but its moral influence was more enduring, and may be traced in the national

[5] Some of the high church clergy also cried out against the theatre. Collier tells us in his "Annals of the Stage," that Archbishop Laud had the comic actor Wilson placed on the whipping-block dressed in a donkey's head, because Wilson had played the part of Bottom in the "Midsummer Night's Dream," on a Sunday, in the house of the Bishop of Lincoln, who also had to pay a fine.

character of the English to this day. Puritanism has many defects, but its virtues are great enough to outweigh them. Its principles not only inspired Cromwell, the greatest ruler England ever had, but also Milton, one of the greatest poets the country possesses, the noblest type of Puritanism, and its glorious standard-bearer in the realm of intelligence.

John Milton was born in London, on the 9th of December, 1608, and received the careful education of a gentleman of that time. He gained his academical honours at Cambridge, where his Latin verses, the first inspirations of his muse, created a sensation. He first thought of taking orders in the Episcopal church, but the eagerness of his theological studies made him dislike the orthodoxy of Anglicanism. When he left the University he spent several years at his father's country place in Buckinghamshire. Inspired by its quiet charms he began to write English poetry, and composed the graceful masque "Comus," and the tender elegy "Lycidas," suggested by the death of a friend. It was the fashion then, as it is now, for gentlemen to complete their education by a continental tour. Milton passed through Paris, where he made the acquaintance of Grotius, the great professor of Law, and went to Italy, with whose language and literature he was acquainted and where he was introduced into the society of men of note, amongst others of Galileo. A sacred drama, representing the Fall of Man, is said to have given him the first idea of the poem which is now one of the greatest ornaments of the literature of his country. His plan was to go from Italy to Greece, but he gave it up on hearing that disputes had arisen at home between the Crown and Parliament. He went to reside in London, and distinguished himself by his writings as a zealous champion of civil and religious liberty. The republican party soon became powerful, and took notice of Milton, but he still remained in humble circumstances. His married life was unhappy, like that of Dante and Shakespeare. In 1643 he had married the daughter of a country gentleman and many disputes arose from the fact that his wife and her family were staunch supporters of the Monarchy. After the execution of Charles I., Cromwell promoted Milton to a secretaryship of the Council of State with the special duty of writing the Latin despatches.

Milton began his career as an author by publishing five tracts " Concerning the Church Government," which appeared in 1641, and were directed against the high church party as the strongest support of political absolutism. Three years later appeared his "Areopagitica, a Speech for the Liberty of Unlicensed Printing," directed against the Presbyterians who on succeeding to power exercised a severe censorship of the press; in this " Speech " the free press is treated of for the first time as the foundation of all political and religious liberty. Before the execution of Charles I., Milton had written a pamphlet on the position of kings and authorities, but it was only published after the execution with some few additions.[6] After that catastrophe the royalists published a pamphlet entitled " The Royal Image " (" Ikon-basilike") which they pretended was composed by Charles himself, containing a justification of his life and actions. Milton was commissioned by the Government to answer this pamphlet, and did it by his " Ikonoklastes" (destroyer of images) which deserves its title. But the most famous of Milton's political writings is his " Defensio pro populo Anglicano " published in 1651 in answer to the " Defensio regia pro Carolo Primo" by Saumaise, a French philologer and rhetorician, in the pay of the Stuarts. Later on Milton published a second and third " Defensio." But his great exertions in the service of his country wore out his eyesight, he became blind ; yet he did not relinquish his duties as a servant of the State, and even a few months before the Restoration he published a pamphlet " A Ready and Easy Way to Establish a Free Commonwealth." The Restoration deprived him of his office, and decreed his imprisonment ; this latter decree, however, was annulled by the House of Commons. Later on the Court offered Milton his former office, but he refused it. His career as a political writer and as a statesman was now closed, and he gave his whole mind to the cultivation of poetry as the solace of his misfortunes. As early as 1645, in the midst of political

[6] Compare Taine, " Hist. de la Littérature Anglaise," 1873, i. 341—352.

excitement, he had published his "Juvenile Poems," a collection of lyrics containing amongst others his famous "L'Allegro" and "Il Penseroso," showing how differently life may be viewed by a cheerful or a melancholy mind. Among Milton's lyrical compositions his Sonnets are particularly noteworthy. They are a series of confessions, memorials of a noble life. He made the same use of the sonnet as Shakespeare. But Milton's poetical genius required a larger field to display its full grandeur, and this he found in "Paradise Lost," where sublimity and energy are combined with deep tenderness and grace.

"Paradise Lost" though completed under the Restoration is altogether a fruit of Puritanism, but of Puritanism in its highest and noblest form. Just as Dante after the fall of his party carried with him into his exile the principles, the love and hatred, the enthusiasm and anger, of the Florentine Ghibellines, and formed from them an immortal poem, so Milton in his solitude fed on the great memories of the Revolution, and those memories furnished him with the inspiration for a poem in which the great struggle between Light and Darkness should, as it were, be fought over again. His subject was the sublimest to which the imagination of his time could rise: the Biblical story of Satan's struggle against God, of the rising of Hell against Heaven, of the sin and fall of the first man. Milton first thought of treating his subject dramatically, but the epic form finally appeared the most suitable, and in 1655 he changed the dramatic plan of the poem for the epic, making use of rhymeless iambics. In 1665 the work was completed, but the royal censor threw many difficulties in the way of publication, on account of the republican principles of the poet. At last, however, in 1667 "Paradise Lost" appeared in ten books, and in the second edition, in 1674, in twelve. The book met with but a cold reception at first from the upper classes, though Dryden, the literary authority of the time of the Restoration, said of the poet of "Paradise Lost," "This man cuts us all." Among the middle classes the poet found more grateful readers, for in 1695 the sixth edition was issued. In the beginning of the eighteenth century "Paradise Lost" was fully acknowledged as a classical national poem in England, and the fame of it had spread to the continent; in Germany especially Milton was much admired.

"Paradise Lost" is a work whose name is in every mouth, and which enjoys a traditional reputation. The course of the epic according to the chronological order of the events, which sometimes deviates from that of the cantos, is as follows: The poet manifests his religious disposition at the very beginning of the poem, for he calls the Muse of Sacred History to his assistance.[7] The events

[7] Sing, heavenly Muse, that on the secret top
Of Oreb, or of Sinai, didst inspire
That shepherd who first taught the chosen seed
In the beginning how the heavens and earth
Rose out of Chaos. Or if Sion's hill
Delight thee more, and Siloa's brook that flow'd

which happened before the creation of man are related to Adam by the archangel Raphael. According to his account God at one time assembled His angels to tell them that He had begotten His only Son, whom they saw sitting at His right hand, and that homage should be paid to Him. But one of the most powerful princes in heaven rebelled at the idea of bowing the knee to one younger than himself and left heaven suddenly in the night, accompanied by his legions, drawing after him the third part of the heavenly host. This wrathful withdrawal of Satan was the beginning of his rebellion against the Lord of Heaven, Who at once made preparation for defence against the rebels : they in their turn hastened to begin the attack. Michael and Gabriel are placed at the head of the heavenly legions and the battle begins after Satan has tried in vain to draw his adversaries over to his side by taunts and allurements. Both parties display the greatest bravery. Michael mows down whole battalions with one stroke of his flaming sword ; he meets Satan in single combat and disables him for the time by wounding him in the side. Night closes the battle but not the struggle, for on the following morning the host of Hell is again in the field with a new and fearful invention, that of artillery—Satan has acquainted his army with the use of gunpowder,

> Fast by the oracle of God, I thence
> Invoke thy aid to my advent'rous song,
> That with no middle flight intends to soar
> Above th' Aonian mount.

and during the night guns and balls have been cast. This new hellish invention makes fearful havoc and the victory seems to be on the side of Satan;[8] but the heavenly warriors rouse themselves to new energy, and the second day ends with such terrible uproar that the very firmament was threatened with ruin. The next morning God says to His Son: "Two days of fighting have passed without result; the third is Thine." Then the Son rises to fight, and ascends the chariot of the Almighty. The description of His going to battle is one of the most magnificent creations of the imagination.[9]

[8] The description of the use and effect of the cannon, book vi. 571—599, is remarkably vivid.

[9]   Forth rushed with whirlwind sound
  The chariot of Paternal Deity,
  Flashing thick flames, wheel within wheel undrawn,
  Itself instinct with Spirit, but convoyed
  By four Cherubick shapes; four faces each
  Had wonderous; as with stars, their bodies all
  And wings were set with eyes; with eyes the wheels
  Of beryl, and careering fires between;
  Over their heads a crystal firmament,
  Whereon a sapphire throne, inlaid with pure
  Amber, and colours of the showery arch.
  He, in celestial panoply all armed
  Of radient Urim, work divinely wrought,
  Ascended; at his right hand Victory
  Sat eagle-winged; beside him hung his bow
  And quiver with three-bolted thunder stored;
  And from about him fierce effusion rolled
  Of smoke, and bickering flame, and sparkles dire:
  Attended with ten thousand thousand Saints,
  He onward came; far off his coming shone;
  And twenty thousand (I their number heard)

Satan's army is unable to withstand such an adversary. The rebels soon give up all resistance, the floor of heaven opening wide rolls back, and an abyss opens into which Satan and his angels are cast. Nine days they fall until they arrive at the bottom of Hell. But God mourns the depopulation of His Heaven and to replace the fallen angels He determined to create a new world with new creatures. Here follows the history of the Creation, a brilliant paraphrase of the Mosaic Genesis. Adam then details to the archangel his sensations and experiences since the first hour of his existence. The account of his marriage with Eve is one of the most graceful and charming passages in the poem.[1]

> Chariots of God, half on each hand, were seen ;
> He on the wings of Cherub rode sublime
> On the crystálline sky, in sapphire throned,
> Illustrious far and wide ; but by his own
> First seen : them unexpected joy surprised,
> When the great ensign of Messiah blazed
> Aloft by Angels borne, his sign in Heaven ;
> Under whose conduct Michael soon reduced
> His army, circumfused on either wing,
> Under their Head imbodied all in one.
> Before him Power Divine his way prepared ;
> At his command the uprooted hills retired
> Each to his place ; they heard his voice, and went
> Obsequious ; Heaven his wonted face renewed,
> And with fresh flowerets hill and valley smiled.

[1]
>   To the nuptial bower
> I led her, blushing like the morn. All Heaven,
> And happy constellations, on that hour
> Shed their selectest influence ; the Earth
> Gave sign of gratulation, and each hill ;
> Joyous the birds ; fresh gales and gentle airs

Meanwhile Satan has recovered from the confusion he experienced on his fall into Hell. The place in which he finds himself is grandly described;[2] a fearful waste, visible darkness exhaling, it reveals to him the full depth of his fall. But his rebellious pride becomes an inexhaustible source of energy, he is—the Prince of Hell. No poet can equal Milton in his delineation of supernatural beings, especially of evil spirits.[3] His Satan is an image

> Whispered it to the woods, and from their wings
> Flung rose, flung odours from the spicy shrub,
> Disporting, till the amorous bird of night
> Sung spousal, and bid haste the evening star
> On his hill top, to light the bridal lamp.

[2] Book i. 56, and succeeding lines.

[3] "The spirits of Milton are unlike those of almost all other writers. His fiends, in particular, are wonderful creations. They are not metaphysical abstractions. They are not wicked men. They are not ugly beasts. They have no horns, no tails, none of the fee-faw-fum of Tasso and Klopstock. They have just enough in common with human nature to be intelligible to human beings. Their characters are, like their forms, marked by a certain dim resemblance to those of men, but exaggerated to gigantic dimensions, and veiled in mysterious gloom."—Macaulay: Milton (Essays).

Compare the following description of Satan ("Paradise Lost," book i. 193—120):

> "With head uplift above the wave, and eyes
> That sparkling blazed; his other parts besides
> Prone on the flood, extended long and large,
> Lay floating many a rood; in bulk as huge
> As whom the fables name of monstrous size,
> Titanian, or Earth-born, that warred on Jove;
> Briarëos or Typhon, whom the den
> By ancient Tarsus held; or that sea-beast
> Leviathan, which God of all his works

full of majesty, creating terror; his character is well defined and maintained throughout. He succeeds in inspiring his comrades with his own courage, rousing them to a further struggle against God. The new-created earth is selected by Satan as the fittest place for its renewal; and while the other evil spirits disperse through Hell to pursue their several occupations or amusements (philosophical disputes are mentioned amongst others), Satan starts to explore the new battle-field. He arrives at the gates of Hell which are secured by threefold doors of brass, iron, and diamond, and here he finds two fearful guards, Death and his daughter Sin, whose delineation again shows the poet's masterly power in such creations.[4] Sin moves her father to open the gate and Satan enters Chaos, a drear abyss, the womb of Nature, and perhaps her grave. The demons of this place show him the way; dawn begins to glimmer and in the radiance streaming from the palace of God,[5] he

> Created hugest that swim the ocean stream:
> Him, haply, slumbering on the Norway foam
> The pilot of some small night-foundered skiff
> Deeming some island, oft, as sea-men tell,
> With fixed anchor in his scaly rind
> Moors by his side under the lee, while night
> Invests the sea, and wished morn delays:
> So stretched out huge in length the Arch-Fiend lay.

Compare, besides, the representation of Satan flying, book ii. 629—643, also book iv. 985—990.

[4] Book ii. 648, and succeeding lines.

[5] The blind poet made use of this opportunity to address a touching apostrophe to light (book iii. 1, and succeeding lines).

sees and enters the Creation so lately wrung from Chaos. The splendour of the firmament with its myriads of stars makes him pause a moment with wonder; but he soon continues his course, first into the Sun. There he meets the archangel Uriel, and that he may not be recognized he takes the form of a stripling cherub, and pretends to be wandering through the universe in order to adore the greatness of the Creator, asking Uriel at the same time to show him the way to the newly created earth. Uriel complies, and Satan arrives in Eden, whose beauties the poet paints in the most exquisite colours.[6] A conversation between Adam and Eve betrays to him that the pair are threatened with death if they eat of the tree of knowledge. Satan in a monologue raises the question whether knowledge could be sin, and whether the happiness of the newly-created pair depends on their ignorance. He determines to destroy that happiness. But meanwhile Uriel begins to suspect the wandering angel and he flies to the earth to put the angels watching over Paradise on their guard against the intruder. They go in search of him and find him in the shape of a toad, whispering evil dreams into the ear of Eve. Upon Uriel's touching him with his sword he is obliged to show himself in his true form, at which the angels step back in amazement. A violent conflict would have ensued, but the Almighty hung forth in heaven His golden scales wherein He weighs all things created. Satan sees his scale

[6] Book iv. 205—355.

rising, and flees murmuring. Meanwhile the dreams inspired by the Evil One have had their effect upon Eve and she longs to taste the forbidden fruit. God foresees the mischief threatening man, but having given man free-will He does not interpose. Yet the fall of man which He foresees provokes the Divine justice and a sacrifice is required to atone for the sin. The Son then offers to become that sacrifice. God also foretells the Last Day, when the number of the accursed shall be complete, and hell closed for ever. The world shall be consumed by fire and out of its ashes shall arise a new heaven and a new earth, the abode of the Blessed.[7] Man, however, has to be warned before he is tempted, and for that purpose God sends Raphael to tell him of Satan's fall and the creation of the world. But the warning proves useless. Satan, who has not left Paradise, again begins his temptations; he adopts the form of a serpent and by flattering Eve he makes her taste the fruit of the Tree of Knowledge. Eve persuades Adam to do the same, and on coming to their senses again the feeling of shame takes hold of them. They know now what is good, and what is evil, and this knowledge first shows itself in mutual reproaches. Their punishment is

[7] The dogmatic conversation between God and His Son takes up the greater part of the Third Book. Such theological investigations are frequent in the poem, and considerabl injure the poetical impression; the frequent use Milto makes of Greek mythological images also annoys the taste of the present day. Both faults are excusable as belonging to the temper of the times in which the poem was composed.

close at hand. The angels flee from Eden; the Son of God appears and pronounces judgment on the guilty pair. Sin and Death leave Hell and take up their abode upon earth. Eve succeeds in reconciling herself to her angry husband after having asked his pardon in the most touching manner.[8] The archangel Michael drives the pair out of Paradise and shows them in a splendid vision the consequences of their Fall, which is to be atoned for by the sacrifice of the Son of God. Eve is comforted by the thought that she should be worthy to be the mother of the Saviour; she succeeds in comforting Adam, and hand in hand they slowly quit Paradise.

This grand poem had not exhausted Milton's pleasure in composing, but it had exhausted his poetical power. He undertook to write a sequel to "Paradise Lost," "Paradise Regained," which was published in 1671, in four books, and in the same metre. Its subject is the temptation of Jesus by Satan in the wilderness, and the frustration of the hellish invention; but it is tedious to wade through the lengthy theological disputations of which "Paradise Regained" chiefly consists.

"Samson Agonistes" (1671), a tragedy, with choruses on the model of the classics, contains some passages of noble diction, but is on the whole an uninteresting composition; Handel has set it to music in the form of an oratorio. Towards the end of his life Milton once more published some political

[8] Book x. 909, and succeeding lines.

pamphlets, at a time when the power of the Court again threatened to become despotic; but he did not long enjoy the victory of his party, for he died in London on the 10th November, 1674. The leaders of the opposition and the citizens of the capital gave him a solemn funeral, which served as a demonstration against the court. A monument was erected to him in the poet's corner of Westminster Abbey in 1737, and a still finer one was raised to his memory by Macaulay in his essay bearing Milton's name.[9]

Milton, it has been already said, was the poet of Puritanism in its sublimest form. But in its re-

[9] "His public conduct," Macaulay says, among other things, "was such as was to be expected from a man of spirit so high and of an intellect so powerful. He lived at one of the most memorable eras in the history of mankind, at the very crisis of the great conflict between Oromasdes and Arimanes, liberty and despotism, reason and prejudice. That great battle was fought for no single generation, for no single land. The destinies of the human race were staked on the same cast with the freedom of the English people. Then were first proclaimed those mighty principles which have since worked their way into the depths of the American forests, which have roused Greece from the slavery and degradation of two thousand years, and which, from one end of Europe to the other, have kindled an unquenchable fire in the hearts of the oppressed, and loosed the knees of the oppressors with an unwonted fear. Of those principles, then struggling for their infant existence, Milton was the most devoted and eloquent literary champion."

The best edition of "Paradise Lost" is by Th. Newton, 1749. There are numerous collective editions of Milton's poetical works. Prose works, ed. by Symmons, 1806. The life of John Milton, by W. Heiley, 1798.

ligious and social forms Puritanism was too ludicrous to escape satire. Only people of a serious turn of mind, indifferent to outward appearances, could help laughing at the majority of the "roundheads"—snuffling crop-eared saints, with their quaint sugar-loaf hats, sad-coloured clothes, and mournful fanatical mien—at their phraseology taken from the Old Testament, at their names sometimes consisting of a whole Bible text, at their monstrous preaching, and at their furious animosity against all social amusements. Samuel Butler, born in 1612 at Strensham, in Worcestershire, laid hold of the scourge of Satire and handled it dexterously and vigorously. His poem, which shows the reverse side of Puritanism, was written and published after the Restoration, but it is a product of the Rebellion and the Commonwealth. It is a comic epos entitled "Hudibras" after its principal character. The first part of the work appeared in 1663, the second in 1664, and the third in 1678, each containing three cantos.[1] In the ninth canto the satire breaks off suddenly; the ungodliness of the poet's party perhaps induced him to leave his work a fragment. Though the royalists and high churchmen were delighted with "Hudibras," they did not alleviate the poet's poverty, and Charles II., who was fond of reciting passages from the poem, gave him only 300*l.* instead of a pension for life as might have been expected. Butler died in em-

---

[1] "Hudibras, by Samuel Butler," ed. by Grey, 1774, 3 vols. "Hudibras," with the life of the author, by Nash, 1793, iii.

barrassed circumstances in 1680. Forty years afterwards a monument was erected to his memory in the Poet's Corner of Westminster Abbey by an admirer of his satire. There is no doubt that the author of "Hudibras" had Don Quixote in his mind while composing his poem, but he has not nearly come up to his model. Hudibras, a Presbyterian knight, sets out with his esquire Ralph, who belongs to the sect of the Independents, to free the country from prelates and other evils. Both characters are vulgar, cowardly, hypocritical, parasitical rascals, on which the poet has heaped all the weaknesses, follies, and vices of which the Cavaliers accused the Roundheads. Of course Sir Hudibras gets the worst of it everywhere, and there is abundance of blows and obscenities in the book. We cannot agree with Hume who praises "Hudibras" as a work of inimitable wit; but we must acknowledge that the poem, viewed in a party spirit, is an excellent satire. At the very commencement a good picture is drawn of the times when people fought for "Dame Religion."[2] The

[2] "When civil dudgeon first grew high,
And men fell out, they knew not why;
When hard words, jealousies, and fears,
Set folks together by the ears,
And made them fight, like mad or drunk,
For Dame Religion, as for punk;
Whose honesty they all durst swear for,
Though not a man of them knew wherefore:
When Gospel-Trumpeter, surrounded
With long-ear'd rout, to battle sounded;

I

satirical delineation of the character of the hero and his esquire is excellent, and many of their burlesque and grotesque adventures are conducive to laughter. Still the poem on the whole is somewhat tedious, and can only be understood by the help of a good commentary, on account of the theological learning and the many local and personal allusions contained in it.

Besides Milton and Butler the great civil war only produced poets of the third and fourth order. Edmund Waller (1615—1687), an inconstant politician, made himself known as an elegant speaker in Parliament, but as a poet he is nothing but a rhetorician. His love-songs to various beauties, amongst whom Dorothea Sydney occupies the first place as "Sacharissa," are elegant but sometimes trifling. A greater epic poem, "The Battle of the Summer Islands," to which he was prompted by a voyage to the Bermudas, was admired on account of its elegant versification. The ode "Upon the Death of the Lord Protector" is considered his masterwork. It had scarcely been written ere he sang the praises of the returning Charles II.[3]

> And pulpit, drum ecclesiastic,
> Was beat with fist, instead of a stick;
> Then did Sir Knight abandon dwelling,
> And out he rode a colonelling."

[3] The king remarked to Waller that the poem dedicated to himself was far inferior to that made on Cromwell; whereupon the poet is said to have answered with the mean flattery: "Poets, sire, succeed better in fiction than in truth."

Abraham Cowley displays greater power and more ideas in his numberless odes and elegies. His epic attempt, "Davideis," was not successful, but he succeeded perfectly in hitting the style of the national ballad in " The Chronicle."

Sir John Denham (1615—1668) ought to be mentioned here because he introduced a new style of poetry in his most famous poem "Cooper's Hill" (1643), a moralizing description of landscapes which has become exceedingly popular in England.

CHAPTER VIII.

The Restoration—Society and Literature—The Stage—Dryden—Tragedy: Otway—Comedy: Wycherley, Congreve, Vanbrugh, Farquhar—Satire: Rochester—Novelists: Boyle, Harrington, Aphra Behn, Mrs. Heywood, Miss Manley, Bunyan—Oratorical, political, and historical prose: Taylor, Barrow, Barnet, Tillotson, Sidney, Whiteloke, Clarendon, Temple.

THE difference between English society during the Commonwealth, and the same after the Restoration, is immense, and can only be explained by the indisputable law of reaction which causes human nature to go from one extreme to the other.

On the 29th May, 1660, the indolent and voluptuous Charles II. was welcomed back to England as a deliverer; but the consequences of the Restoration soon became evident, especially when the direction of public affairs was taken from the careful Clarendon, and left to the mercy of a ministry stigmatized by history under the name of the Cabal,—Clifford, Ashley, Buckingham, Arlington, Lauderdale. English honour, so gloriously represented by Cromwell, was shamefully sold to Louis XIV. England, which had been the bulwark of Protestantism, now became a vassal of France. The public spirit of the country declined rapidly. The policy of the Stuarts agreed with the doctrine of Sir Robert Filmer,[1] who in his writings uphold the absolute power of all kings as a necessity, and required from the people a slavish and passive obedience. Those noble champions of religious and political freedom, William Russell and Algernon Sidney, were sent to the scaffold. Nor did the popular party of the Whigs scruple to employ the worst means for their end: they disgraced themselves especially by the use they made of the "Popish plot," the invention of a rascal called Oates. The debauchery of the Court was a signal for a general demoralization of manners, increased by some fearful public calamities. In 1665 the plague destroyed 100,000 inhabitants of London; in 1666 two-thirds of the houses of the capital were reduced to ashes by a great fire; and the unsuccessful insurrection of the Duke of Monmouth, a natural son of Charles II., incited James II. to the cruel persecution of the popular party, that became known as the "bloody assizes" and has rendered the name of the Chief Justice Jeffreys for ever infamous. Charles II. had acquired the most dissolute habits during his banishment at the French Court, and he did not discontinue them at Whitehall. All classes of the people were infected by his example, and the history of his time furnishes abnormal instances of debauchery, of coarseness and vulgarity of mind, and of revolting dissoluteness

[1] In his books "Necessity of the Absolute Power of all Kings" (1648), "The Anarchy" (1648), "Patriarcha" (1650).

in the tone of conversation. The immorality of Society was the parent of immorality in Literature, which is everywhere and at all times the faithful reflection of the former. The literature of this epoch is despicable, alike from its immorality, its bad taste, and the inhuman spirit breathing through it.[2] The anti-Puritan reaction was carried furthest by the authors who wrote for the stage. Comedy especially was considered by dramatists and actors as an excellent occasion for taking their revenge on the Puritans ; they not only scorned and jeered at the Puritanical edicts by which they had suffered, but they trampled without restraint upon all laws of morality. Polite society encouraged them ; going to the playhouse was the most regular occupation of the fashionable world. The Stage received additional attractions : a complicated scenic machinery, splendid decorations and costumes, and, above all, actresses instead of boys who had until now played the women's parts.

Immorality in every sense of the word is the chief characteristic of the Literature of the Restoration. Another peculiarity was its spirit of negation, of scepticism, and criticism. The poet who wished to excite attention had to write satires and lampoons. Poetry was much more a product of reason than of fancy or feeling ; there is therefore a striking want of good lyrical poetry. Satire in every form

[2] Macaulay : Comic Dramatists of the Restoration.—"Essays."

was the favourite style, especially in a dramatized form, and every poet tried to write satires, whether his talents lay in that direction or not. French manners furnished subjects for the Literature of the Restoration, French rules of art decided its form. The correctness of Boileau's style was the test of good taste in England, and the London coffee-houses were the scenes where literary productions were discussed and criticized. These coffee-houses were imitated from the Turkish places of assembly. The first one was opened during the Commonwealth; they flourished especially in the last forty years of the 17th century, when they took the place of the press and exercised a great influence on public opinion. Each class and profession, each religious and political party, had their special coffee-houses, Will's coffee-house, between Covent Garden and Bow Street, was the acknowledged centre of literary life. Here Dryden sat in the warm chimney corner, uttering those criticisms which his companions received as laws.

John Dryden was born in 1631 at Oldwinkle, in Northamptonshire. He studied at Westminster College, and finished his education at Cambridge. His life was like that of all literary men of his time: being at one time in plenty, at another troubled with debts and care. He was a frequent guest at the king's board, but was obliged to make great efforts in later years to gain a livelihood by his pen. He died in 1700. His tomb in Westminster Abbey is between those of Chaucer and

Cowley.[3] Dryden resembled Waller in his want of character and principle, but his talent is far above Waller's. His first publication was an apotheosis of Cromwell entitled "Heroic Stanzas" (1685); his second, two years later, the "Astræa Redux," a song of joy at the Restoration of the Stuarts. As a reward for this and other literary services, he was made poet laureate and historiographer royal, which dignities were taken from him by the Revolution of 1688. Meanwhile Dryden wrote for the Stage though he had no talent for dramatic composition. From 1661 to 1694 he wrote twenty-eight dramas, tragedies, comedies, tragi-comedies, and operas.[4] To make up for his want

[3] One of Dryden's amiable qualities was his readiness to acknowledge and advance younger talents. When Congreve's comedy "The Double Dealer," was represented in 1694, the clever piece met with a lukewarm reception at first. Dryden, to comfort the poet, addressed a very fine poem to him, whose last lines are most touching :—

"Already I am worn with cares and age,
And just abandoning th' ungrateful stage;
But you, whom every Muse and Grace adorn,
Whom I foresee to better fortune born,
Be kind to my remains; and, oh, defend
Against your judgment your departed friend.
Let not the insulting foe my fame pursue,
But guard those laurels which descend to you."

[4] The beginnings of the English opera are to be found in the masques of Ben Jonson. William Davenant, whose opera, "Britannia Triumphans," was represented in 1637, contributed much towards their development as court poet and theatrical director after the Restoration. He took great pains to improve the mechanism of the theatre. The introduction of movable decorations on the English stage is owing to him.

of invention he borrowed very freely from other dramatic poets both of England (e. g. from Shakespeare) and of other countries. This fault was unpardonable, for however pure and excellent the characters he copied, he sullied them by dragging them through the mire of the immorality of his time. Dryden wrote with extraordinary ease; his plays were but a small portion of his writings. In 1667 appeared his historical poem "Annus Mirabilis;" and soon afterwards his famous "Essay on Dramatic Poesy," written in the form of a dialogue, which raised him to the dignity of chief critic in all matters of literary taste among his contemporaries. He created a still greater sensation by his satire "Absalom and Achitophel" (1681), which two names stood for the Duke of Monmouth and his adviser Lord Shaftesbury, the intriguing leader of the Whigs. The appearance of this striking satire was a political event which contributed much to lower the already depressed spirits of the popular party, and to encourage Toryism. After the accession of James II. Dryden became a Roman Catholic to flatter the fanaticism of the king and published his satirical fable "The Hind and the Panther"—the former representing the Roman church pursued by the panther of Protestantism— a strange and silly invention which was well parodied.[5] In the latter years of his life Dryden was chiefly occupied with translations of ancient classical authors, whose works he succeeded in

[5] By Prior and Montagu's witty fable "The Town Mouse and the Country Mouse."

rendering into English better than any of his countrymen had done before him. In 1693 he published Persius and Juvenal, in 1697 Virgil, and closed his poetical career by his "Fables Ancient and Modern" taken from Homer, Ovid, Boccaccio, and Chaucer, and containing some of the best examples of his powerful and elegant style. This collection also contains "Alexander's Feast, or the Power of Music," which was set to music by Handel Besides these poetical works, of which only the most important have been mentioned, Dryden wrote a great deal of Prose, biographies, critical treatises, translations, prefaces, and letters. There is much ability and clearsightedness in all his writings, and though Dryden was guided by French taste he still has the right instinct of a critic, and knows how to distinguish gold from tinsel.[6] As a poet

---

[6] As a pattern of the æsthetic criticism of that time, and of Dryden's prose, we insert his judgment on Shakespeare (from the "Essay on Dramatic Poesy"):—" He (Shakespeare) was the man who, of all modern and perhaps ancient poets, had the largest and most comprehensive soul. All the images of nature were still present to him, and he drew them not laboriously but luckily. When he describes anything, you more than see it, you feel it too. Those who accuse him to have wanted learning, give him the greater commendation. He was naturally learned; he needed not the spectacles of books to read nature; he looked inwards, and found her there. I cannot say he is everywhere alike; were he so, I should do him injury to compare him with the greatest of mankind. He is many times flat, insipid; his comic wit degenerating into clenches, his serious swelling into bombast. But he is always great when some great

he is at the head of a new School which might be called the critical; its inspiration came from the brain, its poetry was the poetry of reason, its views of the world and of life are sceptical. Didactic and satirical poetry, the comic epos, the comic play, are the favourite literary forms cultivated from the time of the Restoration to the middle of the eighteenth century; lyric, epic, and tragic poetry had but few admirers and cultivators. Dryden's style, both in poetry and prose, has exercised a great and good influence upon the English language. As a prose writer he is clear and decided; his poetical diction is elegant but also powerful and lofty. He was neither a great poet nor a genius, but an elegant writer, didactic, a clever and impressive satirist, and a discerning critic.[7]

Regard for the National Drama was not however quite lost. Thomas Otway (1651—1685), Nathan Lee (1692), and Nicolas Rowe (1718), attempted to oppose the ruling fashion. But Lee and Rowe in their imitations of Shakespeare gave proofs of more good will than talent, and Otway was lost too soon in debauchery and misery to bring his genius to maturity. His tragedy "Venice

occasion is presented to him. No man can say he ever had a fit subject for his wit and did not then raise himself as high above the rest of poets,
"Quantum lenta solent inter viburna cupressi."
[7] Complete edition of Dryden's works: "The Complete Works of John Dryden, with notes historical and critical, and a life of the author," by W. Scott. Lond. 1808, 18 vols.

Preserved" (1685), the subject of which is the famous conspiracy against Venice in 1618, is undoubtedly a work of genius, far superior to any dramatic composition of this period ; it will remain for ever one of the classical tragedies of English literature. But the times were not favourable to such noble compositions. The play-going public would have nothing but comedies, brimming over with frivolity, wit, malice, and immorality. The comedy writer, George Villiers, Duke of Buckingham, who in "The Rehearsal" makes fun of Dryden's dramatic impotence, Thomas Shadwell, George Etherege, Charles Sedley, and the female writers, Aphra Behn and Susan Centlivre, these were the authors whose pieces drew crowds to the playhouses; but yet these were only considered as second-rate writers of comedy. The first rank belonged to William Wycherley (1640—1715), William Congreve (1670—1728) George Farquhar (1678—1707), and John Vanbrugh (1666—1726). Wycherley is the most immoral of the four : " The Country Wife" and "The Plain Dealer" are the wittiest of his comedies. Farquhar's pieces "The Recruiting Officer," " Love and a Battle," and others, are amusing for their unaffected merriment. Vanbrugh's comedies, especially "The False Friend" and " The Provoked Wife," are a very faithful reflection of the conversational language of the time. But Congreve is far above the others in talent and success ; his comedies are sparkling with wit and eloquence, and they are particularly attractive for his diction, which possesses a certain artistic repose. Besides his comedies, "The Old Bachelor," "The Double Dealer," "Love for Love," he wrote a tragedy,"The Mourning Bride,"and his contemporaries then pronounced him to be the first comic and tragic writer of the period.[8] The "spirit of Belial" which inspired the comedy-writers equally influenced the satirists, and their writings were but a mirror of their own lives. The drunkard Rochester was the most shameless of all. His satires are very clever, but so revolting that they cannot be touched upon without producing disgust.[9]

Novels gradually caught this immoral and satirical tone. Immediately after the Restoration, English novelists tried to imitate the romantic sentiment of Mdlle. Madeleine Scudery, as for instance Roger Boyle Earl of Orrery in his "Parthenissa" (1664). Other writers made use of the novel to embody their political republican fancies, as Sir Thomas Harrington in his allegorical novel "Oceana," the subject of which anticipates the false modern theories of democracy and socialism. Towards the end of Charles II.'s reign the comedy-writer Aphra Behn published some very immoral novels, which were imitated by Mrs. Heywood and a little later by Miss Mary Manley, the

---

[8] "The Dramatic Works of Wycherley, Congreve, Vanbrugh, and Farquhar, with biographical and critical notices," by Leigh Hunt. 1840.

[9] Hume says (chap. lxxiii.) that the very name of Rochester is offensive to a pure ear.

indecency of whose novel "The New Atlantis" was mixed with cutting political satire directed against the Whigs. Religious faith, which during these frivolous times increased in strength and depth in some minds, also made use of the novel as a means of influence. The tinker John Bunyan (1628—1688), who was thrown into prison at the Restoration and kept there for twelve years, wrote the famous allegorical novel "The Pilgrim's Progress" during his imprisonment. The extraordinary popularity of the book is easily accounted for; it not only addresses itself to fancy and reason, but also touches the heart, and the subject is one of universal human interest.[1]

The development of English prose advanced considerably during this period. Dryden's influence on it has been already mentioned, and dramatic dialogues, novels, and critical researches helped to make it flexible and smooth, and enriched it with new forms, though often at the expense of its purity, as many of the innovations were imported from the French language. Great care was bestowed upon the

---

[1] The author of the "Pilgrim's Progress" has also left an autobiography, under the title of "Grace Abounding," which is as remarkable from a psychological as from an historical point of view. This book is the best study for the origin and essence of Puritanism. It is a work which, in spite of its being specifically English, has the significance for the seventeenth century that the "Confessiones" of St. Augustin have for the fifth, and the "Confessions" of Rousseau for the eighteenth. In these three books beats the full and living pulse of the times in which they were composed.

cultivation of oratorical prose. Some famous divines and preachers—Jeremy Taylor (+ 1667), Isaac Barrow (+ 1677), Thomas Burnet (+ 1715), and John Tillotson(+ 1694)—shed a lustre over this period; to classical learning they added great eloquence, to which their more serious contemporaries listened with delight, and which captivated the attention even of the frivolous, the companions of Rochester and Wycherley. Political publications were gradually becoming a necessity for English society. Discussions on the politics of the day or on principles of government always found willing listeners. Filmer's theory of slavish submission, which has been mentioned before, received several powerful refutations. Algernon Sidney (executed in 1683) argued against this servile theory in his " Discourses concerning Government."

The age of the Restoration being the period during which the romantic illusions of the middle ages had altogether given way to the realistic tendency of modern times, is also the period in which Historiography, in the true sense of the word, takes its rise. The sober Whitelocke and the high-minded Ludlow wrote " Memorials " of the civil war, and the same subject is treated in the " History of the Rebellion " by Edward Hyde, Earl of Clarendon, an impartial historian, whose work is of classical merit. Bishop Burnet wrote a history of the English Reformation and an excellent " History of his Own Time," 1724—1734, on the reign of the two last Stuarts. The famous diplomatist Sir William

Temple (+ 1699), whose leisure hours were devoted to learned and literary studies, also wrote valuable "Memoirs," letters, and despatches, an " Essay upon Ancient and Modern Learning," and also one " Upon Poetry." [2]

[2] In this Essay Milton is not even mentioned—a proof of the injustice and weakness to which even the most cultivated men of that period were tempted by party-spirit.

CHAPTER IX.

THE AGE OF WILLIAM III. AND MARY; QUEEN ANNE; GEORGE I. AND II.—GENERAL CHARACTER OF THE LITERATURE OF THIS PERIOD.

Realistic philosophy: Locke—Freethinkers: Toland and others—Wits in high life: Shaftesbury and Bolingbroke—Natural Science: Newton—Historians: Hume, Robertson, Mitford, Ferguson, Gibbon, Roscoe—Memoirs: Walpole—Poets: Pope, Gay, Prior, Young—Essayists: Steele and Addison, Swift and Johnson—Letters and epistles on the subjects of worldly wisdom and politics: Chesterfield and Junius—Novel-writers: Family novels of ideal and realistic views: Richardson, Fielding, Miss Burney—Humorous novels: Smollett and Sterne—Pastoral novels: Goldsmith—Novels written for special purposes: Godwin, Miss Edgeworth —Sensational novels: Horace Walpole, Mrs. Radcliffe—Matthew Gregory Lewis.

THIS period comprises from sixty to seventy years. Its political history has several subdivisions, culture and morals also pass through different phases, but yet it may be considered as one period, for the character of English Literature remained essentially the same during this space of time. In many respects it is one of the most brilliant epochs in the history of English literature, for new sources of knowledge were opened up by science that influenced the whole of Europe. The poetry of this period was on the whole only a more perfect continuation of the path traced by Dryden and his contemporaries. Up to the middle of the eighteenth century the characteristics of English poetry remained French in their *esprit*, and subject to rules of art whose watchword was accuracy. English poets, however, were not slavish imitators of the French, they had always more imagination and more feeling ; but, nevertheless, sceptical and critical reasonings played the chief part in their compositions. In the period under consideration the favourite kinds of poetry were still didactic and satirical, the humorous epic, and the moralizing description of nature. The literature of the period adopted wit and satire as its rulers ; these had to take the place, so far as they could, of enthusiasm and the creative power of genius. One branch of poetical literature, however, grew and flourished in England, and became the admiration of the whole of Europe ; this was the poetic novel which called forth numerous imitators on the Continent.

The delight which was manifested on the restoration of Charles II. to the throne of his fathers lasted only during the first years of his reign, for his worthlessness soon became apparent to all. The struggle between the popular party and the Court, between the Whigs and Tories, which had begun under Charles, led to the catastrophe of 1688, by which James II. lost the crown. William of Orange, the son-in-law of this foolish and heartless man, was called to the vacant throne, after he had sworn to maintain the Protestant religion, and had signed the famous Declaration of Rights which embodied the constitutional liberties of the nation. From that time forth the English constitution was never again in serious danger. William was an upholder of the Germanic principles of liberty, in opposition to Louis XIV., who represented those of absolutism. The Prince of Orange was still a youth when he conducted the glorious war that the United Provinces of Holland waged against Louis XIV.'s lust of conquest, and he maintained throughout his life a stedfast resistance to the encroachments of French polity. Under William's government England was again raised to a respected and leading position among the nations of Europe.

·During the reign of his successor, Anne, the younger daughter of James II., Scotland was fully united to England, and the succession was settled on the Protestant house of Hanover.

France had been humbled by England's participation in the Wars of the Succession in Spain. Marlborough's victories on the Continent gave a new impulse to public life in England. A feeble attempt of the favourite party to restore the Stuarts to the throne after Queen Anne's death, was frustrated, and all the later Jacobite rebellions against the Hanoverian dynasty shared the same fate.

The victory gained by Protestant and Whig principles in the Revolution of 1688 caused a remarkable change in public morals, chiefly amongst the middle classes who returned to the milder forms of Puritan tradition. The Court of William and Mary was very pure, and exercised a corresponding influence on society. An opposition was formed against the immorality of literature, especially of the drama. In the year 1698 Jeremy Collier, a minister of the Anglican church, published " A Short View of the Immorality and Profanity of the English Stage," which created a great sensation, and exercised an important and lasting influence. Collier only expressed what the great majority of the nation had long ago felt; disgust at the demoralizing abuse of the stage, an institution which might and could have produced a very different effect. Congreve's feeble defence could not silence the applause which Collier received, and which was the greater as he attacked his adversaries with their own weapons of scorn and satire.

During the reigns of the two first Georges a lower tone was reintroduced into English society. Both princes were deficient in mind and cultivation, and their family quarrels did not tend to increase decorum. The powerful minister of these two kings, Sir Robert Walpole, governed by means of a system of corruption, by which membership of Parliament and other offices could be bought; and this naturally exercised an immense influence on social morality. What the manners and morals of this time were may be gathered from the letters of the witty and eccentric Lady Mary Wortley Montagu (1690—1762), who was intimately mixed up with the literary life of that time and who was rendered famous by her travelling adventures in Turkey.[1] At the head of society was Sarah Jennings, wife of the Duke of Marlborough, a woman of great beauty and energy, but a coarse-spoken she-dragon, who made life very troublesome to her husband and children, to Queen Anne, and to everybody. Nor was there a lack of fully "emancipated" women, such as the Ladies Townshend, Oxford, Vane, Petersham, and others, who took care that the "chronique scandaleuse" should never be at a loss for materials. The corruption of high life thus furnished plenty of food for satire, but Methodism, introduced by Wesley and Whitfield, also found an entrance into society, though as a less welcome guest. Its influence, however, was unable to effect a sudden change in a society given to drinking, gambling and other fashionable vices. The great merit of the followers of Wesley and Whitfield was their unselfish devotion to the lower classes of the people, whose minds had been up to this time entirely neglected.

Science and literature were but little encouraged by the Court during this whole period. William III. took no part whatever in the intellectual life of Eng-

[1] "The Letters and other Works of the Right Honourable Lady Mary Wortley Montagu," 1803, 5 vols.

land. His heart was in Holland and he looked upon his government in England as a heavy duty, which, it must be confessed, he fulfilled most honourably. Queen Anne was of limited understanding; she preferred the scandal and small talk of her Court to literature. George I. was a Hanoverian country squire, only caring for material enjoyments. George II. was also indifferent to literature, and George III. had very peculiar notions on the subject. But English literature did not any longer require the encouragement of a Court; it had emancipated itself and become a power in the state, supported by the influential writings of men like Steele, Addison, and Johnson. The introduction of literature into society had also taken another form; the coffee-houses were no longer the chief centres of literary conversation, as they had been in Dryden's time. They were rivalled by assemblies attracted by the talents, wit, and beauty of some famous woman like Lady Mary Horsley Montagu, Mrs. Vesey, Mrs. Thrale, Mrs. Boscawen, and Mrs. Chapone, in imitation of the Parisian *bureaux d'esprit* of Madame du Deffand, Mademoiselle de l'Espinasse, and others, and there all questions relating to intellectual or literary life were discussed.

England contributed largely to the enfranchisement of science which began in the seventeenth century, and which was a natural product of the advancing civilization of Europe. The Frenchman Descartes may be considered as the father of modern philosophy; he entirely broke through the method practised up to his time, set aside all theological and philosophical premisses, and carried the human understanding back to its original sources. His system is a bold protest against everything that had been presented to the human mind as truth coming from without; it rests upon the principle of consciousness; and recognizing the opposition of mind and matter, of existence and thought, treats the annulment of this opposition as the problem of philosophy. Baruch Spinoza undertook to solve this problem by means of his grand pantheistic system, according to which everything partial and finite is absorbed by the infinitude of the Divine substance. But he was not quite successful in demonstrating the connexion between the Ideal and the Material, and the tree of modern philosophy, planted by Descartes, was now divided into two great branches, Idealism on the one hand and Realism (sensualism, materialism) on the other. Idealistic principles were developed in Germany by Leibnitz; the realistic, ending in France in the extreme materialism of the eighteenth century, first received a scientific foundation in England, in the seventeenth century, from John Locke, who was born in 1632, at Rusford, near Bristol, educated at Oxford, and by his travels, and involved in the party struggles of his time. He died at Oates, in Essex, in 1704. He trained his mind on the principles of Descartes, and published the results of his independent activity in his famous "Essay concerning the Human Understanding," in four books; the first edition appeared in 1689. His philosophy is nothing but a Theory of Perception, and may be summed up in the negative proposition that the mind possesses no innate ideas, and its corresponding affirmative that experience is the source of all the understanding and knowledge we possess. Locke's realism is strongly opposed to supernaturalism, and its consequences. In his other writings, especially in his three famous Letters on Tolerance, he drew the practical conclusions from the principles embodied in his chief work, and has by these greatly contributed to the free investigation and tolerance in matters of belief of later times. Locke's Philosophy of Experience, and the violent attacks that were directed against superstition by Lord Herbert of Cherbury, a contemporary of Lord Bacon, called forth a considerable number of more or less gifted assailants of the orthodoxy of the Church. They were called "Freethinkers," "Deists," and even Atheists, because they not only rejected the doctrine of the Triune God, but of a personal God altogether. The chief among these were Charles Blount (died 1693), John Toland (died 1722), Anthony Collins (died 1729), Thomas Woolston (died 1731), Peter Annet (died 1768), Matthew Tindal (died 1733), Thomas Chubb (died 1747), Thomas Morgan (1743), and the Scotchman David Hume (1711—1776), of whom we have still to speak as an historian.

The merit of their writings varies a good deal; Toland's "Christianity not Mysterious,"[2] and Hume's "Essays"[3] may be mentioned as the most important. Their endeavours to establish a *modus vivendi* between faith and knowledge, dogma and reason, called the clergy to arms and most of the freethinkers were severely persecuted. But their views, which were drawn up in an easy popular form, made proselytes among the middle classes. These views were also propagated among the upper classes by two members of the aristocracy, Anthony Ashley Cooper, Earl of Shaftesbury (1671—1713) and Henry St. John, Viscount Bolingbroke (1672—1751). Shaftesbury—not to be confounded with the celebrated party leader during the Restoration—was a keen observer of men and morals, but the style of his letters, and that of the essays in which he recommends a morality founded upon reason, is affected.[4] Bolingbroke, who played a notorious part in the politics of his time, was an accomplished man of the world, clear-sighted and clever in his capacity

[2] "Christianity not Mysterious, or a treatise showing there is nothing in the Gospel contrary to reason or above it, and that no Christian doctrine can be properly called a mysterie," 1696.
[3] "Essays Moral and Philosophical," 1740. "Essays on Human Understanding," 1741. "Essay on Miracles," 1750. "Natural History of Religion," 1755. "Philosophical Works," 1826.
[4] His chief work: "Characteristics of Men, Manners, Opinions, Times," 1773, 3 vols.

as a statesman, an author, and as a member of society. During his involuntary retirement from business, as the great enemy of Walpole, he wrote political pamphlets and popular philosophical works. The writings of Locke and Boyle had trained his scepticism, and it was he who first touched upon the most important problems in a tone of easy and graceful mockery—a style imitated by Voltaire and in which Bolingbroke became a master. His chief work, "Letters on the Study and Use of History," is of great merit on account of its critical disregard of all conventional traditions.[5] How powerfully science was influenced by the

[5] In the preface to his book, " The English Deists " (1853), the German Noack gives the following concise characteristic of their various views. " Toland stripped Christianity of its mysteries, which, he said, had only been a means of education and civilization. Collins acquired for the deists the name of " freethinkers," and refuted the ordinary proofs of the prophecies and miracles which are given in support of supernatural revelation. Shaftesbury considered the chief and eternal truth of Christianity to consist in morality, upon which happiness is eternally and necessarily dependent. Woolston and Annet joined Tindal in his refutation of prophecies and miracles. Tindal, the great apostle of the deists, declared Christianity to be as old as the creation and identical with the natural religion of reason, consisting in the fulfilment of our duties towards God and man. Chubb tried to prove this to be the express teaching of Christ, while Morgan applied the deistic principle to the Old Testament, and Bolingbroke introduced it among the cultivated classes. Hume's scepticism brings the deistic development of England to a close by declaring the proof of a divine revelation an impossibility and by calling faith itself a miracle opposed to and contradicted by reason."

principles of modern philosophy is proved by the great achievements of Isaac Newton (1642—1727). Having discovered the law of gravitation his genius roamed over all the various fields of natural science and drew the dark veil from the laws of Nature.[6]

Doubt is the parent of inquiry, and the investigation of tradition the origin of historical science. In England history, entering the paths traced by the realism of Locke and the scepticism of Bolingbroke and Hume, shone with extraordinary lustre in the second half of the eighteenth century. Hume himself turned from the investigation of theology to that of history, and the immense success of his history of the Stuarts (1754), encouraged him to write the history of England under the Tudors, the Plantagenets, the Normans, Saxons, and Britons, and thus gradually he completed his great national work the " History of Great Britain," which is carried down from the earlier times to the year 1688. It still occupies a chief place among English histories, and rightly so, for it is based on the careful study of original sources, the materials are fully mastered and clearly developed, and due attention is paid to the lessons history teaches ; persons and times are represented from an impartial point of view on the whole, and the style is fascinating throughout.

Hume found a rival in his countryman William Robertson (1721—1793), who ably relates the

---

[6] " Nature and nature's laws lay hid in night ;
God said : ' Let Newton be !' and all was light."—Pope.

history of Scotland, as well as that of America, and the history of Charles V.[7]

Amongst the English historians of this time, who chose Ancient History for the subject of their study, must be mentioned William Mitford, who wrote the "History of Greece," and Adam Ferguson, who wrote the "History of the Progress and Termination of the Roman Republic." But both are thrown into the shade by Edward Gibbon whose famous " History of the Decline and Fall of the Roman Empire " is not only the crowning work of English historiography, but of that of the eighteenth century as a whole. Gibbon was born at Putney, in Surrey, April 27th, 1737, and died in London in 1794. When twenty-seven years of age, in 1764, he undertook a journey to Rome and there made up his mind to write his great work.[8] The first volume of it appeared in 1776, the second and third in 1781, and the last in 1788. Whatever may be said against Gibbon's religious views,[9] his work must be considered as one of the greatest triumphs

---

[7] "History of Scotland during the reigns of the Queen Mary and of King James VI.," 1759. "History of Charles V.," 1769. "History of America," 1777. Besides Hume and Robertson, and immediately after them, the histories of England, Scotland, and Ireland were investigated by Smollet, John Dalrymple, David Dalrymple, Henry, Macpherson, Stuart, Pinkerton, and Laing.

[8] His memoirs are contained in his "Miscellaneous Works," 1796.

[9] Concerning Gibbon's relation to Christianity, compare the chapters xv., xvi., xxi., and xlvii. of his work.

of the Art and Science of History. William Roscoe is a good biographer in his histories of the Medici,[1] and Horace Walpole is to be distinguished among the memoir-writers of that time. In his memoirs of the times of George II. and III., as well as in his letters to his friend Mann, which furnish a lively picture of the society of that time, he regards history from the point of view of a clever talker—and this is indeed what Walpole was.[2]

The poetry of this period has been characterized in the beginning of this chapter. On the whole it was the poetry of the learned for the learned; it was impregnated by the spirit of the time—by reason, scepticism, and criticism—and tried to compensate by a refined poetical form for what it lacked of truly poetical elements. Mythological images were its favourite ornaments, and the history and literature of antiquity its continual resource, for it was wanting in original and innate power. It was cultivated by many, but it would be useless to enumerate their names.

The poet of the epoch was Alexander Pope, born in London in May 1688. He was a weakly boy, and reading early became his chief amusement and pleasure; his insignificant and deformed figure, which was a source of much grief to his not inconsiderable vanity, made him prefer a literary career to any other. He was a Roman Catholic and

---

[1] "The Life of Lorenzo de Medici," 1795. "The Life of Leo X.," 1803.
[2] Memoirs, 1822. Letters to Sir Horace Mann, 1832.

received his education partly in the seminary at Twyford, and partly from private tutors. He began very early to write verses and was only twelve years of age when he composed his "Ode on Solitude." He formed his style upon that of the Italian and French poets, and among English authors Spenser, Waller, and Dryden were his models. When sixteen years of age he wrote his "Pastorals;" these procured admittance for him into those exclusive circles of high life for whose applause he cared so much. A didactic poem, "An Essay on Criticism" (1709), increased his reputation. Two years later he wrote the beautiful elegy "On an Unfortunate Lady," inspired by the suicide of a young girl who had been betrayed; this is the most touching of all his poems. Of much less value is his famous "Ode on St. Cecilia's Day," meant to rival that of Dryden, and an allegorical poem, "The Temple of Fame," which reminds us of Petrarch, Chaucer, and Spenser, but to the disadvantage of the imitator. Soon after this he wrote his comic epic "The Rape of the Lock" (1711), which was most strikingly adapted to the taste of his contemporaries.

The somewhat too practical gallantry of a certain Lord Petre, who cut off one of the much admired curls of the beautiful Miss Arabella Fermor, was the incident on which Pope founded his poem. It was read with delight. At its first appearance it only consisted of two cantos, but was afterwards spun out into five. "The Rape of the Lock" is indeed a pretty composition in Pope's most finished and popular style; it has also the merit of being playful and humorous without containing any ambiguities or obscenities. Not only this poem but all Pope's writings tended to introduce a more decorous tone into literature after the lawlessness of the Restoration, and no common talent was required to accomplish such a change successfully.

In 1713 he wrote "Windsor Forest," a poetical description of nature, in which the episode "Lodona" is particularly tender; an elegy, "From Eloisa to Abelard;" and then he began his translation of "Homer." The "Iliad" appeared in 1715 —1720, the "Odyssey" in 1725. Pope became a rich man by this translation; it is in verse, and is valued even in our days, though it is far from a truthful rendering of the greatest of all great poets. Nor is Pope's edition of Shakespeare's works a success. The sphere in which Homer and Shakespeare shone could not be Pope's. He had besides many weak points which laid him open to the attacks of his adversaries. But he did not allow any one to attack his literary talent with impunity, and his satire the "Dunciad," published in 1729, dealt a sharp thrust to all who had dared do so. The fruit of Pope's friendship with Lord Bolingbroke is a famous didactic poem on the nature and destination of man, the "Essay on Man," which appeared in 1732—1734, in four epistles. The first—another proof of Pope's brilliant versification—treats of the nature and position of man with regard to the world; the second considers man as an individual, the third as a member of society, the fourth develops his claims to happiness and defines the nature of that happiness. All this is discussed in a mild and persuasive manner, according to the principles of deistic rationalism, and with due regard to the views of the world on the subject. This philosophy in verse speaks much of God and of virtue, but it is decidedly a philosophy of egotism. The service of God and the good of humanity are not to be the aim and end of life, but our own personal comfort is to be that object, and therefore sacrifice and examination of self are considered foolish. The "Essay on Man" was attacked by the orthodox party; Pope answered by his "Universal Prayer," and later on by his "Moral Essays," in four poetical epistles which, however, are only variations on the "Essay on Man." His antagonists did not succeed in ruining his position in those circles for whose applause alone he cared. He died in the full enjoyment of his fame, in May 1744, at the age of fifty-six and was buried at his favourite country seat at Twickenham.[3]

We have before said that this whole period is void all originality and power in matters of poetry, but there was no lack of talented persons who cultivated the formal and conventional poetry of the time, such as Philips and Blair, who wrote didactic poems; Parnell, Collins, and Penrose,

[3] "Works," ed. by Warburton, 1751, 9 vols.; by Warton, 1797; by Bowles, 1806.

lyrics; Tickell and Shenstone, elegies; Churchill, satires; and many others who rank as minor poets. John Gray (born 1688) distinguished himself by his Fables by idylls; such as "The Shepherd's Week," and by descriptive poems; such as " Rural Sports;" he also wrote the famous " Beggars' Opera," in 1727. Matthew Prior (1664—1741) is tedious in his serious didactic poem " Solomon," but more pleasing in his humorous " Alma," which discusses the question of the seat of the human soul. There is a good deal more wit and philosophy in his four poetical tales, " The Ladle," " Protogenes and Apelles," " Paolo Purgenti," and " Hans Carvel." Prior's brightness and vivacity form a great contrast to the grave melancholy of Edward Young (1681 —1765), who first became famous by his satires which appeared separately, and which he afterwards collected under the title of " Love of Fame " (1728); but his best work is his moral poem, " The Complaint, or Night Thoughts," which he wrote in a fit of wild melancholy.

These poetical contemplations, which appeared in 1741, mark a great turning-point in the manner of thought of English society. They were diametrically opposed to the fashionable philosophy of Pope and Bolingbroke : in them the Germanic seriousness of the English mind for the first time broke through the superficial culture of the French school. The language of the poem is also Germanic; in lofty pathos it laments the transitory nature of all things earthly.

It has been said above that the literature of England had become at this time an independent power. Such a power required organs for its diffusion, and those organs were supplied by the famous weekly periodicals of the eighteenth century, whose place is occupied in our time by the different "Reviews." These literary and critical periodicals contained papers on the most varied subjects, and have vastly contributed to extend the sphere of mental culture; but they did not rise above the fashion of the times as regards literature, poetry, and philosophy. Richard Steele (1671—1729), called "Dicky" by his friends, a clever pamphleteer, an adventurer in politics and literature, was the first who thought of publishing a periodical which was to contain news from foreign countries, accounts of the theatres, summaries of the conversations at the literary coffee-houses, characteristics of morals and manners, and anecdotes of the day. This periodical was to appear on the days on which the post left London for the various counties. According to this plan Steele founded the "Tatler" in 1709. Soon afterwards he obtained the assistance of Addison in publishing the "Spectator," which took the place of the "Tatler," and became the favourite paper of that kind, upwards of 20,000 copies being required. Steele received the honour of knighthood on the accession of George I. Joseph Addison (1672—1719) became famous while at Magdalen College, Oxford, by his elegant Latin verses and then by the description of his journey to Italy. His poem on the battle of Blenheim (1704) made his fortune. He was commissioned by the Tories to write on this subject, though Addison was himself a Whig. His poem was nothing but an account of the battle in rhyme, but the very absence of fancy caused it to be admired by many, and the author was brilliantly rewarded by the Government with a pension of 200*l*. Addison's poetry in general is rhetorical prose in verse; a striking proof of this is his tragedy "Cato." It was performed at Drury Lane in 1713, and the immense applause it called forth bore witness to the deterioration of dramatic taste in the native country of Shakespeare.

As a prose writer Addison really deserved the respect and admiration of his contemporaries. His essays are better than any that had previously been written, his diction is easy, clear, and graceful; his wit is good-humoured and refined. Addison was very humane, and he saw not only the ridiculous but also the noble side of human nature. The plan of the "Spectator" was well imagined. The "Spectator," an eager observer of men and things, a student of the Temple, a clergyman, a soldier, a merchant, an old country baronet, and an old libertine, form a club in which the most various subjects are discussed. The description of the members of the club is in itself charming, an excellent picture from real life. Steele and Addison were also joint editors of the "Guardian," and each wrote some political paper, which, however, were soon discontinued as well as the literary "Guardian." [4]

In opposition to the French urbanity of Addison's *esprit*, two thoroughly English characters, Jonathan Swift and Samuel Johnson, represent the native English temper. Swift and Johnson were as staunch Tories as Steele and Addison were steadfast Whigs. Swift, in opposition to Addison's periodicals, published his " Examiner." Johnson's " Rambler," which appeared in 1750—1752, is considered as much a standard work as the " Spectator." Swift has been compared to a rosebud whose calix was changed into thorns by unfavourable circumstances. But it would be difficult to discover anything of the nature of a rose in Swift's writings ; still less in his life, which consumed itself in bitterness and selfishness and ended in madness. No, Swift was unquestionably a thorn, a thorn in the flesh to all religious, political, and literary pedantry and indolence. Contradiction was the essence of his nature, and unsparing satire the tendency of his talent ; wherever he attempts to be serious or pathetic he becomes pompous and stilted, as in his poetical tale " Cadenus and Vanessa " which, under a flimsy disguise, treats of one of his own two famous love-affairs. Swift was

[4] "Works of Joseph Addison," ed. by Hurd, 1811, 6 vols. Macaulay's Essay on Addison is written in his most beautiful style, but his Whig principles have caused him to be too much of a panegyrist. Addison was the first professional author who rose so high as to be made Secretary of State.

not at home in the region of the ideal. As a pamphleteer, a political and theological satirist, he aimed to be popular, but is often vulgar. His most witty satire is the "Tale of a Tub" (1704), in which he attacks with great bitterness the priesthood of the Roman Catholic, Lutheran, and Calvinistic churches. "The Battle of the Books,"[5] which is added to the "Tale of a Tub," is a very amusing satire on the philological and æsthetic pedantry of the time. But Swift's European reputation rests chiefly on his satirical novel, "Gulliver's Travels,"[6] in which the author represents the public and social life in England and France. The work is full of gigantic caricatures and is profoundly cynical; it has been translated into all languages and has even been changed into a story-book for children; but the real meaning of its satire can only be rightly understood by those who are intimately acquainted with the persons and state of society of the author's time.[7]

Johnson, after the publication of his "Rambler" and of his famous "Dictionary,"[8] occupied a position like that which had belonged to Dryden;

[5] An account of a battle between the ancient and modern books in St. James's library.

[6] Lemuel Gulliver's travels into several remote nations of the world, 1727.

[7] "Works, with a life of the author, and notes," edited by Scott, 1815, 19 vols.

[8] "Dictionary of the English language: in which the words are deduced from their originals and illustrated in their different significations by examples of the best writers;

he presided over the literary circle assembled at Mrs. Thrale's house and wielded his critical sceptre with sublime rudeness. He presented "common-sense" in the most prosaic sense of the word. His edition of Shakespeare's works was not more successful than Pope's. His Satires, "London" (1749) and "The Vanity of Human Wishes" (1749), as well as his didactic novel, the "History of Rasselas," are sensible and well-written, but there is an entire absence of poetry in them. At the age of seventy he undertook to write an important work, "The Lives of the most eminent English Poets." [9]

On the whole English aristocratic society at the time of the two first Georges preferred the refinement of French philosophy, and the language of Voltaire, Bolingbroke, and Pope, to the views and language of Swift or Johnson. A remarkable document illustrative of the tone and views of the great world are the "Letters" which the well-known statesman, Philip Dormer Stanhope, Earl of Chesterfield (1694—1773) wrote to his son Philip Stanhope, with the view of forming him into a courtier, statesman, and man of the world. The moral of Chesterfield's instructions how to get on

---

to which are prefixed a history of the language and an English grammar," 1755, 2 vols. fol.

[9] Johnson's own life was written by his friend Boswell in two stout quarto volumes. It is the work of an almost idolatrous admirer, but otherwise a rich mine of information as to the state of English society at that time.

in the world is shortly this : almost everything is allowable, but it must be done in a becoming manner. Before these letters were published, other epistles of a very different kind were absorbing the attention of the public. During the years 1769—1773 a series of letters appeared in the "Public Advertiser" written with Swift's polemical bitterness, and giving proofs of the unknown author's intimate acquaintance with the affairs and the leading ministers of state. They were signed "Junius" and the impenetrable secrecy which the author succeeded in maintaining tended to heighten the effect they produced. "Junius" criticized the whole administration more deeply and severely than was ever done before or since this time. His master-stroke is the letter to George III., dated December 19th, 1769. Rarely, if ever, has a king been told the truth in such a manner.[1]

[1] Letters of Junius, complete edition, 1812. The secret of the authorship seems to have been discovered by Macaulay, who asserts—in his Essay on Warren Hastings—that Junius could not have been anybody else but Philip Francis. The proofs he gives for his assertion appear to us to be convincing. Byron in his "Vision of Judgment" makes Junius appear as a witness against George III., and insinuates the mystery surrounding that great pamphleteer in the following manner :
"The shadow came—a tall, thin, greyhair'd figure,
  That looked as it had been a shade on earth ;
  Quick in its motions, with an air of vigour,
  But naught to mark its breeding or its birth :
  Now it waxed little, then again grew bigger,
  With now an air of gloom or savage mirth ;
  But as you gazed upon its features, they
Changed every instant—to *what*, none could say.

Before closing this period we have still to glance over a broad field of the literary productions of this time, that of Novel-writing. It has been said on a former occasion that in Queen Elizabeth's time the chivalrous novels of the middle ages were supplanted by the Arcadian pastoral novels, and that these had to give way to those of gallantry and adventures, of allegories and satires, during the period of the Restoration. These varieties were imitations from foreign models. Even novels of adventures in travel, such as Daniel Defoe's famous " Robinson Crusoe " (1709), and Swift's " Gulliver's Travels," were imitations, especially of Greek novels of the kind. But now a thorough change was taking place in this respect, and English literature produced novels which became in their turn models for continental writers. The beginning of these original compositions must undoubtedly be traced back to the " Spectator," which first sought the materials for novelistic delineations in the reality of natural English life. Thirty years later the English popular novel was founded by Samuel Richardson (1689—1761) who from a printer had risen to be an author. His first production was " Pamela," which was succeeded by " Clarissa Harlowe " and the " History of Sir Charles Grandison." He introduced the epistolary style into novels, and found a very grateful public. He started from a didactic point of view, and represented men as they ought to be within the social circumstances of the England of his time. His fluency is extraordinary, but his composition is monotonous. In " Pamela," the ideal virtue of the heroine is victorious over the seducing arts of the libertine who pursues her, and accomplishes the miracle of converting him. In " Clarissa Harlowe " the same fiction is brought to a negative ending, as the virtuous heroine at last falls a victim to the brutality of Lovelace. " Sir Charles Grandison " is the ideal of a perfect gentleman, but this ideal is only a " faultless monster." As has been wittily remarked, the situation in which he is placed, that of having to choose between two sisters of equal beauty, virtue, and devotion to him, reminds one of Buridan's ass, who had to choose between two bundles of hay. Richardson has been much over-valued by his contemporaries ; Rousseau placed him on a par with Homer![2] Henry Fielding (1707—1754), whose first publication was " Joseph Andrews," a novel (1740). His second, " Jonathan Wild," in which he indulges the taste of his countrymen for stories of thieves and highwaymen, owes his literary importance to his famous novel " Tom Jones, or The History of a Foundling." This excellent work is generally regarded exclusively as a comic novel, but wrongly so, for " Tom Jones " is as much serious as comic. It is the first realistic, national, popular novel of English literature. The author represents men as they are,

[2] Diderot expresses himself no less enthusiastically ; he places Richardson on a par with Moses, Sophocles, and Euripides—a strange juxtaposition. D'Israeli has called Richardson the Shakespeare of prose-writers.

and departs widely from the insipid idealism of Richardson, who portrays nothing but the most impossible perfection or the direst corruption. Fielding represents the characters and circumstances of real life in firm, telling outlines, and the conceptions of his plot and the manner in which he carries it out are equally masterly. It is true, the ideal side of human nature receives little attention; but this want is fully compensated by the deep insight the book gives us into the manners and morals of the time. We also meet with delineations of real life in the novels of Frances Burney (Madame D'Arblay, 1752—1840), in "Evelina," "Cecilia," and "Camilla;" she describes real men and real passions, and she is the first female writer in English literature who undertook such a task. It was only after she had set the example that other ladies dared to write on this subject, which had until then been considered unsuitable for them.

Fielding's rival in public favour was Tobias Smollett (1721—1771) whose chief novels are "Roderick Random," "Peregrine Pickle," and "Humphrey Clinker." He is full of wit and humour, but his humour is too broad and occasionally rather coarse. Smollett, however, is not only comic, he also possesses wonderful power for the representation of the pathetic and the horrible. The most original and the most carefully written of his novels is "Humphrey Clinker;" its leading idea is the well-known moral axiom, that the happiness of mankind does not depend so much on outward circumstances as on the qualities of the heart and mind.

Extremes are found in close connexion in literature as elsewhere: beside Smollett, who goes to the utmost limits of realistic humour, we find Laurence Sterne as the representative of the most extreme idealistic humour. Sterne is the humorist par excellence. Material objects fall entirely out of view before his reflection, which, coming from a mind overflowing with love, makes him burst into smiles and tears at the same moment. His famous novel, "Tristram Shandy" (1759), is not really a novel; the thin thread of the story is only used to connect innumerable bursts of humour, his only plan is to have no plan; the most significant things are treated as a joke and trifles with the greatest importance. The action in "Tristram Shandy" is very poor, but Sterne's humour is inexhaustible; he is, however, not very particular in regard to decorum. A year before Sterne's death appeared his famous "Sentimental Journey through France and Italy," the journal of a humorist who describes his travels in a very different manner from other people. The book is a product of the sentimentalism which infected the upper classes of that time; it is for England what Goethe's "Sorrows of Werther" were for Germany, the most remarkable illustration of a social sickliness produced by satiety and inactivity.

Another of the great English novel-writers of

the eighteenth century is Oliver Goldsmith (1728—1774). He was not only a poet, but also a popular historian, and his histories of England, Greece, and Rome are not without merit; that he is still greater as a critic is proved by his collection of "Essays." His prose and verse are classical. His plays belong to the standard drama, the two poems, "The Traveller" and "The Deserted Village," are perhaps the best loved of all. The latter shows the contrast between the over-refinement of civilization, and the peace of more natural country life. In it Goldsmith decidedly outstripped his time and entered on the succeeding period of English literature. His famous idyllic novel "The Vicar of Wakefield," which has been translated into every language, is another proof that Goldsmith would have nothing to do with Pope's poetry of reason.

Two other kinds of novels have still to be mentioned, before coming to later developments of that branch of literature. In the eighteenth century we meet with novels whose tendency is to reform society, and others in which a revival of the romance of the middle ages is attempted. William Godwin (1756—1836), in his novel "The Adventures of Caleb Williams" (1794), unites a faithful delineation of manners and morals with the most intimate knowledge of the human heart, with the

[3] John Forster's "Life and Times of Oliver Goldsmith" (1854) is one of the best literary biographies in English literature.

intention of showing society to itself as in a mirror, and especially of throwing a bright light on the defects of the administration of justice in his country. There is extraordinary force in the description of the pangs of conscience endured by the high-bred Falkland, whose innocent secretary, Caleb Williams, is threatened with death for a crime committed by his master. The tendency of the novel is that of a revolutionary age, a struggle against existing facts. The same tendency is traceable in the novels of Miss Edgworth, though in a milder form, and combined with moral and religious views. The revival of romance led to unsuccessful attempts. The great turning-point of universal history, the epoch of the Revolution and Restoration, had to be passed, before poetry could again feel at home in the charmed scenes of knighthood and times long past. As yet the false notion prevailed that the romantic and the horrible were identical. In this spirit Horace Walpole wrote his novel "The Castle of Otranto" (1764), which is intended to excite a shudder, but whose incidents —an enormous helmet in which the hero of the novel is locked up, a statue whose nose drops blood, a sword that can only be lifted by the combined strength of a hundred men, &c.—only raise a sceptical smile. Ann Radcliffe (1764—1823) handled the horrible with greater dexterity in her novels; she worked upon the excitement of the coarsest sensations of the mind, and for some time her books found an immense number of readers.[4] In the novel "The Monk" (1795), by the highly gifted Matthew Gregory Lewis (1773—1818), Mrs. Radcliffe's characteristics have been exaggerated into a convulsive climax of horrors.[5] Charles Robert Maturin in his powerful romances, "Melmoth, the Wanderer," and "Bertram," attempted even to outdo Lewis. And thus we see the spirit of romance deteriorating sadly almost as soon as it had been revived.

[4] The three favourites were : "The Romance of the Forest," 1791 ; "The Mysteries of Udolpho," 1794 ; and "The Italian," 1797.

[5] Byron, in his journal of Dec. 6th, 1813, condemned "The Monk" in the following terms: "These descriptions ought to have been written by Tiberius at Caprea ; they are forced —the 'philtered' ideas of a jaded voluptuary. It is to me inconceivable how they could have been composed by a man of only twenty—his age when he wrote them. They have no nature—all the sour cream of cantharides."

CHAPTER X.

A new life—Its forerunners : Thomson, Glover, Gray, Chatterton, Cowper—Macpherson's "Ossian"—Percy's "Reliques"—Revival of Shakespeare's plays : Garrick, Kemble, Mrs. Siddons—The theatre : Lillo, Foote, Sheridan— The most brilliant period of parliamentary eloquence : Pitt, Burke, Sheridan, Fox, the younger Pitt, Grattan— Scotch popular poetry : Burns, and his successors—The transition from the eighteenth to the nineteenth century: from the poetry of reason to that of romantic sentiment —Crabbe, Montgomery, Rogers, Campbell.

IN the great battle between ancient and modern times, which was fought during the eighteenth century, England gradually acquired her position as the first of the great powers of the world. The wars of the Spanish and Austrian Succession had weakened the two great absolute monarchies of the Continent, France and Austria, while they had increased the public consideration for constitutional England, which for a century to come exercised a decisive influence on the politics of Europe. Absolute princes indeed tried their best to annihilate this influence. In the Seven Years' War absolute France and absolute Russia formed a coalition with the very evident purpose of uprooting

Protestanism by destroying its representative, aspiring Prussia, and thus robbing England of her constitutional ally. But the genius of Frederick the Great and the gold of England frustrated this plan. Pitt, the "Great Commoner," whose administration gave such a glorious impulse to the power of England, assisted Prussia with English gold, and raised the English fleet to a state of such efficiency that France and Spain were kept in subjection, and the English flag waved triumphant in the most distant parts of the world. At the same time the advantages of a constitutional government were demonstrated by England, which prospered in spite of her kings. Neither George II. or III. were able or willing to give such an impulse to English energy, and when George III., in the commencement of his reign, outstripped the limits of his constitutional rights by interfering in politics, an ominous change took place in them. The Peace of Paris (1763), brought about by the ministry of the favourite Bute, was not only a breach with Pitt's system, but also a change to that policy which under Grenville and North opposed the independence of the American Colonies, and under the younger Pitt the movement of the French Revolution, and which eventually, under Castlereagh, culminated in a reaction.

But, during the time under consideration, the immense excitement of the Continental revolutionary wars had not yet subsided in England. Although George III. was, as the poet represents him, an antagonist of liberty,[1] public opinion was true to the spirit of the century, and fully entered into its phases of development. Rousseau, the inspired advocate of Nature and of Liberty, who opposed the sceptical egotism of Voltaire and his followers,[2] gained numerous proselytes in England. Then also began a warfare against everything affected and artificial, both in life and literature, and amidst the noisy party struggles raised by the demand of the American Colonies for independence, a great reformation in literature set in. The declaration of American Independence indeed reminded the English aristocracy of the results which liberal ideas might produce, and they accordingly gave them up; but some amongst them remained steadfast adherents to the reformatory principles, and even the terrors of the French Revolution could not prejudice them against the idea of nature and liberty. In literature this idea had been powerful enough to open the eyes of the nation to the want of genial life in Dryden's and Pope's poetry of reason. The verdure and wild flowers of a new spring began to overgrow the stiff garden-cultivation. Long-forgotten sources of true poetry were resorted to

[1] " He ever warr'd with freedom and the free :
   Nations as men, home subjects, foreign foes,
   So that they utter'd the word ' Liberty !'
   Found George III. their first opponent. . . ."
                    Byron : "A Vision of Judgment."
[2] " La nouvelle Heloïse," 1759 ; " Contrat Social," and " Émile," 1762.

for the nourishment of the growing germ, and a national pulse again began to beat in English literature which had for so long done homage to the French fashion.

Forerunners of this new life were not wanting. We have seen how, in the early part of the eighteenth century, opposition had already been made against the conventional style of literature. All the great novel-writers, beginning with Richardson, as well as Young and Goldsmith, may be placed in the ranks of this opposition. To these we may add James Thomson (1700—1784), Richard Glover (1712—1785), Thomas Gray (1716—1771), Thomas Chatterton (1752—1770), and William Cowper (1731—1800).

Thomson first attempted to write descriptive—didactic poetry,[3] and allegories in imitation of Spenser;[4] he was less successful in his tragedies. His first work remained his best, the poem "The Seasons," is written in blank verse. His poetical description of nature is faithful and thus denotes great progress; the work still abounds with mythological figures and images, but they do not spoil it. Passing through the circle of the Seasons the poet gracefully points out the mutual relations between the life of nature and the life of man; his descriptions of nature are finest where he is a true son of the north, rendering the changes which take place in the air and on the earth at the passage

---

[3] "Upon Liberty."
[4] "The Castle of Indolence."

from autumn into winter, and of winter into spring.[5] Thomson also is the author of the famous national hymn "Rule Britannia."

Glover's chief merit resides in two epic poems. In one of these, "Leonidas," he attempts to give an epic form to a great historical event, the battle of Thermopylæ, without making use of the marvellous; its serious and manly tone forms a pleasant contrast to the smooth ornamental poetry of those days. The same may be said of his beautiful ballad, "Admiral Hosier's Ghost," which is a thoroughly national composition.

Gray's letters about Italy are written in a charmingly natural style. His poems fill one small volume, but a very important one. His odes are noble inspirations, and his far-famed "Elegy written in a Country Churchyard" is a most splendid proof that a new life was beginning for English literature. Gray's beautiful elegy is void of all false sentiment, but full of true and deep feeling, and the impulse it gave to English poetry may be traced even in the works of the Lake poets. The name of Chatterton recalls one of the saddest events in the history of

[5] Compare book i., Spring, the passage :—
"The north-east spends his rage; he now shut up
Within his iron cave, th' effusive south
Warms the wide air," &c.
And book iv., Winter, the passage :—
"When from the pallid sky the sun descends,
With many a spot, that o'er his gloomy orb
Uncertain wanders, stain'd; red fiery streaks
Begin to flush around," &c.

English literature. This "prodigy," as Wordsworth called him, poisoned himself because he was starving, after vain appeals to the heartless Horace Walpole, to save his genius from the most profound distress. Chatterton wrote his poems in antiquated language and published them under the name of Rowley, supposed to be an old monk. His genius was capable of great sweetness and tenderness, but it shows to greatest advantage where he gives a loose rein to his powers. His description of the battle of Hastings is wildly magnificent, and his ballad "Dethe of Sir Charles Bawdin" ranks with the finest heroic lays of the old English and Scotch ballads.

Cowper largely contributed to restore true feeling and a natural style to the poetry of his country. He did this in the quiet manner peculiar to him and was all the more successful. Bad health and disappointed hopes strengthened the religion of his soul, and a deep religious feeling is the characteristic note of his poetry, which does not prevent him from enjoying fun, or from being a devoted patriot. He first published a volume of poems (1782) whose contents are indicated by the titles: Table-talk—Progress of Error—Truth—Expostulation—Hope—Charity—Conversation—Retirement. Two years later appeared his chief work "The Task."[6] There is a wonderful variety

[6] The peculiar title originated in a lady-friend's asking the poet for a poem in blank verse on the subject of the "sofa." Cowper accomplished this task by writing one of the best

of objects and of thought in this poem; it may be called a universal composition, for the poet gathers up all the phenomena of life, nature, and society, and the colours with which he paints the bright and the dark sides of all things are as brilliant as they are true.[7] His humorous talent is proved by his ballad, "The diverting History of John Gilpin." These amusing adventures of a respectable London citizen are pleasantly familiar to young and old.

The works of men like Thomson, Gray, Chatterton, and Cowper could not but tend to undermine the dominion of French taste in England, but its fall was also hastened from another quarter, though in a less direct manner. The national romance, banished from the literary coffee-houses and drawing-rooms of London, had gathered new strength on the hills of Westmoreland, in the

---

didactic poems in existence. Southey seems to me to have judged Cowper's poem in the best and most concise manner: "'The Task,' was at once descriptive, moral, and satirical. The descriptive parts everywhere bore evidence of a thoughtful mind and a gentle spirit, as well as of an observant eye; and the moral sentiment which pervaded them gave a charm in which descriptive poetry is often found wanting. The best didactic poems, when compared with 'The Task' are like formal gardens in comparison with woodland scenery."

[7] Some of the most famous lines of the "Task" are those comparing the country to the town, at the close of the first canto:
"God made the country, and man made the town," &c.
and in the second canto, the address to England, beginning:
"England, with all thy faults I love thee still."

highlands of Scotland, and in the vales of Ireland, and reappeared now that the public mind began to be more and more dissatisfied with the poetry of Pope. But the romantic muse was still distrustful of the times and hid herself behind a mask at her first reappearance; in other words, a literary imposture of the most extraordinary kind first turned the public attention to the treasures of the old national poetry. A Scotch scholar named James Macpherson (1713—1796) began to publish fragments of poems of an epic-elegiac character which he gave out to be translations from the Gaelic, fragments from the Songs of Ossian, son of Fingal, who was said to have lived in the Scotch highlands in the fourth century. The matter created a great sensation and a learned feud resulted from it with numberless arguments for and against the authenticity. It has now been decided that Macpherson's " Ossian " was indeed not genuine, for its author, though he made use of the old Gaelic national poetry, had transformed it so arbitrarily that it was not to be recognized. So soon as the public was convinced of the great deception, the great admiration for Ossian's songs which had been aroused in England and Germany, and even in France and Italy, abated. So long as the halo of antiquity surrounded these poems they met with immoderate veneration, but when their author was known to be a simple Scotch scholar instead of a mythical prince of poets, they were most unsparingly criticized. Still Macpherson's "Ossian" is a decided proof of poetical inspiration. There is a want of epic formation, everything is nebulous; figures and events glide past like shadows, and the story loses itself in a sentimental description of nature. But this description has a sweet and melancholy charm; the soul is tuned to compassion by the gentle complaint at the fall of an heroic age which is shown to us in shadowy outlines, and the ear revels in the soft flute-like rhythm.[8]

The " Reliques of Ancient English Poetry," published in 1765 by Bishop Thomas Percy, produced a purer and more lasting effect than Macpherson's " Ossian." They are the fruit of the industry of a loving and careful collector, and proved to every susceptible mind that the essence of poetry is not to be found in formalism, and in sober reflection, but in true and strong feelings. In Percy's " Reliques " we again meet with undisguised nature, with simple feeling, and with energetic action; they are the poetic reflection of an age of national heroes and whose traditions are closely interwoven with English thought and feeling. Hence the powerful and rapid influence these ancient relics of minstrelsy acquired in England and Scotland, an influence which may be traced in the development of English poetry down to our own days.

[8] Especially beautiful are " The songs of Selma," which Goethe has rendered as beautifully in " Werther's Leiden :" " Star of descending night ! fair is thy light in the west ! thou liftest thy unshorn head from the cloud: thy steps are stately on the hill," &c.

The theatrical revival of Shakespeare's plays also belongs to this time of literary reform. The comparatively excellent edition of them by Lewis Theobald in 1733, paved the old master's way to a stage from which the hollow declamations of the French school had driven him. An actor of genius, David Garrick (1716—1779), presented to the English public a series of Shakespearean characters, and in such a manner that it was easy to feel the difference between these undying creations of poetical genius, and the plays composed on French models. Garrick indeed treated Shakespeare's plays very arbitrarily, leaving out, condensing, and altering freely; but if his undertaking was to be successful, and if he wanted to create sympathy for Shakespeare's genius, he had to consider the perverted taste of his contemporaries ; and he was successful.

It remained for a later time, and for the æsthetics of the German school of art, to show to England and to the whole civilized world what a poet Shakespeare really was. Meanwhile the public interest in the poet increased so rapidly, that under Garrick's management a Shakespearean Jubilee was enthusiastically celebrated at Stratford-on-Avon in September 1769 ; but yet the criterion by which the great master was judged was that of his correctness in those rules of artistic composition which had been formulated in the age of Queen Anne. Old Ben Jonson had said of Shakespeare that he was the poet of nature *par excellence*, but a mere bungler in artistic composition ; and the same criticism was now repeated by Samuel Johnson, the highest critical authority of the century. This was believed, and Shakespeare's influence on the English stage remained insignificant for a time. But matters changed towards the close of the century, when German literature and German criticism became known in England, when Garrick's great successor, John Philip Kemble, at the head of Drury Lane Theatre, revived the representation of the masterpieces of the national stage, and his sister, Mistress Siddons, the greatest tragic actress England ever had, made her majestic beauty and her splendid talent shine through the characters of Shakespearean heroines. Meanwhile the playgoing public were content with dramas of very doubtful value. The London goldsmith George Lillo (died 1739) had introduced into England the so-called tragedy of private life, meant to touch and to produce tears; this, and French melodramas and vaudevilles, long remained in favour. Satirical farces next came into fashion; these were taken from the every-day life of London society by Garrick's rival, the actor Samuel Foote (died 1777). Many of Foote's jokes are dubious and frivolous, but on the whole a much more decorous tone began to pervade the upper classes, owing to the influence of George III.'s love of refinement and great propriety.

Richard Brinsley Sheridan reintroduced a more elevated style into the comic drama. As a writer of comedy he may be compared to Congreve, but to

Congreve purified. Sheridan is quite his equal in wit and humour, in accurate observation and comic power. His comedy "The Rivals" was first placed upon the stage (1775), then, amidst increasing applause, the farce "St. Patrick's Day," the comic opera "The Duenna," in the year 1777 the comedy "The School for Scandal," and, soon after, the farce "The Critic." The "School for Scandal" and the beautiful "Monody on the memory of Garrick" (1779) are Sheridan's best poetical productions. "The School for Scandal" will always rank as a standard comedy, and all future generations in England will be amused by Lady Teazle and Lady Sneerwell.

The name of Sheridan also recalls the most brilliant period of the parliamentary eloquence of Great Britain, whose constitution secures a vast influence to the noblest of human faculties, the power of speech, which is an echo of the mind. The political eloquence of England had its first training during the Long Parliament, and from that time the practice of public speaking has been a necessity for men in public life. A characteristic distinction was always noticeable between the eloquence of the House of Lords and that of the House of Commons. The former is solemn and dispassionate, while in the Lower House the debate runs through the whole scale of emotions, from the most unpolished sarcasm mingled with personal invective, to oratorical pomp and pathos. In the first half of the eighteenth century Robert Walpole and his opponent William Pulteney were known as good debaters ; but an artistic management of parliamentary speaking began somewhat later, and was brought to perfection by the elder Pitt, Burke, the younger Pitt, Fox, and Sheridan. William Pitt, created Earl of Chatham, but immortalized in the history of his country and of humanity by the title of "The Great Commoner," was born in London in 1708, and expired at his country seat at Hayes in 1778, while saying to his friend Camden, " Dear Camden, save my country!" He was the first who governed public opinion, the parliament, and the reluctant Court, by the power of speech, and obliged two kings to yield to his political views of freedom and of glory. He always fought on the side of the oppressed, and glorified the evening of his life by his steadfast resistance to those shortsighted measures which brought about the independence of the American Colonies. In January 1766, at the great debate on the duties imposed upon the Americans by the Grenville administration and maintained by that of Rockingham, Pitt exclaimed that he was glad to hear America was determined to resist this unjustifiable demand. On that occasion, and in a speech delivered nine years later in the same cause, his eloquence once rose to its full power. Edmund Burke (1730—1797), more the noble and highly-gifted Irishman, also gained his first laurels as an orator in the North American cause. On the occasion of the notorious

Tea Act, Burke delivered his " speech on American taxation," in the House of Commons, April 19th, 1774, which put him in the foremost rank of the great parliamentary speakers.

A second great speech, delivered December 1st 1783, was directed against Fox's East India Bill. Burke had hitherto been a partisan of Fox. His oratorical activity was most effective in the famous lawsuit which in 1786 was carried on before the Lords against Warren Hastings, the great Governor-General of India. Burke stood at the head of the members which the House of Commons had commissioned to conduct the accusation to the effect that extortion had been practised, that the princes and peoples of India had been oppressed, that the English name had been disgraced by injustice and cruelty. Westminster Hall had never witnessed a greater spectacle than was offered by this lawsuit, and never since the days of Demosthenes and Cicero had the power of speech produced a more brilliant effect. Not long afterwards Burke deserted his post, his party, and the good cause, and the speech he delivered February 9th 1790, was the beginning of his action against the French Revolution, which he carried on with the passionate heat of an apostate, and by which he gained the favour of the Court. In the lawsuit against Warren Hastings Sheridan had been on the side of Burke. The speech of accusation which the writer of the "School for Scandal" delivered before the House of Lords concerning the imprisonment and spoliations of the Begums (princesses) of Oude by the Governor-General of India, has been handed down to us but imperfectly, for stenography was unknown at that time; but according to the testimony of contemporaries it must have been the finest production of this highly-gifted man. All say that the impression this speech produced has never been equalled. When Sheridan had finished Westminster Hall rang with uproarious applause, and the excitement was so great that the debate had to be adjourned. The commotion spread through the whole town; a bookseller offered 1000*l.* for the speech if Sheridan would put it on paper ready for print, and for years it was the subject of delighted recollection. The most famous of Sheridan's political speeches is perhaps that one which he delivered in the House of Commons after the peace of Amiens, December 8th, 1802, concerning Bonaparte's designs upon England, it is as witty as the Begum speech is pathetic.[9] Charles Fox (1749—1806)

[9] Sheridan died in poor circumstances, for he had always been a bad manager of his own affairs. He was buried in Westminster Abbey on the 14th of July 1816, and his pall was carried by a duke, two earls, two viscounts and a bishop. In Lord Byron's journal of the 17th of December 1813, we read : " Lord Holland told me a curious piece of sentimentality in Sheridan. The other night we were all delivering our respective and various opinions upon him and other 'hommes marquants,' and mine was this :—Whatever Sheridan has done or chosen to do has been *par excellence* always the *best* of its kind. He has written the best comedy ('School for Scandal'), the best drama ('The Duenna'), the best farce ('The Critic'), and the best address ('Monody on Garrick'),

was elected a member of the House of Commons when only nineteen years of age, and was numbered with the parliamentary celebrities of that time after having won his spurs in the American cause. In his youth he was a careless tippler and spendthrift, and throughout his life he did not care for money or material advantages; he was always in debt, often embarrassed for want of a guinea, and well acquainted with usurers and bailiffs; but with all this so pleasant and cheery a companion that Burke, his early friend and subsequent antagonist, might say with truth "Fox was born to be loved." Indeed his friends idolized him; and at the famous Westminster election in 1784, duchesses paid with kisses for votes in favour of their friend Fox. He merited such devotion, not only by his personal amiability, but also for his faithful devotion and attachment to his own high-minded principles. In his political career he was rather a cosmopolitan than an Englishman, and that explains his desire to be at peace with France, just reviving after the Revolution, and the support he gave to the cause

and delivered the very best oration (the famous Begum speech) ever conceived or heard in this country. Somebody told Sheridan this the next day, and on hearing it he burst into tears. Poor Brinsley! if they were tears of pleasure, I would rather have said these few, but most sincere words, than have written the 'Iliad,' or made his own celebrated philippic." The same noble feeling which breathes from these lines also inspired Byron with his beautiful "Monody on the Death of Sheridan."

of freedom wherever support was asked for or
required. But, although he was an enthusiast
for the improvement of mankind, his eloquence
tended to convince reason rather than to please
fancy. There was no declamation in his speeches,
but much logic, and a logic whose demonstra-
tions were conveyed in the language of a man
of true and kindly feeling. His last great speech
was delivered shortly before his death; in it he
prevailed on the House of Commons to assent to
the abolition of slavery.[1] The great antagonist
of Fox was William Pitt (1759—1806), the famous
son of a famous father. He entered the House of
Commons in 1781, and made his maiden speech in
favour of a motion introduced by Burke for a
more economical organization of the royal household. At his second appearance, Fox praised him
warmly, and Wilberforce, the noble champion
of the abolition of slavery, prophesied that the
young man would one day fill the first place in the
kingdom. That prophecy was soon fulfilled, for
Pitt was not twenty-five years of age when he
became First Lord of the Treasury and Leader of
the House of Commons. This lofty position he
maintained with an interruption of only a few
years, until the day on which he was gathered to

[1] "The Speeches of the Right Hon. Charles James
Fox," 1815, 6 vols. Fox's unfinished "History of the Reign of
James II." appeared after his death, 1808. Fox's widow
received for it the greatest price which had been paid by
bookseller up to that time, namely 4500*l.*

the great dead in Westminster Abbey. He was a thoroughly English politician; from the point of view of a patriotic aristocrat, he guided the state in an anti-revolutionary direction, and armed the coalitions of monarchical Europe against the French republic, in spite of all the efforts of the Whig party. Great presence of mind and clearness and ease of expression distinguished him as an orator.[2] Henry Grattan (1750—1820), a countryman of Sheridan's, had also great oratorical powers, but can hardly be placed on a level with those already mentioned. With him and Sheridan, Fox and the younger Pitt,[3] two great generations of statesmen and parliamentary orators, who had directed the fate of Great Britain from the days of Frederick the Great to those of Napoleon, were laid in the grave. The English historian may well be proud when he tells the story of his countrymen of that epoch. Genius and energy vied with each other to serve their country in the parliamentary arena; the loftiest ideas of humanity were discussed there, as well as the interests of the nation ; and while the Continent yielded to the boundless ambition of a despotic upstart, England maintained her national independence, to her own advantage and glory, and as an example to other nations.

[2] "The Speeches of the Right Hon. William Pitt," 1808, 3 vols.
[3] Compare on these two the beautiful parallel in Scott's "Marmion:"—
"Oh, think, how to this latest day,
When death just hovering claimed his prey," &c.

Literature experienced the influence of this glorious development of national power. Great events elevate man and teach him the language which his soul utters in its loftiest flights, the language of poetry. The rise of the Italian Republics in the middle ages produced a Dante, the period of the great German Emperors a Wolfram v. Eschenbach and Gottfried v. Strassburg, the age of Queen Elizabeth a Shakespeare, the Seven Years' War was succeeded by the classical period of German literature, the Revolution trained Béranger, the most national poet of France, and in the struggle which England maintained against the Revolution, arose Burns and Byron.

Neither Pope with his smooth verses, nor Lord Bolingbroke with his sceptical wit, nor Dr. Johnson amid his worshippers, gave forth the first truly original note which announced a new phase in the poetry of Great Britain: from the banks of the Doon, out of a cottage in Scotland, rosethe woodlark who uttered it.

Scotchmen had been more faithful in their love for the romance of the middle ages than the English. The Scotch countrypeople especially clung fondly to the heroic history of their ancestors, as it had been handed down from one generation to another. Like a thread of gold, poetry winds through the poor and troubled life of the Scotch peasant, from times long past to our own days, in spite of the Puritan principles of his Presbyterian church. While the popular songs have sadly degenerated among

N

civilized nations, they have remained fresh and productive in Scotland and have improved without ceasing to be simple. Since the seventeenth century love-ballads and political songs were preeminent among the popular poetry, and in the eighteenth century the political song still flourished, fed by the insurrections of the Stuarts against the House of Hanover.

Burns, who breathed a new life into the popular poetry of his country, and whose compositions have exercised such a powerful influence on English literature, was not without predecessors. Beginning with Allan Ramsay, who died a year before Burns was born, a number of Scotch poets attempted with more or less success to compose popular and national songs. The best of this kind is undoubtedly the beautiful ballad of "Auld Robin Gray," written by Lady Ann Lindsay (Lady Barnard) in 1771.

Robert Burns was born January 25th 1759, in the parish of Alloway, in a poor cottage on the banks of the Doon. Burns has given an attractive picture of his home life—which was religious, poor, but full of humour—in his poem "The Cottar's Saturday Night." The Scotch country-people, as a class, are advocates for education and instruction, and the poor farmer tried his best to have his children taught by the itinerant teachers of that time. Young Robert learned English, French, and geometry. After an unsuccessful attempt to earn his bread by flax-combing, Burns became a farmer as his ancestors had been. But this did not prevent him from continuing his education. When twenty-one years of age he founded a club for young farmers in the village of Tarbolton, to give them the opportunity "for recreation after their work, to promote sociability and friendship, and to improve their minds;" the rules for this club were laid down by Burns, and he begins by saying that "the great aim of human society is to become wiser and better, and that this should also be the aim of every man in every rank." These words contained the idea of that high-minded consciousness which Burns has expressed in so many of his songs, especially in the beautiful "A man's a man for a' that," the last verse of which prophesies the brotherhood of all men. In the last part of his stay at Tarbolton, Burns made the acquaintance of Mary Campbell, who was a milkmaid at Colesfield Castle. This is the "Highland Mary," loving and beloved, whom Burns has immortalized, as Dante has immortalized his Beatrice, Petrarch his Laura, Goethe his Gretchen. Burns says, " One day, after having been sure of our mutual love for some time, we met by agreement on the banks of Ayr, to say farewell before Mary went to the western highlands where she was to settle everything for our impending marriage. At the close of the succeeding autumn she came back, but had scarcely landed when she was seized by a malignant fever, and my dear girl died before I heard of her illness." [4] After

[4] Robert Chambers, in his edition of the "Life and Works

his father's death Burns and his brother Gilbert became joint tenants of Mossgiel near Mauchline. Here he married Janet Armour, in patriarchal Scotch fashion, according to which the mutual consent of the betrothed is sufficient to unite them; and he has written songs on his wife as he did of his "Highland Mary." The publication of his first collection of poems (1786) procured for him a reputation, and brought him into connexion with the aristocratic and literary world of Edinburgh. For one winter he was the "lion" of these circles; but he behaved sensibly, and was wise enough to return to his plough. With the produce of his poetical firstfruits he took a larger farm in Nithsdale. But poor Burns was not made to get on in the world. He was too much of a poet to be a good farmer, and the death of the flowers which he tore up with his plough inspired him with the dark presentiment that he himself would ere long sink into the furrow of the grave, uprooted by the ploughshare of misfortune.[5] At the close of the year 1791 Burns gave up his farm to save himself from ruin, and went to Dumfries, where his friends had procured him some employment in the excise. But his hopes of rising in the public service were not realized. He was too much of a Scotchman

of Burns" (vol. i. page 248), tells of a deeply poetical moment in this farewell scene: "The lovers stood on each side of a purling brook; they laved their hands in the limpid stream, and holding a Bible between them pronounced their vows to be faithful to each other .... they parted never to meet again"

[5] See the beautiful poem "Stanzas to a Mountain Daisy."

to hide his antipathy to the Hanoverian dynasty, and on the other hand he was too fond of liberty to make a secret of his sympathy with the revolutionary ideas of France. His sincerity got him into serious trouble ; his health began to give way ; poverty and cares and the dread of being imprisoned for debt increased his illness. He died on the 21st of July 1796, at the age of thirty-seven years and six months.[6]

Burns was entirely a poet of the people. His genius attempted but very few compositions of any length ; his " Tam o' Shanter," however, is a masterpiece of poetic narrative, and Sir Walter Scott says that, "with the exception of Shakespeare, no poet ever showed such power in exciting the most varied feelings by passing rapidly from the sublime to the ridiculous.[7] But Burns was preeminently

[6] Burns was buried with military honours, and the nation provided for his destitute family. Forty-eight years after his death (1844), thousands were gathered on the banks of the Doon where a monument had been erected to the poet to celebrate his memory. On this occasion Lord Eglintoun said, in proposing a toast to Burns, "At his name every Scottish heart beats high. He has become a household word in the palace and in the cottage."

[7] In "Tam o' Shanter" Burns introduces the famous image of the transitoriness of human joys :—
 "But pleasures are like poppies spread,
  You seize the flow'r, its bloom is shed !
  Or like the snowfall in the river,
  A moment white —then melts for ever ;
  Or like the borealis race,
  That flit ere you can point their place ;
  Or like the rainbow's lovely form,
  Evanishing amid the storm."

a lyric poet, the first after a long interval in Great Britain who expressed in his songs the feelings of his own heart. This is why his songs have such a wonderful freshness, and are so noble in their great simplicity. In their outward form they closely resemble the ancient popular airs. A virtue as of green fields and mountain air, says Carlyle, breathes from the poems of Burns; there are tears in them, but also a destroying fire, hidden like lightning in the drops of the summer clouds. His teachers were nature and life alone, but it is extraordinary how well his poetry combines the truth of reality with ideal conception. It has been truly said of him that in his heart there was a tone for every shade of human feeling. Very few poets have, like Burns, poured the entire fulness of their existence into their songs. Liberty, which is the vital spring of modern culture, was the ideal of Burns's existence, and taught him to understand life in its fulness. The fire of his soul consumed him prematurely, but the works he left behind him were sufficient to breathe a new life into the literature of his country and to delight distant nations.[8] The names of more than a hundred

[8] The first complete edition of Burns's works we owe to his biographer Currie (Lond. 1800, 4 vols). Carlyle's well-known Essay on Burns, was called forth by Lockhart's "Life of Burns," 1828, and first published in the December number of the "Edinburgh Review" of the same year; it was afterwards reprinted in Carlyle's "Critical and Miscellaneous Essays." In Byron's journal of December 13th, 1813, we read the following: Lord Holland has lent me a

poets might be mentioned who since the death of Burns have cultivated the national Scotch song. The most eminent belong to the lower classes, with the exception of Joanna Baillie (died 1851), who not only wrote songs but also tragedies, and with such success that Lord Byron said of her that she was the only woman who understood how to write tragedies.

There is the weaver Robert Tannahill (1774—1810), and the sheriff's clerk William Motherwell (1797—1835), both surpassed only by Burns himself; then Allan Cunningham (1784—1842), who from a bricklayer became an eminent man of letters; Robert Nicoll (1814—1857), the son of a journeyman, who unfortunately died young, and who composed the beautiful songs "Thoughts of Heaven" and "We are brethren a';" and finally James Hogg (1772—1835), called the "Ettrick Shepherd," for he was a shepherd by profession, and the cottage in which he was born stood near the Ettrick forest. His songs do not compare with those of Burns and Motherwell, but his fairy tales and ballads are excellent. His best compositions of that kind he collected under the general title " The Queen's Wake " (1813).[9] The finest of this collection are

quantity of Burns's unpublished, and never-to-be-published, letters. They are full of oaths and obscene songs. What an antithetical mind !—tenderness, roughness—delicacy, coarseness—sentiment, sensuality—soaring and grovelling, dirt and Deity—all mixed up in that one compound of inspired clay!"

[9] Hogg imagines his tales and ballads to be recited by

the delicate fairy tale, "Kilmeny," and the magnificent ballad "The Witch of Fife," one of the most fanciful productions of Scotch heaths and mountains. "The Queen's Wake" obtained great and well-deserved fame for the Ettrick Shepherd, none of his later works are equal to it, but there is true poetry in most of them, especially in the fairy tale "The Pilgrims of the Sun" (1815), in which the passages describing the wild wanderings of a planet are worthy of Milton.

Whenever the literature of a nation enters upon a new phase, we always meet with some poets who occupy an intermediate position, inasmuch as they try to accommodate the new spirit to the accustomed forms of the conventional taste. The merit of these transition poets is often greater than we are inclined to acknowledge when the new movement has been victorious. Man is a creature of habit, and the Germanic nations especially do not like sudden transitions, but prefer to be prepared for a change, and to receive new ideas under accustomed forms. It is different with the Scotch, whose Celtic nature makes them fond of change and innovation; this characteristic, and their national pride contributed to the enthusiastic acknowledgment Burns found in his country. In England the poetical revival of literature was effected more slowly and more methodically. The realistic and national spirit which was to revive

minstrels on Christmas Eve at the Court of Mary Queen of Scots ; the title of the work is owing to this fiction.

English literature entered it as early as Johnson's time; but before it could prevail, reasonable consideration had to be paid to the existing taste and ideas. The four poets mentioned below had this regard for existing ideas, and therefore are to be considered as intermediate between the poetry of reason of the eighteenth and the romantic poetry of the nineteenth centuries. They are George Crabbe (1754—1832), James Montgomery (born 1771), Samuel Rogers (died 1832), and Thomas Campbell (1771—1843).

Crabbe was a protégé of Burke's, and his patron procured an independent position for him by having him appointed to a country vicarage which gave him facilities for following his tastes by observing the life of the country-people. He committed his observations to writing, and formed them gradually into poems. In 1783 appeared "The Village," in 1807 "The Parish Register," in 1810 "The Borough," after that the "Tales in Verse," and lastly the "Tales of the Hall," in 1819, in which two brothers meet after a long separation and communicate their experiences to each other.

Crabbe is a poet of reality, and of the reality of everyday life. His style is like Dutch genre painting; but it is wrong to call him the Hogarth of poetry, for Crabbe does not caricature. He is very serious and truthful in his delineations of life. Like an unsparing anatomist he has dissected the body of society, and points out its great blemishes with frigid calmness and without irony.[1] It would be vain to look for any ideality in Crabbe's works; it was his intention to reflect reality alone, and he has throughout remained faithful to his purpose. For that reason his descriptions produce a dismal and even terrible impression; but their stern truthfulness has helped to banish conventional Arcadian falsehoods from English literature.

James Montgomery was brought up at a Moravian seminary, and his poems have an essentially religious tone. When a youth he expressed his sympathy with the French Revolution so loudly that he was twice imprisoned; but his revolutionary enthusiasm soon grew cold, and in 1806 he describes the reverse of the great movement in his poem "The Wanderer of Switzerland." Description is the chief element of Montgomery's works,[2] but he combines with it such vividness of fancy and warmth of feeling that his poems leave a very different impression from the reasoning poetical descriptions of the preceding century. Of his shorter poems "The Common Lot" is the best and the most famous.

Rogers and Campbell brought the didactic-descriptive poetry of England to a most brilliant

---

[1] "Crabbe! poetical anatomist of woe!"—Sharon Turner.
[2] "The West Indies," "The Pelican Island," "Greenland," "The World before the Flood." In the last-mentioned poem there is the beautiful passage on the power of poetry:
"There is a living spirit in the lyre,
A breath of music, and a soul of fire," &c.

close. The didactic poem of the former, "The Pleasures of Memory" (1792), and that of the latter, "The Pleasures of Hope" (1803), deserve their great reputation; both works combine brilliantly correct diction with expression full of the power and fancy of the new school, and both embrace a vast sphere of thought, and are rich in magnificent and deeply-touching passages. Rogers' later poems are also didactic and descriptive in kind; so is his poem "The Human Life" (1819), in which he describes the happiness of married and family life with a depth of feeling which can only be found in the poetry of Germanic nations; so is also his poem of travels, "Italy" (1822), which contains a beautiful passage on Lord Byron.[3] In his poetical narrative "Jacqueline," which is full of tender melancholy, Rogers attempted to approach the modern style of poetry, but he was less successful than Campbell, whose ballads "Lochiel and the Wizard" and "O'Connor's Child," as well as his poetical tale "Gertrude of Wyoming," are sufficient proofs that he had fully imbibed the spirit of the modern romantic school. "Gertrude of Wyoming" consists of three cantos, and treats of a tragical subject taken from the history of the North American colonies; it introduced the romance of the virgin forest with its red warriors into European literature more than ten years before

[3] ". . . . . Much had pass'd
Since last we parted; and those five years,
Much had they told!" &c.

Cooper wrote his Red Indian novels. The most admired of Campbell's lyrical poems are two warlike poems, " Hohenlinden " and " The Battle of the Baltic," as well as his darkly magnificent composition of fancy " The Last Man ;" but the most popular of all is his sailor-song " Ye Mariners of England."

CHAPTER XI.

Scott and Moore.

THE French Revolution, which at first seemed to be a struggle for the common cause of humanity, did not keep its grand promise. With the rise of Napoleon, its cosmopolitan tendencies assumed a purely French direction, and then, passing into a new phase, broke out again in the old and barbarous lust of conquest. French nationality, stripped of its cosmopolitanism, increased in wantonness as it increased in power, from the time of Napoleon's first Italian campaign, and other countries felt their national sentiments hurt and irritated. European civilization, which had tended towards cosmopolitanism in the eighteenth century, now began to reassume a national character. In opposition to the levelling despotism of the last great conqueror, specific nationality rose in defiance everywhere ; and since the idea of the Revolution could not gain a general acknowledgment, the nations of Europe began jealously to cultivate the idea of their nationality as the foundation of their further development. And so it happened naturally that the several nations turned with a new interest to their own histories. To know their way in the present, and to fix their hopes of the future, they investigated their past in every direction ; the historical and antiquarian sciences entered upon a fresh phase, and European society found a new pleasure in the ideal of the middle ages—the Romance of Chivalry.

This movement soon found its expression in literature. Goethe was the last great poet of the historical epoch now drawing to a close, Schiller the last great humanitarian prophet. The latter had even made several attempts to blend the new national and romantic with the humanistic and cosmopolitan principle.[1] Then arose in Germany the romantic school of poetry, whose two chief tendencies, the romantic and national, and the natural and philosophical, found their expression in English literature, the former in Walter Scott and his imitators, the latter in the poets of the Lake school. The influence of German literature on that of England at this time cannot be denied ;[2] and though we do not mean to say that the great

[1] Especially in the " Maid of Orleans " and " William Tell."
[2] Already in 1786 Goethe's " Werther" was produced on the London stage by Reynolds, which was however a mistake. In 1792 Schiller's " Robbers " appeared in an English translation ; 1793, Goethe's "Iphigenie ; " 1794, Lessing's " Emilia Galotti ; " 1795, " Fiesko," and " Cabal and Love ; " 1796, " Don Carlos ; " 1798, " Stella," and " Clavigo." Up to the present time, twenty and more English translations have been made of Goethe's " Faust."

change in English poetry had been brought about by the example of Germany, it must be acknowledged that several leaders of the new literary movement in Great Britain have received a stimulus from Germany. On the whole, however, the similarity of the German and English literatures in the nineteenth century has a deeper cause than the admiration which any English author may have felt for German poetry; we must look for that cause in the Germanic genius of both nations, which has stimulated them to similar activity, in opposition to French arrogance. Only Germany, England, and Scandinavia have produced important works of modern romance; in Spain and Portugal it never rose above imitation, the same, with few exceptions, may be said of Italy, while the modern romance of France is mixed with foreign and impure elements. It is natural enough that it should be so, for the romantic ideal of beauty had sprung from the union of the Germanic spirit with Christianity, and if grand conceptions of it may be found in the modern literature of Poland, in the poems of Miekiewicz, Garezyuski, and Krasinski, the fact is to be explained by the extraordinary power of appropriation possessed by the Sclavonic race : their poets assimilated the spirit of German and English romance with their own national recollections.

In Great Britain a Scotchman had been the first to oppose original and national lyrics to the stiff and formal reflective poetry of England ; and it was another Scotchman who gave to his nation the epic poetry of romance, and who, by his compositions in verse and in prose, made for a time the Historical Romance the chief element in the literary movement of the world.

WALTER SCOTT

was born in Edinburgh on the 15th of August, 1771. He was a sickly boy, lame of one foot, and his schoolfellows had a poor opinion of his intellectual powers. But people of better judgment, like Burns, and one of his masters, the well-known preacher and critic Hugh Blair, prophesied that the pupil who was esteemed so lightly would grow up to a more brilliant future than any of his comrades. Even his schoolfellows admitted that he was a good story-teller, and his reputation stood high in the playground, for his courage was unconquerable in spite of personal defects. By degrees his health became robust. His father designed him for the legal profession and made him his clerk for five years, during which time he continued his historical and imaginative reading, revelling in old popular songs, romances of chivalry, and the history of his country during the middle ages. At twenty-one he was called to the bar and became a lawyer at the highest court of justice in Edinburgh; later he entered on other offices of consideration, but his favourite residence was a place which he had purchased not far from Edinburgh, called Abbotsford, on the banks of the Tweed, in 1811, and which he enlarged and beautified by degrees. Walter Scott's life does not offer any surprising or romantic incidents. His was of a sober disposition; the careful father of a family, a true Scottish gentleman, one who loved hunting and hospitality, a kind neighbour and a faithful friend. The misfortune that came upon him in his later years by the colossal bankruptcy of his publishers, he tried to retrieve by unwearied activity, and, productive as Lope and Calderon, he died, as it were pen in hand, on the 21st of September 1832, aged sixty-one years. Abbotsford was secured to his family by a national subscription.[3]

Scott's genius was silent until he had grown to manhood. In the German poet Bürger's ballads, in Goethe's "Götz," he found a spirit similar to his own; he translated Goethe's first great drama, "Götz von Berlichingen;" he rendered "Lenore," "The Wild Huntsman," and "The Erlking" into English. He then proceeded to original compositions and wrote his first ballads (1801) among which "Glenfinlas" and "The Fire-King" are proofs of a master-mind. In 1802-3 appeared his "Minstrelsy of the Scottish Border" in three volumes, a fruit of the poet's wanderings through

[3] "Memoirs of the Life of Sir Walter Scott," ed. by Lockhart, 1837, 7 vols. "The Domestic Manners and Private Life of Sir Walter Scott," by J. Hogg, 1835. "Abbotsford and Newstead Abbey," by W. Irving, 1835,

"Complete Works, including all his poetical works, life and correspondence, notes, additions, corrections, and various readings," 1839, 52 vols.

the Scottish border-country, the home of national ballads, which he collected from the mouths of the people and which he edited most tastefully and conscientiously. The work made his name known all over Great Britain, it renewed and completed the effect of Percy's "Reliques."

In 1805 Scott published his "Lay of the Last Minstrel," which was received enthusiastically. Its circulation immediately became immense; within ten years fifteen editions were called for, and it has since then exceeded the circulation of any other English poem. It is an epic descriptive of the romantic border-feuds and composed of ballads supposed to have been sung by an old minstrel, the last of his race. Scott could dare to publish such a fiction, for he was able indeed to make old minstrelsy rise from its tomb. In the "Lay of the Last Minstrel" he gave new life to legendary romance, as he did in "Marmion" to the romance of history. The subject of the poetical tale of "Marmion," published in 1808, is the battle of Flodden Field, fought in 1513 between Henry VIII. of England and James IV. of Scotland. But Scott's greatest triumph was his "Lady of the Lake" (1810), a magnificent poem which introduces us to the wild and picturesque scenery of the Scottish highlands. There is a powerful charm in Scott's descriptions of landscape; he has succeeded in making all the civilized world feel at home on the mountains and heaths of his native country. His later epic poems, "Rokeby" (1813), the scene of which is laid in England during the time of the civil wars, and the " Lord of the Isles " (1814), a story of adventure by sea and land, are rather novels in verse. " The Bridal of Triermain " and " Harold the Dauntless," written still later, are much inferior to his former poems in power and beauty, and were received the more coldly since Byron, the greatest master of poetic narrative, had begun to publish his glowing compositions in that style. Scott perhaps felt that no more laurels were to be won on this field and therefore turned to another, to the Historical Novel, in which he gained popularity more quickly and fully than any author in ancient or modern times.

Scott may unquestionably be considered as the real founder of the Historical Novel, for all attempts of the kind which had been previously made had proved unsuccessful. Scott was the first who showed the poetry of history in all its grandeur. His novels are faithfully historical in their descriptions of manners and customs, his characteristic art is perfect, his morality of the highest order, and his works have the peculiar characteristic of being equally appreciated by all classes of society ; they were read with delight by the aristocracy of Europe, in the log-huts of the Far West, and in the cottage of the German peasant.

Scott had begun to write his first novel as early as 1805, but it only appeared in 1814, anonymously, under the title of "Waverley, or 'Tis Sixty Years Since" (the time of the Jacobite insurrection in

1745). It was not an attempt but a masterpiece of its kind, and from that time the Waverley Novels followed each other in close succession and gave to their author the name of "The Great Unknown." "Guy Mannering" appeared in 1815 ; "The Antiquary" and the first series of the "Tales of my Landlord" in 1816 ; "Rob Roy" and the "Heart of Midlothian" in 1818 ; the "Bride of Lammermoor" in 1819 ; "Kenilworth" in 1821 ; "Quentin Durward" in 1822 ; the " Tales of the Crusaders" in 1825 ; "Ivanhoe" and "Woodstock" in 1826 ; the "Fair Maid of Perth" in 1828. The whole series of seventy-four volumes was closed in 1831, with "Count Robert of Paris" and the "Castle Dangerous." Amongst the tales of chivalry proper "Ivanhoe," "Quentin Durward," and "Kenilworth" are rivals in excellence. The "Fortunes of Nigel," "Woodstock," "Peveril of the Peak," and "Old Mortality" form a most interesting cycle, descriptive of manners and customs before the Revolution, under Cromwell, and during the Restoration. The most humorous of the novels is the "Antiquary." "Guy Mannering," "Rob Roy," and "Waverley" are pre-eminent in delineation of character. The "Bride of Lammermoor" and the "Heart of Midlothian" are the most powerfully poetical.

Scott kept the secret of his authorship until 1827, but his friends had guessed the truth long before.[4]

[4] In the spring of 1815 Walter Scott was in London. The prince regent, afterwards George IV., who knighted the poet,

On the 23rd of February of that year a great dinner was held in his honour at Edinburgh, and there circumstances induced him to acknowledge himself as the author of these compositions; he closed his speech with the modest words: " Now the charm is broken and the wand buried. May my hearers allow me to say with Prospero, 'It was your gentle breath which filled my sails.'"

But even the astonishing activity which we have recorded does not show us the whole of Scott's productive powers. He edited some older authors, such as Dryden and Swift; he wrote the " Tales of a Grandfather " to make his grandchildren familiar with the history of their country; he published antiquarian researches, and wrote some excellent biographies, " Lives of the Novelists." But his "Life of Napoleon Buonaparte" (1829), in nine volumes, was prejudicial to his fame; it is much rather an apology for English Toryism than an historical work, and it is altogether wanting in that justice which characterizes Scott as a poet.

Walter Scott is essentially a national poet, and a specifically Scotch one. His view embraces a large sphere, but his point of view is ever that of a Scotchman. He was inspired by love of his country, and whenever his poetical impulse soars highest it is in praise of his native land. No poet

---

gave a banquet in his honour, and on that occasion proposed a toast to him as to the author of " Waverley." But Scott answered evasively.

has so glorified the country of his birth as Scott.[5] He is also essentially an epic poet and his dramatic compositions—for he also wrote plays [6]—are only epics in the form of dialogue. His characters are those of an epic poem, that is to say, they rise with plastic precision from the background of the scene in which they are placed, and do not move and act by their own free will, but according to the will of their creator. The plastically realistic delineation of men, landscapes, and events, is Scott's most characteristic feature, and enters with equal power into the different styles of his works. The stag-hunt in the beginning of the first canto of the "Lady of the Lake," the description of the cave Coir-uan-Uriskin in the third, the household of a Highland robber in "Waverley," the banquet in the castle of a chief in "Montrose," the entrance of Elizabeth into Kenilworth, the tournament in "Ivanhoe," the meeting of Louis XI. and Charles the Bold in "Quentin Durward," the noise of the battle in "Marmion"—how comprehensively and clearly is all this brought before our eyes! There

[5] "O Caledonia! stern and wild,
    Meet nurse for a poetic child!
    Land of brown heath and shaggy wood,
    Land of the mountain and the flood,
    Land of my sires! what mortal hand
    Can e'er untie this filial band,
    That knits me to thy rugged strand!" &c.
                "Lay of the Last Minstrel," vi. 2.
[6] "Halidon Hill," "Macduff's Cross," "The Doom of Devorgvil," "The Auchidane Tragedy."

might be a little more historic calmness in Scott's figures here and there, but his delineation of scenery is perfect throughout, and it is truly marvellous how he renders not only the outward form, but the very spirit of the locality. Scott has been called the poet of the aristocracy, for by means of his fascinating gift of narration he has made the romance of the feudal world exceedingly popular. He has not, however, confined himself to one class, but has placed all classes in dramatic relation to each other, not as classes, but as individuals; for his figures are not cut out from a pattern but taken from real life and from history, and thence the mass of original characters which he introduces. Scott might as well be called the poet of the people, for no poet has drawn to such perfection the power, sense, and faithfulness inherent in the people. Indeed the chief charm of his novels rests with his popular characters: Cuddie Headrigg, Richie Moniplies, Monkbarns, Dandy Dinmont, Andrew Fairservice, Harry of the Wynd, Edie Ochiltree, Meg Merrilies, Madge Wildfire, and others; and none of his queens and ladies are surrounded with such a glory of poetry as Rebecca, the daughter of the despised tribe of Israel, and Jeannie Deans, who undertakes the dangerous journey from Edinburgh to London on foot, to implore the wife of George II. to save her sister Effie who is sentenced to death.[7]

[7] Scott had a whole host of imitators. His school was one of the most extensive that ever existed. One of its oldest members is Horace Smith ("Brambletye House," "Tower

At the time that Walter Scott awakened the sympathy of England and of all the civilized world for his Scottish home, another brilliant writer did the same, though in a somewhat less degree, for Ireland, "the emerald gem of the Western world." It had long been customary in England to look upon Ireland as a country to be put to profit and to be disliked, and on the Irish as on an entirely inferior race, though more than one highly gifted Irishman had crossed St. George's Channel. Thomas Moore was the first Catholic Irishman who became incorporated with the national literature of England, and the English are obliged to acknowledge that he is one of its most important representatives in modern times. He was born May 28th 1780, in Dublin, at the University of which city he also pursued his studies. On his coming to England his Anacreontic songs caused him to be received at the merry parties of the Prince Regent; he was then intrusted for a while with some office in the Bermudas, and from

Hill"), its most productive one G. P. R. James ("Darnley," "Richelieu," "Mary of Burgundy," &c. &c.) who now and then comes up to his model. Thomas Grattan is another of the better writers of historical novels ("The Heiress of Bruges," "Agnes de Mansfeldt," &c.). Lady Morgan, famous as a writer of travels ("France," "Italy"), has cultivated in her novels ("O'Donnel," "The O'Briens, and O'Flahertys," &c.) the romance of her native country, Ireland. The same may be said of her countryman John Banim ("Tales of the O'Hara Family," "The Battle of the Boyne," &c.). W. H. Ainsworth delights in the romance of highwaymen and is not sparing of horrors ("Rookwood," "Jack Sheppard," &c.).

the time of his return to that of his death (1851) he lived in retirement in the country, devoted to poetry and historical studies. Moore was not like Scott a national and romantic poet from the beginning. He began by writing playful lyrics and satires, as was the fashion in Queen Anne's reign. He translated the pretty " Songs of Anacreon," which he published under the name of Tom Little, in allusion to the shortness of his person, and after his return from the Bermudas he published epistles satirizing North American Yankeeism. But the powerful national spirit of the time came upon him also, and reminded him of his duty towards his unhappy country. He drew "the harp of his country"[8] from its dark resting-place and sang those immortal songs which, forming the text of national airs, are known by the name of " Irish Melodies." They had a great success and have given comfort to, and awakened sympathy for, the country from which they sprang. There is Celtic softness and melancholy in these songs, the plaintive, elegiac tone prevails in them, and thus they are diametrically opposed in character to Scott's powerful and chivalrous manliness. Moore in looking on his "green Erin" saw nothing but decay and all the misfortunes of servitude ; he had but little occasion to feel any of that pride with which Scott looked

---

[8] "Dear harp of my country ! in darkness I found thee!
The cold chain of silence had hung o'er thee long,
When proudly, my own Island harp ! I unbound thee,
And gave all thy chords to light, freedom, nd song."

on the past history of his nation. Nor is he an epical and descriptive poet like Scott; his style is lyrical; he does not take scenes and characters from the history of his country, but only moods and feelings which find their utterance in those lyrical songs many of which are unequalled in their sweet and melancholy charm.[9] Moore's lyrical

[9] "As a beam o'er the face of the waters may glow
While the tide runs in darkness and coolness below,
So the cheek may be tinged with a warm, sunny smile,
Though the cold heart to ruin runs darkly the while.

One fatal remembrance, one sorrow that throws
Its bleak shade alike o'er our joys and our woes,
To which life nothing darker or brighter can bring,
For which joy has no balm and affliction no sting!

Oh! this thought in the midst of enjoyment will stay,
Like a dead, leafless branch in the summer's bright ray;
The beams of the warm sun play round it in vain,—
It may smile in his light, but it blooms not again!"

"Come, rest in this bosom, my own stricken deer!
Though the herd have fled from thee, thy home is still here;
Here still is the smile, that no cloud can o'ercast,
And the heart and the hand all thy own to the last!

Oh! what was love made for, if 'tis not the same
Through joy and through torments, through glory and shame?
I know not, I ask not, if guilt's in that heart,
I but know that I love thee, whatever thou art!

Thou hast call'd me thy angel in moments of bliss,
And thy angel I'll be, 'mid the horrors of this,—
Through the furnace, unshrinking, thy steps to pursue,
And shield thee, and save thee, or—perish there too."

Of these and others of the Irish melodies Byron used to say that each one of them was worth more than all the heroic

talent also shows in his "Sacred Songs" and "National Airs."

But even his first works prove that softness was only one side of his talent, that satire was another. He made use of it, in publishing under the name of James Brown, his "Intercepted Letters, or the Twopenny Postbag," in 1810. Here Moore was no longer the Anacreontic sharer of the orgies of the Prince of Wales, but the Irish patriot hitting hard at the English Tories. Of more lasting satirical value are his "Letters of the Fudge Family in Paris" (1818), which paint the joys and sorrows of an English family during their residence in the French capital. A year before the publication of that satire appeared Moore's "Lalla Rookh," an Oriental romance, which was received with admiration. This is the poet's chief work.

The spirit of romance naturally felt drawn to the East, for there was the home of its leading idea, the idea of the struggle between mind and matter, between God and the world, between this world and a future state. In Germany it was Friedrich Schlegel who first pointed to the East as to the fountain-head of romance, and German poets as well as German men of science soon found there a rich field for study and inspiration. In England the study of the East had begun

poems which had appeared in his time. Hogg, the Ettrick Shepherd, thought rather differently about Moore: "His notes are too sweet," he said, "too artificial: mine are just right."

already in the eighteenth century and had become of great practical importance, since a society of English merchants, the "East India Company," ruled more or less directly over a hundred million Eastern people. Byron's Oriental tales tended to increase the delight taken in the poetry and imagery of those countries and the Eastern romance became a rival of the romance of chivalry. Just about this time, when the attention of the public had been drawn to the East by Warren Hastings' lawsuit and Burke's brilliant speeches on the occasion, Moore published his "Lalla Rookh," and it excited universal pleasure and admiration. Men who knew the East well, praised Moore for his faithful rendering of local colouring, and said that he had painted with the colours of Hafis and Dschami. Even the "Edinburgh Review," at this time under the severely critical direction of Jeffrey, the Dr. Johnson of this time, was full of Lalla Rookh's praise. He said ("Edinburgh Review," 1817): "It is the finest Orientalism we have had yet. The land of the sun has never shone out so brightly on the children of the North, nor the sweets of Asia been poured forth, nor her gorgeousness displayed so profusely, to the delighted senses of Europe. The beauteous forms, the dazzling splendours, the breathing odours of the East seem at last to have found a kindred poet in that green Isle of the West whose genius has long been suspected to be derived from a warmer clime, and now wantons and luxuriates in these voluptuous regions as if it felt that it had at length regained its native element." The praise bestowed on the poem is justified. "Lalla Rookh" is composed in a truly Oriental spirit, abounding in gorgeous pictures, wrapt as it were in a haze of magical brilliancy, and calling forth feelings of Oriental dreaminess. The poem consists of four romances: The Veiled Prophet of Khorassan, Paradise and the Peri, The Fire-Worshippers, The Light of the Harem. A short tale in prose connects these poems. Lalla Rookh (Tulip-Cheek), the daughter of Aurungzebe, ruler of India, is engaged to be married to the crown prince of Bokhara. An embassy from Delhi is sent to fetch the bride. At the resting-places of the caravan a young minstrel recites these poetical tales to the princess; and though the chamberlain of the harem, Fadladeen, criticizes him most severely, the grace of his person and delivery arouses a secret inclination in the heart of the bride who has not yet seen her husband. At the end of the journey the minstrel proves to be the princely bridegroom himself, who has won the heart of his bride under this mask, and the story closes with a happy wedding. The first of Feramorz's romances tells the tragical story of a pair of Persian lovers, Azim and Zelika, who are mixed up with the fate of the Veiled Prophet of Khorassan, Mokanna. The second, a poem of great beauty, describes the expiation of a Peri driven from Paradise, who has to regain entrance by bringing to the gate of Eden the gift most precious to Heaven. She first procures a drop of blood from the heart of a youth fallen in the defence of his country; then the last sigh of a maiden who would rather die with her lover than live without him; and finally the tear of repentance of a robber and murderer who has been converted by the sight of a praying child. The third romance, the most powerful as regards its subject and its execution, relates the unhappy and mutual love of the Gheber chief Hafed and of the emir's daughter Hinda, drawing a rich and poetical picture of the historical catastrophe by which the power of Islam suppressed the Persian fire-worship. The fourth romance, "The Light of the Harem," is merely a graceful trifle.[1] Another epic poem of Moore's,

[1] Taine ("Hist. de la Litt. angl." iii. 479,) pronounces a most severe judgment on Moore's and Southey's Eastern romances, but we must agree that there is some truth in his words:—"Cette fantasmagorie est bien brillante; par malheur elle sent la fabrique. Si vous voulez en avoir l'image, figurez-vous que vous êtes à l'opéra. Beau spectacle! on en sort ébloui, assourdi; les sens défaillent sous cette inondation de magnificences; mais en rentrant chez soi, on se demande ce qu'on a appris, ce qu'on a senti, si véritablement on a senti quelque chose. Après tout, il n'y a guère ici que des décors et de la mise en scène; les sentiments sont factices; ce sont des sentiments d'opéra; les auteurs ne sont que d'habiles gens, manufacturiers de livrets et de toiles peintes, ils ont des talents et point de génie; ils tirent leurs idées non de leur cœur, mais de leur tête. Telle est l'impression que laissent 'Lalla Rookh,' 'Thalaba,' 'Kehama.' Ce sont de grandes machines décoratives appropriées à la mode. La marque propre du génie est la découverte de quelque large région inexplorée dans la nature humaine, et cette marque leur manque; ils témoignent seulement de beaucoup d'habileté et de savoir."

"The Loves of the Angels" (1823), treating a subject taken from the sixth chapter of Genesis, which also attracted Byron, is equally Eastern in its imagery, but does not come up to the splendour of "Lalla Rookh." Later on Moore's poetical muse yielded but one other production, "The Epicurean" (1827), a somewhat forced representation of the conflict between Christianity, the priestly religion of Egypt, and Greek philosophy; and the poem "Alciphron," which is a variation of that novel in verse.[2] Moore then returned to the cause of his native country, and advocated it as eloquently in prose, by his "Memoirs of Captain Rock," as he had done in verse by his "Irish Melodies." The book contains a somewhat exaggerated description of the sufferings of Ireland brought about by English oppression. He is a more objective historian in his masterly "History of Ireland,[3] which unfortunately is only carried up to the time of the English invasion. Moore also wrote some very good biographies, the most important of which are those of Byron and Sheridan.

[2] "The poetical works of Thomas Moore," collected by himself, 1841, 10 vols., contain: "Odes of Anacreon," "Juvenile Poems," "Poems relating to America," "Satirical and Humorous poems," "Irish Melodies," "National Airs," "Sacred Songs," "Legendary Ballads," "Set of Glees," "Miscellaneous Poems," "Lalla Rookh," "Political Poems," "Fables for the Holy Alliance," "The Fudge Family in Paris," "Rhymes on the Road," "The Loves of the Angels," "The Fudges in England," "The Blue Stockings." "The Epicurean," "Alciphron." "Memoirs, Journal, and Correspondence of Thomas Moore," ed. by the Right Hon. Lord John Russell, 1852. [3] London, 1835, 3 vols.

CHAPTER XII.

The Lake School : Wordsworth, Coleridge, Southey, Wilson.

ENGLISH literature has been very fortunate in its modern development, having been guarded from uniformity and monotony by its Germanic genius —which is ever anxious to encourage and cultivate individuality—in contradistinction to the French love of centralization and uniformity. The works of Scott and Moore were rich and beautiful in themselves, but there was a danger in both, and their imitators fully proved it. Scott's historical romance might turn into the mere mechanical process of putting history on the stage, and Moore's Eastern romance might degenerate into revelling among meaningless images. A wholesome counterpoise to this weakening of the spirit of poetry, as well as to its over-stimulation by Byron's poetry of passion, we find in the tendency of the so-called Lake School.

This group of poets is considered to consist of Wordsworth, Coleridge, Southey, and Wilson, though the latter is but slightly connected with the others. The three former may be said to form a

School inasmuch as they started from the same principles, and tried to realize them in part by common efforts; they were also intimate personal friends. The origin of their collective name, that of "the Lake poets," is to be found in the circumstance that Wordsworth, Coleridge, and Southey resided for some time by the charming lakes of Cumberland and Westmoreland, and that country, so rich in beautiful waters and mountains, became a favourite subject of their poetical descriptions of nature. Wilson, a Scotchman, stood in no familiar relation to the others; he may only be called a Lake poet because his poetical principles were similar to those of the Lake School. But the three others also deviated from each other in many ways as they grew older; and Southey even became a thorough apostate from the principles of philosophical and political freedom which he had embraced so enthusiastically in his youth. Wordsworth and Coleridge were never unfaithful to the cause of freedom and humanity, though they chose different paths as poets in their more mature compositions; Wordsworth being guided by philosophical reflection while Coleridge followed his somewhat fanciful imagination.

William Wordsworth (1770—1850) began his poetical career by descriptions in verse of his walking tour among the Swiss Alps and English lakes, and then he and Coleridge published a volume of "Lyrical Ballads" (1798). In 1807 appeared his

P

"Miscellaneous Poems." In the preface to the lyrical ballads he makes a full exposition of his principles of composition. He there requires a poet to possess: "1st. the powers of observation and description, i.e. the ability to observe with accuracy things as they are in themselves, and with fidelity to describe them, unmodified by any passion or feeling existing in the mind of the writer, whether the things depicted be actually present to the senses, or have a place only in the memory," &c. "2nd. Sensibility, which, the more exquisite it is, the wider will be the range of a poet's perception," &c. "3rd. Reflection, which makes the poet acquainted with the value of actions, images, thoughts, and feelings, and assist the sensibility in perceiving their connexion with each other. 4th. Imagination and fancy, to modify, to create, and associate. 5th. Invention, by which characters are composed out of materials supplied by observation," &c. "And lastly, judgment, to decide how, where, and in what degree each of these faculties should be exerted," &c.

On closer reflection we must confess that little is to be gained by this pedantic and incomplete analysis of the poetical talent, which might have come from the pen of Addison or Pope. And yet Wordsworth and the other Lake poets were diametrically opposed to the style of Pope and his time; they stood in the front ranks of the poetical reformers, their watchword was: Nature. Poetry was to be found in nature, in everyday life; and its spirit was to speak the language of nature, and to call things by their proper names. Such a tendency contained the danger of degenerating into prosiness, from which the Lake school has not always been free.

In the autumn of 1798, Wordsworth went to Germany with his friend Samuel Taylor Coleridge (1772—1834). Both were anxious to go there from a feeling of consanguinity with the German nation, which induced them to make themselves familiar with the manners and customs, the views, and the literature of the Germans. Their stay there was undoubtedly of great moment, in bringing about more intimate literary relations between the two countries. Coleridge made an excellent metrical translation of Schiller's "Wallenstein" and thus made known to his countrymen the masterpiece of the most ideal poet of the German race.

At the time that these two poets stayed in Germany, Schelling's philosophy of nature, which had originated in the mind of the philosopher Fichte, was gaining ground there. Those views brought about a new epoch in the study of natural science, and were embraced by Wordsworth and Coleridge. Organic and inorganic nature was looked upon by them as one vast harmony, whose largest and smallest portions were mysteriously connected with the Divine Soul of the World, and all intellectual and moral power was imagined to be diffused by millions of veins through the physical organism of the world. But these pantheistic dreams of the poets did not prevent them from remaining orthodox Trinitarians.

Wordsworth has carried out the idyllic simplicity and philosophical tendency of the lake-school with great consistency, and has left a lasting monument to those principles in the chief work of his life, the poem " The Recluse " (1814), the first part of which is entitled " The Excursion," and the second " The White Doe of Rylstone." " The Excursion " offers the fullest exposition of what may be called Wordsworth's religious, moral, and social theory. The plan of the poem is as follows : a pedlar who passes through the mountainous parts of the north of England meets the poet near a ruined cottage on a solitary heath ; both wander on together, meeting a discharged military chaplain, the wife of a distressed weaver, a servant, and other persons of low rank, with whom they converse on the changeful fate of human life. In these conversations the relation of man to God, to nature, to his fellowmen, and to his own self, is considered from all points of view. In his poem " The Old Beggar," Wordsworth has warmly expressed his belief that nature is one perfect organism, in which everything is assigned to a certain place and fulfils a certain purpose. Many of his shorter poems are charming idyllic pictures, and his sonnets—he has written about 400—contain many excellent thoughts clearly expressed. His influence was felt but gradually, but it was penetrative and beneficial in many respects ; nevertheless his compositions cannot produce purely poetical impressions on account of the philosophical and moralizing tendency, which is too strongly pronounced in most of them.[1]

Coleridge took more trouble than Wordsworth to bring the reformatory views of the Lake school to bear on the busy life of politics and society. He introduced into England public lectures on æsthetics and literary history, as was the fashion in Germany, and was busy throughout his life as an essayist. In his lyrical poems[2] Coleridge has remained faithful to the principles of the Lake school; but he forms a great contrast to the sobriety and simplicity of Wordsworth inasmuch as he chose the wildest and strangest subjects for his poetical treatment and interwove the Lake idyll with romantic traditions. This is specially the case in his admired romance "Geneviève." His drama "Remorse" was represented on the stage in 1813, and was received favourably. But his genius shows most originality in the poetical tale "Christabel" (1816), which he appropriately called a vision, and in his ballad "The Ancient Mariner." "Christabel" was to consist of five cantos, but only two were completed. The fragmentary character of the poem does not injure its effect, it rather increases its peculiar and vague horror. In this poem, as well as in the wildly beautiful ballad of "The Ancient Mariner," the mysterious operation of demoniacal

[1] "Poetical Works of William Wordsworth," Lond. 1833, 4 vols.
[2] "Juvenile Poems," "Sibylline Leaves," "Miscellaneous Poems."

powers in nature is made to be felt so vividly that we are seized with horror at the tale of the old sailor and of his fearful adventures. The chief idea of the poem is that man should be gentle and grateful towards inferior creatures, so as not to excite the anger of the mysterious powers, whose rule is shown by the dreadful punishment inflicted on the crew of a vessel in consequence of their wantonly killing an albatross. The fantastic contents of the ballad form an effective contrast to the conciseness of the style; descriptions—such as of the calm, and of the appearance of the spectre-bark, on whose deck Night-mare and Death are casting dice for the crew destined to destruction [3]—are powerfully impressive. Coleridge in an

[3] "The western wave was all a-flame,
The day was well-nigh done!
Almost upon the western wave
Rested the broad bright sun;
When that strange shape drove suddenly
Betwixt us and the sun.
And straight the sun was fleck'd with bars
(Heaven's mother send us grace!),
As if through a dungeon-grate he peer'd
With broad and burning face.
Alas! (thought I, and my heart beat loud)
How fast she nears and nears!
Are those her sails that glance in the sun,
Like restless gossameres?
Are those her ribs through which the sun
Did peer as through a grate?
And is that Woman all her crew?
Is that a Death? and are there two?
Is Death that woman's mate?

autobiography gives an interesting description of the literary life of his time, and of the position he occupied in it.[4]

Robert Southey (1774—1843), the third of the Lake poets, had such extreme religious and political views in his youth, that he not only enthusiastically expressed his sympathy with the French Revolution, but European society appeared to him too narrow for his ideal of freedom, and he intended to go to America with his friend Coleridge to found in the forests of the new world a truly free and humane state.

These views made him choose Wat Tyler for the subject of his first work, which is a dramatic glorification of that revolutionary character. But soon Southey's inclinations and opinions took an entirely

> Her lips were red, her looks were free,
> Her locks were yellow as gold ;
> Her skin was as white as leprosy,
> The Nightmare Life-in-Death was she,
> Who thicks men's blood with cold.
>
> The naked hulk alongside came,
> And the twain were casting dice ;
> 'The game is done! I've won, I've won!'
> Quoth she, and whistles thrice.
>
> The sun's rim dips ; the stars rush out :
> At one stride comes the dark ;
> With far-heard whisper, o'er the sea,
> Off shot the spectre-bark."

[4] "Biographical Sketches of my Literary Life and Opinions," 1817. "Poetical Works," 1828, 3 vols. Compare : "Memoirs and Letters of Sara Coleridge," ed. by her Daughter, 2 vols. 1873.

opposite direction, and after he had been made poet laureate (1813) his apostasy became complete. He has had much to suffer on account of this, especially from Lord Byron, who heaped the bitterest sarcasms on him on every occasion. We must not, however, be tempted to consider these as a criterion of Southey as a poet. Southey *was* a poet, and one of the most imaginative and productive that England ever possessed. His poetry has been compared to the solemn harmony of an organ; and we may add, that the instrument was played by the hand of an artist. In his first lyrical attempts he did homage to the style of the Lake school, but he soon turned to epic poetry, for which he was more gifted, and he has essentially enlarged and enriched the sphere of the romantic epic founded by Scott. His first epic poem was "Joan of Arc" (1797), and it was succeeded by a number of brilliant compositions of powerful fancy touching both hemispheres. In 1804 appeared his "Metrical Tales" and his Arabian narrative "Thalaba the Destroyer;" then followed "Madoc" (1805), the subject of which is the legend of the discovery of America by a Welsh chieftain in the year 1170; then "The Curse of Kehama" (1813), gathering up the life of India into a brilliant picture; and lastly, "Roderick, the Last of the Goths" (1814), written in powerful blank verse—a truly heroic poem on the decline of the Gothic power in Spain by the invasion of the Arabs. All these poems reveal an abundance of fancy and of truly poetical conception, rendered in a style rich in images, and yet lucid and clear. Southey's style shows itself to still greater advantage in his ballads, several of which, such as "The Old Woman of Berkeley," "Lord William and Mary," "Mary the Maid of the Inn," are among the best poems of this kind. Southey's epic talent also made him successful as an historian. His " History of Brazil ' (1810), and "History of the Peninsular War" (the war of Spanish independence, against Napoleon) are distinguished by impressive combination, and by clear representations of the movements of the masses, and his "Biography of Nelson" (1813) will always remain an ornament among English biographies. Southey was also an active critic, but his judgment is often biassed by political prejudice.[5]

John Wilson (born 1789) has been called a Lake poet without sufficient reason; his descriptive poem "The Angler's Tent," and his novels,[6] which are most true to nature, might perhaps entitle him to the name. Both the poem and the novels bring about a graceful connexion between the prose of life and poetry, without giving evidence of the intention. Wilson attempted a loftier style of poetry in "The City of the Plague," which describes the desolation of London by the plague in touching but by no means disgusting traits; also

[5] "Poetical Works of Robert Southey," 1820, 14 vols.
[6] "Lights and Shadows of Scottish Life," "The Trials of Margaret Lindsay," "The Foresters."

in his charming fairy-tale "Edith and Nora," and in his poetical narrative "The Isle of Palms," which first established his reputation. The story of the poem is simple: two lovers suffer shipwreck in the Indian Ocean; they are cast on an uninhabited island, live there seven years; is born to them a child, and they at last return home on a vessel landing by chance. Wilson's imagination had full scope in such a subject to revel in descriptions of tropical nature, and of an idyllic life under palm-trees.

CHAPTER XIII.

Byron.[1]

AT the time that Scott had reached the zenith of his glory in the romantic epic, that Moore sang his

[1] "The Works of Lord Byron, in one volume, with notes by Moore, Jeffrey, Scott, Heber, Rogers, Wilson, Lockhart, Ellis, Campbell, and Milman," 1842. "The Life and Prose Works of Lord Byron, including his Letters and Journals, with notices of his Life," by Thomas Moore, 1842. "Conversations with Lord Byron," ed. by Medwin, 1824. "Lord Byron en Italie et en Grèce," ed. by De Salvo, 1825. "Lord Byron and some of his contemporaries," ed. by Leigh Hunt, 1828. "Conversations with Lord Byron," ed. by Lady Blessington, 1834. "Lord Byron, jugé par les témoins de sa vie," par la Comtesse Teresa Guiccioli, 1868.

To avoid repetitions in the text, here follows the chronology of Byron's works :—

1807.—Hours of Idleness.
1809.—English Bards and Scotch Reviewers.
1812.—The two first cantos of Childe Harold.
1813.—The Waltz. The Giaour. The Bride of Abydos.
1814.—The Corsair. Lara. Hebrew Melodies.
1816.—The Siege of Corinth. Parisina. The Prisoner of Chillon. Monody on the Death of Sheridan. The Dream. Darkness. Prometheus. The third canto of Childe Harold
1817.—Manfred. The Lament of Tasso. Beppo.
1818.—Ode to Venice. The fourth canto of Childe Harold. Mazeppa. The two first cantos of Don Juan.

finest Irish melodies, that Southey planned the most brilliant creations of his fancy, that Coleridge worked at his "Christabel," and Wordsworth at his "Excursion"—at that time a meteor rose on the literary sky of England, which, splendid and fearful like a comet, darkened all other stars to the end of its course, and causing during its existence a feeling of mingled admiration and terror, left at its disappearance an indelible track of flame.

The life of George Gordon Byron is a modern novel with an heroically romantic ending. Many have been tempted to write the history of a creature who is strangely made up of a poet, a voluptuary, and a hero; but none have come up to the reality of its poetry. Byron's life is the best commentary on his works. It cannot be said of him as of other poets, that his works are his life, but they certainly can only be explained by it.

Byron was born in London on the 22nd of

1819.—Don Juan (Cantos III., IV.).
1820.—The prophecy of Dante. Marino Faliero. Don Juan (Canto V.).
1821.—Sardanapalus. The two Foscari. Cain. Vision of Judgment. Heaven and Earth.
1822.—Werner. The Deformed Transformed. Don Juan (Cantos VI.—XI.).
1823.—The Age of Bronze. The Island. Don Juan (Cantos XII.—XVI.).

Byron's shorter poems, except the "Hours of Idleness," have been collected under the titles "Domestic Pieces," and "Occasional Pieces." The bitter satire "The Curse of Minerva," written at Athens in March 1811, was only published in 1828.

January 1788, the offspring of an unhappy marriage. His father, who died when the boy was only three years old, had been known in the dissolute circles of London by the name of "Mad Jack," and was a spendthrift, who left his wife and children in reduced circumstances. Nor was George, independent of this, a child of fortune, for he was born with a club-foot, which became a subject of insurmountable vexation to his irritable temper. His mother, who had the strangest ideas about education if she had any at all, took the boy to her native country, Scotland, and lived in the Highlands with him for a time. Here his young imagination received the first poetical impressions, which may be found later on in several of his poems. His mental cultivation made but slow progress under the rule of his mother, who changed inconsistently from exaggerated tenderness to exaggerated severity, but his physical development was rapid and healthy. In spite of his lame foot he became a bold swimmer when still a child, and later on an excellent rider, boxer, fencer, and pistol-shot. He was very proud of these accomplishments, and an almost boyish conceit of them characterized him throughout life. Ten years after his birth Byron became a member of the aristocracy of his country, by inheriting a peerage and the family seat, Newstead Abbey, from his great uncle, William, who was notorious for his eccentricities. At this change in his fortunes his mother took him back to England, and he was entered at Harrow School. In the last year of his stay there, and while spending his holidays with his mother in Nottingham, the boy became acquainted with Miss Mary Chaworth. The girl's feelings were those of cool friendship, but in the soul of the growing poet was kindled the blazing flame of first love. Miss Chaworth, whose grandfather had been killed in a duel by Byron's great-uncle, preferred an insignificant country gentleman to the "lame boy," and led a very unhappy married life. But the name of Mary remained sacred to Byron for ever,[2] and many years after his rejection by her he loved so passionately, he celebrated her memory by the most deep-felt utterances of his heart.[3] He entered Trinity

---

[2] Compare "Don Juan," canto v., stanza 4 : "I have a passion for the name of Mary."

[3] "As the sweet moon on the horizon's verge,
The maid was on the eve of womanhood ;
The boy had fewer summers, but his heart
Had far outgrown his years, and to his eye
There was but one beloved face on earth,
And that was shining on him ; he had look'd
Upon it till it could not pass away ;
He had no breath, no being, but in hers :
She was his voice ; he did not speak to her,
But trembled on her words : she was his sight,
For his eye follow'd hers, and saw with hers,
Which colour'd all his objects :—he had ceased
To live within himself ; she was his life,
The ocean to the river of his thoughts,
Which terminated all : upon a tone,
A touch of hers, his blood would ebb and flow,
And his cheek change tempestuously . . . ."
　　　　　　　　　　　　"The Dream," ii.

College, Cambridge, in 1805, and there became notorious for his eccentricities: he kept a tame bear in his room (throughout life he was very fond of animals), gave himself up to wine and gambling, and was pleased to make a show of greater debauchery than he was really guilty of. He left Cambridge before he had attained his nineteenth year, and lived alternately in London and at Newstead Abbey. The latter became the noisy gathering-place of a band of like-minded friends who filled the halls of the former convent with the noise of all kinds of pranks. But Byron's ambition began to stir, and in the spring of 1807 he published a first collection of poems, "Hours of Idleness." These poems were not exactly bad, but they did not by any means foreshadow the further development of his genius. The addition on the title-page, by "a Minor," induced the "Edinburgh Review" to pounce on the little book with a bitter and sneering critique. Byron says that when he first read this abusive article pain and rage almost maddened him, and that he could not find any rest until he had taken his revenge. He did it by his satire " English Bards and Scotch Reviewers" which presented the whole literary life of Great Britain at that time in a ridiculous light. This poem, however, gave proof of undeniable power, and from the time of its appearance public attention was ceaselessly occupied with its author. Of course in such a work of revengeful bitterness many unjust and over-hasty judgments were pronounced. Byron suppresed most of them in the later editions of the satire, and entered into friendly relations with several of the men whom he had attacked the most severely, such as Moore, Scott, and Lord Holland. Æsthetic criticism was altogether one of Byron's weakest points; we can scarcely believe our eyes when we read the praises which he bestows upon Pope, at the expense of Shakespeare and Milton.[4]

In January 1809 he attained his majority, and in March he took his seat in the House of Lords. But a political career had no charms for him; his imagination drew him to the sunny countries of the East, and in June he embarked with his friend Hobhouse for Lisbon, from whence he went by Seville, Cadiz, and Gibraltar to the Levant. He landed in Albania, in whose wildly beautiful mountains he visited the court of Ali Pasha, a despot of Eastern grandeur. There, among those foreign surroundings, the first canto of Childe Harold was begun. From Albania he went by Patras, Mount Parnassus, Delphi, and Thebes, to Athens, where he wrote his famous song "The Maid of Athens,"[5]

---

[4] In his literary quarrel with Bowles about Pope, Byron wrote to Moore, May 3rd 1821 : " As to Pope, I have always regarded him as the greatest name in our poetry. Depend upon it the rest are barbarians. He is a Greek temple, with a Gothic cathedral on one hand, and a Turkish mosque and all sorts of fantastic pagodas and conventicles about him. You may call Shakespeare and Milton pyramids, if you please; but I prefer the Temple of Theseus or the Parthenon to a mountain of burnt brickwork."   [5] Teresa Makri.

in February 1810; then on to Smyrna, where the second canto of "Childe Harold" was completed. On the journey from Smyrna to Constantinople the poet visited the plain of Troy, and swam across the Hellespont between Sestos and Abydos, to show that he could equal Leander, even without a Hero. After a few months' stay at Constantinople he returned to Greece, travelled through Morea, paid another visit to Athens, and in the summer of 1811 he returned to England by Malta: his mother died soon after his arrival.

On the 27th of February 1812 Byron delivered his maiden speech in the Upper House. It raised expectations, but the poet only spoke twice afterwards, he did not care for parliamentary debate. Two days after Byron's first speech in the House of Lords appeared the first two cantos of "Childe Harold's Pilgrimage." The success was unexampled; the edition was sold immediately, and the impression the poem created was as deep and lasting as it was general. Byron said quite candidly that he attributed much of his success to his rank. He did not yet know the nature and power of his own genius. Besides "Childe Harold" he had brought from his travels the didactic and satirical Essay "Hints from Horace," and the satire "The Curse of Minerva,"[6] and set great value on the publication of the former, a rather indifferent production.

[6] Directed against Lord Elgin, who had robbed Athens of its antiquities, and sold his spoil to the English Government for 35,000*l.*

His friend Dallas had great trouble in persuading him to publish "Childe Harold" first, and only the delight of the public proved to the author the worth of the poem, and pointed out the course his genius was to take. Byron called the Pilgrimage "a romaunt," but the epic element is quite subordinate in the poem. Through the thin and transparent mask of the hero we always recognize the features of the poet. The poem is written in the Spenserian stanza, and is a poetical diary of travel which presents in magnificent pictures the impressions which the poet received in Spain and in the Levant. The form therefore is not new, for descriptive poetry had been used before now in narratives of travels, as e.g. in Goldsmith's "Traveller." The originality of "Childe Harold" consists in the way in which Byron made use of the old form. He raised descriptive poetry to the loftiest style of the lyric, expressing in words of fire a high-minded sympathy with everything great and noble, and mingling indignation at irrationalism and tyranny, with plaintive notes of the deepest melancholy at the decline of the beautiful, and at the sufferings of the nations. In a word, passionate feeling was the characteristic note of "Childe Harold." Since Shakespeare there had been no poet who could give utterance to passion as Byron did; what Shakespeare did as a dramatist, Byron did as a lyric poet.

In March the following year Byron published, under the name of Horace Hornem, the satire

"The Waltz," a bitter and witty expression of his annoyance at his club-foot which prevented him from waltzing. Two months later appeared "The Giaour," relating the tragical fate of a Turkish slave Leila, who, on account of her love to a Venetian, an infidel (giaour), is thrown into the sea by her master, on whom her lover takes a bloody revenge. The poem sparkles with the glowing colours of the East, and the enthusiasm of love [7] as well as the violence of hatred are drawn with wonderful power. To "The Giaour" succeeded in rapid succession "The Bride of Abydos," "The Corsair," "Lara," "The Siege of Corinth," and "Parisina," five poetical tales, in which Byron reached the perfection of this kind of composition. It had always been popular in England and Chaucer had already made it famous. The form of poetic narrative was particularly well adapted to Byron's genius, for in

---

[7] The most beautiful passage in the praise of love is the following:—
"Yes, Love indeed is light from heaven;
A spark of that immortal fire
With angels shared, by Allah given,
To lift from earth our low desire.
Devotion wafts the mind above,
But heaven itself descends in love;
A feeling from the Godhead caught,
To wean from self each sordid thought;
A ray of Him who form'd the whole,
A glory circling round the soul."
Compare: "Childe Harold" (iv. 121): "O love, no habitant of earth thou art," &c., and "The Island" (ii. 16): "The devotee lives not in earth," &c.

it the lyrical element can occupy a great place and the individuality of the poet finds ample room for subjective utterance. The sombre magnificence of these compositions increased the enthusiasm of general society for Byron, while at the same time his "Hebrew Melodies" won for him the approval of gentle and religious minds.

In the beginning of the year 1816 the poet had attained the zenith of popularity with his countrymen. A great change then took place in the favour of the public, on account of an incident in the private life of the poet. In the early part of the year 1815 Byron had contracted a marriage with Miss Anne Isabella Milbanke, without real inclination on either side, as is shown by letters relating to the subject. The harmony between husband and wife, which had never been more than a superficial one, was soon destroyed, and the more so as Byron's financial affairs were in great disorder at the time. Byron being one of the directors of Drury Lane theatre often came in contact with actresses, and in this circumstance his wife found cause for jealousy; nor was Byron's conduct ever of a kind to please the very cold temperament of his wife. She left the house of her husband with her only child, a little daughter, never to return to it, though even on her journey to the country-seat of her parents she wrote him a letter beginning with most affectionate terms, in which not a word is said of a permanent separation from him.

But steps for a divorce were taken immediately. Byron attributes the mischief to his mother-in-law. The matter, however, has never been fully explained. Byron gave the papers concerning it into Moore's keeping, and he considered it better not to publish them. Byron wrote to his wife his touching " Fare thee well! and if for ever," but this only increased the scandal and the malice of his enemies.

The state of aristocratic society in England in the time of the Prince Regent was most corrupt. The head of the State set the example of every kind of debauchery. Brummell, a man skilled in the arts of the toilet, generally called Beau Brummell, ruled the world of fashion with a tyrannical sceptre, and was the oracle of the proudest aristocracy of Europe. Dukes and earls stood respectfully round his toilet-table while he made experiments in a new tooth-powder, or initiated them into the secret of tying the bow of a neckcloth. Such dandyism was the harmless side of the fashionable world; very much worse things have been told us: one nobleman was a notorious " Greek," that is to say he cheated at cards, and gained by it one and a half million pounds sterling during his life. Another peer was entered in the betting book of a club, as the first rogue that should be hanged in Great Britain; and so on. Byron's diary of December 1813 also furnishes characteristic facts.

Such was the society which had surrounded

Byron by every temptation, and which now pronounced sentence of condemnation on him. He determined to go abroad to seek warmer climes and warmer hearts; he sold Newstead Abbey, and on the 25th of April 1816 he left England, never to return.

He visited the battle-field of Waterloo and went up the Rhine to Switzerland. On this journey the third canto of " Childe Harold," in which the beauty of the noble German river is so warmly acknowledged, was begun. He spent the summer in intimate intercourse with Shelley, who also lived in voluntary exile, and whose friendship Byron had lately acquired; they lived in the Villa Diodati, near Geneva, and made tours in the Bernese Alps, whose peerless magnificence he has described in his diary of 1816, and of which he has made use in the scenery of " Manfred." He was still working at " Childe Harold " and at this time also composed the " Prisoner of Chillon," a hymn to liberty in the form of a poetic narrative; the two beautiful elegies, " Monody on the Death of Sheridan " and " The Dream," the bold address to " Prometheus," and the night-piece " Darkness," whose grandeur is unequalled even by Dante's " Inferno." In the autumn he went across the Alps to Venice, and during the winter which he spent there " Manfred," which he had begun in Switzerland, was finished. The hero of this metaphysical drama belongs to the race of Faust—a grand nature, weighed to the ground by some fearful guilt, irretrievably given up to the powers of darkness. Manfred has loved his sister more than a brother should, and his love has caused his sister's death. It is in vain that he makes the world of spirits subservient to himself to atone for a remembrance which consumes his life without being able to break his pride. The impression of a sultry stormy sky seems to rest upon this composition; only here and there the heavy clouds are rent, and a splendid ray falls on the scenes of Alpine grandeur to which Manfred has carried his pain.

In the spring of 1817, Byron made a pilgrimage to the prison in Ferrara where the poet of "Jerusalem Delivered" had suffered, and there the deeply touching rhapsody "Tasso's Complaint" was inspired. Returning to Venice from an excursion to Rome "Beppo" was written in stanzas of eight lines, a sort of preliminary practice for "Don Juan." At the same time the poet began and finished the fourth and last canto of "Childe Harold," beginning with the famous stanzas on Venice. In the course of that poem Byron dropped the thin epic mask more and more, and in the fourth canto he is quite himself. Of all Byron's creations this leaves the purest and grandest impressions. The contemplation of the monuments and historic memories of Italy inspire him with lyrical strains, whose noble wrath, passing into touching sadness at last, rises to a pathos whose truth and power call forth the deepest sympathy for the poet. In the second half of the year 1818 Byron composed the sad "Ode to Venice," a variation on the theme " There is no hope for nations ;" also the poetical tale "Mazeppa," which rushes along in wild power like the courser of the Ukraine, bound on whose back the hero accomplishes his horrible ride, and the beginning of "Don Juan." This modern heroic epic, which resembles no other poem, is in its form a triumph of the English language. The diction is as bold as it is graceful and unwavering ; now it revels in the sweetest and most caressing tones of love, now it shrieks with hatred and anger ; here, it delights in painting the most voluptuous situations, there, storms at sea, shipwrecks, and battles are thrown out in plastic force ; now it expresses a bitterly satirical disdain of men, and then again it rises to a pathos that would teach, if possible, " the stones to rise against earth's tyrants."[8] "Don Juan" is the practical summing up of Byron's nature : ardour and scepticism, hatred and love, weary satiety and enthusiasm, all the various feelings of this rich and powerful mind are here mingled; to these is added the irresistible charm of humour.

Το first cantos of this remarkable poem are a poetical reflection of the voluptuous and dissipated life which Byron was leading at the time. Venice, the centre of all pleasures before Paris took away its reputation, exercised its luxurious influence on

[8] Canto viii. 135.

the poet too. The palace he inhabited was the scene of voluptuous orgies, in which the wild Venetian Margharita Cogni played a conspicuous part. At that time Byron seemed to look upon intellectual and material life as on an orgie which had to be passed through as quickly as possible in order to get to the end of it. A beautiful female character began to exercise her influence on him at this time, and restored a more serious and noble tone to his life. In April 1819 he first saw Teresa Gamba; she had been married to Count Guiccioli at the age of sixteen; she was eighteen years old at this time, her girlish beauty unimpaired, and she seemed made on purpose to be the mistress of a poet.[9] At the close of the year Byron followed her to Ravenna; in his intercourse with her and with the two Counts Gamba, Teresa's father and brother, Byron first experienced the charms of domestic life, which he, like every Englishman, knew how to appreciate. His life at Ravenna was very different from that at Venice. It was taken up with work, with a lively interest in the patriotic plans of the Carbonari, into which

[9] There exists a letter from the Countess in which she speaks of her first meeting with Byron in the drawing-room of the Countess Benzoni. She there says, speaking of Byron's personal appearance, "His noble and exquisitely beautiful countenance, the tone of his voice, his manners, the thousand enchantments that surrounded him, rendered him so different and superior a being to any whom I had hitherto seen, that it was impossible he should not have left the most profound impression upon me."

the Gambas had initiated him, and with deeds of charity and benevolence, on the subject of which his enemies at home took good care to be silent.[1]

Teresa Guiccioli asked Byron for a poetical ode to Dante's memory, similar to that which he had written on Tasso. In answer to her request he wrote "The Prophecy of Dante," which remained unfinished, but which is a homage not unworthy of the greatest poetic genius of Italy. Teresa's influence may be traced in the seriousness and grandeur which characterize Byron's poetry from the time he became acquainted with the refined and intellectual Italian. Even the continuation of

[1] In her memoirs the Countess Guiccioli speaks of Byron's life at Ravenna in the following manner: "This sort of simple life he led until the fatal day of his departure for Greece, and the few variations he made from it may be said to have arisen solely from the greater or smaller number of occasions which were offered him of doing good, and from the generous actions he was continually performing. Many families (in Ravenna principally) owed to him the few prosperous days they ever enjoyed. His arrival in that town was spoken of as a piece of public good fortune, and his departure as a public calamity; and this is the life which many attempted to asperse as that of a libertine. But the world must at last learn how, with so good and generous a heart, Lord Byron, susceptible, it is true, of the most energetic passions, yet, at the same time, of the sublimest and most pure, and rendering homage in his *acts* to every virtue— how he, I say, could afford such scope to malice and to calumny. Circumstances, and also, probably, an eccentricity of disposition (which, nevertheless, had its origin in a virtuous feeling, an excessive abhorrence for hypocrisy and affectation) contributed perhaps to cloud the splendour of his exalted nature in the opinion of many."

Don Juan became less sensuous and less extravagant. In Ravenna he wrote two tragic dramas, taken from the history of Venice, " Marino Faliero " and " The Two Foscari." They are dramatic only in form, but a language of extraordinary power somewhat compensates for the lack of dramatic action.[2] In consequence of these two pieces, Byron's dramatic talent was denied at once, and he himself did not object to the verdict. Indeed he lacks two essential qualities of the dramatic poet—the capability of creating different characters, and the art of representing these characters in their development. With very few exceptions his characters are fully developed at their first appearance, and they are always, the men at least, Byron himself. Byron was as essentially a lyric, as Shakespeare was a dramatic poet. All his poetry is only the expression of his powerful individuality. Nevertheless he composed a tragedy at this time which fully deserves to be called one, " Sardanapalus." Byron's daring alone could chose such an infamous subject for a tragedy, and only a first-rate poet could make of it a poem of such exceeding beauty. In " Sardanapalus," as well as in the tragedy " Werner," finished soon after the former,

---

[2] The speech in which the Doge Faliero, within view of the block and the axe, curses degenerate Venice, and devotes it to the powers of destruction—" I speak to Time and to Eternity "—is of overpowering grandeur. Jeffrey might well say of it : " His last speech is a grand prophetic rant ; something strained and elaborate, but eloquent and terrible."

weakness of character is raised to a tragical element of power.[3] Besides that, love in its highest conception reigns in "Sardanapalus," personified in the slave Myrrha, who is not inferior to any female character of Shakespeare's or Goethe's, and who is the most beautiful flower in the rich garland of Byron's female figures, which far excel his delineations of the other sex. At Ravenna, in 1821, he wrote also the two other dramatic compositions, "Cain," and "Heaven and Earth," which he entitled "mysteries," in commemoration of the Biblical plays of the middle ages. "Cain" is the most complete and finished work of the poet, and we cannot contradict Shelley when he calls it the greatest of Byron's poems. Cain is a Titanic Manfred, a creation similar to Job and Prometheus. The spirit of Æschylus seems to breathe in the poem, and with the exception of a few passages in "Paradise Lost" and in "Faust," modern poetry has produced nothing similar in boldness and in grandeur to Cain's flight with Lucifer through

---

[3] Rosenkranz, a German critic on æsthetics, characterizes Byron's two tragedies as follows: "The subject of Byron's Sardanapalus and Werner is weakness. In "Sardanapalus" we see a noble, but too humane, too indulgent nature, rise step by step from the careless enjoyment of life to the truly royal dignity, to the heroic courage, to the sublimity of self-sacrifice—a psychological painting of incomparable depth and beauty. In "Werner," on the other hand, the poet has shown how the weakness of an originally noble nature may degenerate into vulgarity, and poison the rest of life by the shameful remembrance of its transgression."

illimitable space,[4] and the conversations of the two in Hades.[5] In England the poem was appreciated by few at first, and Byron called it jestingly "the Waterloo of his popularity."[6] But it is an æsthetic truth that the creation of Satan in "Cain" must be considered as one of the greatest achievements of modern poetry. There are altogether only four poets who have succeeded in portraying Satan: Vandel, Milton, Goethe, and Byron. Vandel's Satan was created fourteen years before that of Milton; it is a powerful conception, and undoubtedly the greatest poetical figure which Holland has produced. Goethe's Mephisto is such a peculiar impersonation of the Satanic idea that he cannot be compared to the others. Byron's Satan ranks next to Milton's. Dante's detailed delineation only produces a somewhat ridiculous monster which leaves us perfectly indifferent, while Milton's and Byron's Satan is a colossal extension of the human form surrounded by a darkness as of thunder-clouds, and exciting our terror as well as a feeling of sympathy. But Byron's conception of Satan is distinctly twofold. In the "Vision of

[4] Act ii. Sc. 1, "I tread on air, and sink not," &c.
[5] Act ii. Sc. 2, "How silent and how vast are these dim worlds!" &c.
[6] "Even I . . . .
Was reckon'd a considerable time
The grand Napoleon of the realms of rhyme.
But 'Juan' was my Moscow, and 'Faliero'
My Leipsic, and my Mont Saint Jean seems 'Cain'"
"Don Juan," xi. 55.

Judgment" he writes of him, "His brow was like the deep when tempest-tossed" &c., and in this the impression which the appearance produces is materially fearful. In "Cain" Lucifer only seems as it were to impress the mind. The passage where Cain sees Satan approaching for the first time, "Whom have we here?" &c., is unequalled by anything that has ever been written of spirits.

Meanwhile the poet had been induced to change his abode. Teresa's father, in whose house she lived, was obliged to leave the Papal States on account of the trial of the Carbonari. In November 1821 Byron followed his friend to Pisa. In Ravenna he had also written the "Vision of Judgment," being irritated by what Southey had said of him in the preface to his poem of the same name. Byron's "Vision of Judgment" is a critique of the Government of George III., sparkling with wit and passion. He inflicted similar chastisement a year later, by the satire "The Age of Bronze." While in Pisa Byron received the news of Shelley's death, and mourned his friend deeply. In September 1822 he went to Genoa and there wrote his last poem of any length, the poetical narrative "The Island." It differs greatly from Byron's former poems of the kind : it is not a volcanic eruption of genius, but the work of the artist. The interesting fable is presented in soft colouring and with quiet grace ; it has not a Byronic ending—that is to say, it does not close with a discord ; the faith of the heroine Neuha, a native of an island of the

South Pacific, triumphs over the fate which threatens to rob her of her beloved white man. The poem impresses us with the idea that at the time of its composition the proud and rebellious heart of the poet had been calmed by the love and friendship of those who surrounded him. But his mind was directed to great aims. The deathlike stillness which the Holy Alliance had spread over Europe was interrupted in the three southern peninsulas. Spain demanded an immense sacrifice from a prince who had no equal in infamy; Italy in fetters gnashed her teeth; Greece began to break the yoke of a barbarous tyranny. Byron, sympathizing with every rebellious feeling, determined to change his poetry into action, and to sacrifice himself and all he had to the cause of Greece. He entered into relations with the Greek chieftains and with the Philhellenic Society in London, and in July 1823 he set sail for Greece with the brother of his mistress and other friends. He was received at Missolonghi with enthusiasm, formed a brigade of Suliotes at his own expense, and was just going to take the command of an expedition which the Greek Government was sending against Lepanto, when a fatal fever seized him. On his thirty-seventh birthday, January 22nd 1824, he had written his last poem, and the last wish he there expressed was for a soldier's grave.[7] It was not to be fulfilled. His

[7] " Seek out—less often sought than found—
A soldier's grave, for thee the best;

illness increased; on the evening of the 18th of April he spoke his last words: " I must sleep now," and on the following day he passed away. The Greek Government accorded military honours to the great deceased, and acknowledged their irreparable loss by ordering a public mourning. His corpse was taken to England and buried in the village church of Hucknall Torkard, near Newstead Abbey. Poets of all nations have rendered due homage to his genius.[8]

    Then look around, and choose thy ground,
        And take thy rest."

[8] The poetical homage rendered to Byron by Rogers and Bulwer in England, by Lamartine and Hugo in France, by Goethe, Zedlitz, Müller, and others, in Germany are well known. Less so is the beautiful passage on Byron in Robert Pollok's (1799—1827) religious and didactic poem "The Course of Time." Pollok was a strictly orthodox member of the Scotch Kirk, but he could not withhold his tribute of admiration for Byron's genius. In Book iv of the poem occurs the following passage:—
" He touched his harp, and nations heard, entranced.
As some vast river of unfailing source,
Rapid, exhaustless, deep, his numbers flowed,
And opened new fountains in the human heart.
Where fancy halted, weary in her flight,
In other men, his, fresh as morning rose,
And soared untrodden heights, and seemed at home
Where angels bashful looked. Others, though great,
Beneath their argument seemed struggling, whiles
He, from above descending, stooped to touch
The loftiest thought: and proudly stooped, as though
It scarce deserved his verse. With Nature's self
He seemed an old acquaintance, free to jest
At will with all her glorious majesty.

The real essence of Byron's poetry is despair—
despair of the world, of mankind, of himself. He

> He laid his hand upon 'the Ocean's mane,'
> And played familiar with his hoary locks;
> Stood on the Alps, stood on the Apennines,
> And with the thunder talked, as friend to friend,
> And wove his garland of the lightning's wing
> In sportive twist—the lightning's fiery wing,
> Which, as the footsteps of the dreadful God,
> Marching upon the storm in vengeance, seemed:
> Then turned, and with the grasshopper, who sang
> His evening song beneath his feet, conversed.
> Suns, moons, and stars, and clouds, his sisters were:
> Rocks, mountains, meteors, seas and winds, and storms,
> His brothers, younger brothers, whom he scarce
> As equals deemed. All passions of all men,
> The wild and tame, the gentle and severe:
> All thoughts, all maxims, sacred and profane:
> All creeds, all seasons, Time, Eternity,
> All that was hated, and all that was dear:
> All that was hoped, all that was feared, by man,
> He tossed about as tempest-withered leaves:
> Then smiling, looked upon the wreck he made.
> With terror now he froze the cowering blood,
> And now dissolved the heart in tenderness:
> Yet would not tremble, would not weep himself:
> But back into his soul retired, alone,
> Dark, sullen, proud, gazing contemptuously
> On hearts and passions prostrate at his feet.
> So Ocean, from the plains his waves had late
> To desolation swept, retired in pride,
> Exulting in the glory of his might,
> And seemed to mock the ruin he had wrought.
> As some fierce comet of tremendous size,
> To which the stars did reverence as it passed,
> So he, through learning and through fancy, took
> His flights sublime, and on the loftiest top

R

lived at a time when an immense void had been created in the minds of men by the destructive philosophy of the eighteenth century, which, arising in England, was popularized and propagated by France, and became in Germany, through Kant, the dignified herald of scientific liberty. The result of this philosophy was the French Revolution, its non-success was an immense disappointment : a great languor took possession of the minds of men. The idea of nationality, which pointed out to the nations in what direction practical development was possible after the cosmopolitan ideal had failed, was recognized so dimly at first, and led to so many errors, that a man of genius could not find in it an aim for his thoughts and deeds. Byron's position as an Englishman and a peer increased the difficulty of the position for him. He could not divest himself of his nationality, and yet it did not satisfy him ; he was an aristocrat by birth, and by personal inclination, but at the same time his blood boiled when he saw how Castlereagh's politics opposed the principles of national liberty. Thus Byron's great intentions could not find a distinct aim : his idealistic expectations in life had met with early disappointments. Placed on the boundary-line which separated a sinking society from one that

> Of fame's dread mountain sat : not soiled and worn
> As if he from the earth had laboured up,
> But as some bird of heavenly plumage fair
> He looked, which down from higher regions comes,
> And perched it there to see what lay beneath."

was still forming, he was restlessly driven from one doubt to another, and at last despaired of everything. The world appeared to him as it did to Hamlet, like an unweeded garden full of things rank and gross in nature, and the life of men "weary, stale, flat, and unprofitable."[9] His utter weariness and satiety would have ended in suicide if a restless love of work had not counterbalanced it.[1] To get rid of his ennui, Byron committed his poems to paper. They are as true as his sufferings. He gave utterance to the pain of his time, as his "Manfred" found a voice for the pangs of his soul.[2] His cry of despair had such a powerful and majestic tone that the poets of doubt and negation of other nations, such as Heine and Lenau, George Sand, Puschkin, and Lermontoff, seem only the echoes of Byron's voice.

[9]
                "O God! O God!
How weary, stale, flat, and unprofitable
Seem to me all the uses of this world!
Fye on't! O fye! 'tis an unweeded garden,
That grows to seed; things rank and gross in nature,
Possess it merely."   "Hamlet," i. 2.

[1] "What is the reason that I have been, all my lifetime, more or less '*ennuyé*'?"—Journal of January 6th, 1821.

[2] The words which Manfred adds (Act ii. Sc. 2), exactly apply to his author:—
              "From my youth upwards
My spirit walked not with the souls of men,
Nor looked upon the earth with human eyes;
The thirst of their ambition was not mine;
The aim of their existence was not mine;
My joys, my griefs, my passions, and my powers,
Made me a stranger."

CHAPTER XIV.

Shelley.[1]

BYRON in his diary once asked the question: "What is poetry?" and answered it in the following manner: "Poetry is the Feeling of a past and of a future world." This thought offers a good criterion for Byron himself: he only expressed one phase of poetry; he doubted all traditions, political, religious, and social, and attacked them all at different times, but he was not able to emancipate himself from them. He sang the dirge of an epoch of history that was gradually sinking below the horizon, a song ringing with the demoniacal joy of annihilation; but he did not rise to the faith in a better future. The poetry of his friend Shelley, on the other hand, is the feeling of a future world. Shelley broke entirely with tradition, and freed himself from it more thoroughly than any other Englishman of his time. The ideal cultivation of his mind was so much in advance of his time that only very few of his countrymen could follow the flight of his thoughts; he was pitied by a few, but the

---

[1] "Works," 1824. "The Shelley Papers," by F. Medwin, 1833. "Memoirs and Correspondence of Percy Bysshe Shelley," ed. by Mary Godwin (Mrs. Shelley), 1842.

majority detested and cursed him. His poetry is
a beautiful dream of the future, whose sparkling
images fade away in a metaphysical atmosphere.
His was a mind of bold speculation, and realism
could not but be opposed to it, the more so as
Shelley did not pay the slightest regard to the
establishments of Church and State.

Percy Bysshe Shelley was born August 4th
1792, at Field Place, near Warnham in Sussex.
At Eton his precocious mind was out of its element, and he had to leave the college on account
of his insubordination. The treatment he had
received at Eton increased the independence of his
character and inspired him with a burning hatred
of every form of oppression. He fared worse at
Oxford. He had come to the conclusion that
the priesthood was the source of all the misery
of mankind, and he identified priesthood with
religion. Religion, he contended, was guilty
of every horror in history, and with this view he
wrote his essay on the " Necessity of Atheism."
The heads of the university did not take the trouble
to find out that Shelley was a pantheist rather than
an atheist; he was called upon to make an uncon-
ditional recantation, and as this was decidedly
refused they expelled the youth from the university.
From that moment Shelley was an outcast from
English society, and so remained throughout his
life.

His family forsook him. He lived in London in
grinding poverty. He was exceedingly delicate,

and under a combination of want and physical suffering he was only kept alive by the enthusiasm which forces genius to make itself known. He had tried before now to give a poetic form to the wild dreams of his youth, and before he was sixteen he had written an epic poem, "The Wandering Jew," and two novels, "Tasterozzi," and the "Rosicrucian." Now, at the age of seventeen years, he composed "Queen Mab," an extravagant expression of his zeal for the improvement of the world, full of vague fantastic notions, but also, like all his poems, replete with delicate, lofty, and brilliant ideas. The book, published by a treacherous bookseller against the poet's wish, was condemned. Shelley had excited persecution especially by the notes he had added to the text. These notes, which contain an argument against Christianity, revealed great youthful incompetence; he forgot that it would be simple folly to deny the effects of Christianity in the history of the world. Contemplating the fatal results of bigotry, he came to the conclusion that the apparent cause of bigotry, Christianity, was to be rejected also. To speak of the poem itself: it does not belong to a particular class; it is a series of sketches, lyrical, descriptive, polemic, didactic, in changing metres.[2] Mab, the

[2] Byron especially admired the first lines of the poem on Death and Sleep :—
 "How wonderful is Death,
 Death and his brother Sleep !
 One, pale as yonder waning moon
 With lips of lurid blue ;

fairy-queen, carries along with her in her car the soul of Ianthe, who has lost on earth her faith in a wise and good God, and carries it through the spaces of the universe to reveal to it the purpose of the world. The fairy makes her protégée look back into the past and survey the present, both equally terrible and discouraging. But at last she also reveals to Ianthe, who turns shudderingly from this labyrinth of folly and vice, the future when the earth will be the reality of heaven, as bright an Utopia as the fondest enthusiast can picture in his most enraptured visions.[3] This presentiment of the future is not only expressed in "Queen Mab," it is, as has been said, the essence of Shelley's poetry.

About this time Shelley began to look in real life for that love whose glad tidings he preached as a poet; but his loving and longing heart was doomed to a great disappointment. He eloped with Miss Harriet Westbrook, and was wedded to her at Gretna Green; but this union was not a happy one, and three years later husband and wife consented to a separation. Shelley then went abroad, in 1814, provided with very moderate means, and roamed

> The other, rosy as the morn
> When, throned on ocean's wave,
> It blushes o'er the world:
> Yet both so passing wonderful!"

[3] "O happy Earth! reality of Heaven!
To which those restless souls that ceaselessly
Throng through the human universe, aspire;
Thou consummation of all mortal hope!" &c.

through France and Switzerland. He was of age when he returned, and became possessed of a property the produce of which he gave up to his father for the yearly sum of a thousand pounds. The summer of 1815 he spent in a house near Windsor forest, and here he wrote his beautiful poem "Alastor, or the Spirit of Solitude," describing the dreamy twilight-life of a youth, a poet, whose restless longings to find the ideal of his soul realized in the wanderings in all climes, is driven to an early grave—a half-conscious, half-unconscious transfiguration of Shelley's own life.[4] The pantheistic revellings in nature of the poem are of exceeding charm and beauty.

In 1816 Shelley became acquainted with Mary Godwin, the daughter of the author of "Caleb Williams," and herself in later times an eminent novel writer,[5]

---

[4] In the following verses from "Alastor" the poet may easily be recognized :
"By solemn vision and bright silver dream
   His infancy was nurtured. Every sight
   And sound from the vast earth and ambient air,
   Sent to its heart the choicest impulses.
   The fountains of divine philosophy
   Fled not his thirsting lips ; and all of great,
   Or good, or lovely, which the sacred past
   In truth or fable consecrates, he felt
   And knew."

[5] "Frankenstein," "Valperga," "The Last Man." "Lodore." "Frankenstein, or the modern Prometheus," is a composition of extraordinary boldness of thought and execution. Rarely has a woman attempted so grand a subject, and still more rarely carried it out in so masterly a manner.

a female nature able to understand and to love him. She left England with Shelley, and her love aroused him from his melancholy resignation to renewed faith in the future. They went to Switzerland and spent a happy summer by the Lake of Geneva. There Shelley and Byron became friends. Many a summer-night they spent in their boat on the lake, exchanging plans and ideas, and their communion was a powerful stimulus for both. Shelley was chiefly occupied at this time with his translation of Æschylus's " Prometheus." He also translated fragments of Goethe's " Faust," and made Byron acquainted with that great German poem. On his return to England a painful shock awaited him : his wife committed suicide in an attack of madness. He wished to have his two children to live with him, but the "radical" and the "atheist" was not considered fit to bring them up. At the instigation of the Lord Chancellor Eldon, the author of "Queen Mab" was declared incapable by law of exercising the duties of a father. Deeply wounded, Shelley retired into the solitude of country life, and under the shades of the beech-woods of Becham he composed the twelve cantos of " The Revolt of Islam," in the Spenserian stanza.[6]

[6] "This poem," Shelley says in the preface, "is an attempt, an experiment on the temper of the public mind, as to how far a thirst for a happier condition of moral and political society survives among the enlightened and refined. I have sought to enlist the harmony of metrical language, the ethereal combinations of the fancy, the rapid and subtle

In May 1818 Shelley left England with his second wife, never to return. Pecuniary difficulties, brought about by his untiring benevolence, and an attack on the chest, made it advisable to go to a

transitions of human passions, all those elements which essentially compose a poem, in the cause of a liberal and comprehensive morality; and in the view of kindling within the bosoms of my readers a virtuous enthusiasm for those doctrines of liberty and justice, that faith and hope in something good which neither violence nor misrepresentation nor prejudice can ever totally extinguish among mankind. . . The poem is narrative not didactic, a succession of pictures illustrating the growth and progress of individual mind aspiring after excellence and devoted to the love of mankind; its influence in refining and making pure the most daring and uncommon impulses of the imagination, the understanding, and the senses; its impatience at all the oppressions that are done under the sun; its tendency to awaken public hope, and to enlighten and improve mankind; the rapid effects of the application of that tendency; the awakening of an immense nation from their slavery and degradation, to a true sense of moral dignity and freedom; the bloodless dethronement of their oppressors, and the unveiling of the religious frauds by which they had been deluded into submission; the tranquillity of successful patriotism, and the universal toleration and benevolence of true philanthropy; the treachery and barbarity of hired soldiers; vice not the object of punishment and hatred, but kindness and pity; the faithlessness of tyrants; the confederacy of the rulers of the world, and the restoration of the expelled dynasty of foreign arms; the massacre and extermination of the patriots, and the victory of established power; the consequences of legitimate despotism,—civil war, famine, plague, superstition, and an utter extinction of the domestic affections; the judicial murder of the advocates of liberty; the temporary triumph of oppression, that secure earnest of its final and inevitable fall; the transient nature of ignorance and error, and the eternity of genius and virtue."

warmer climate in which English prices did not prevail. He went through France and Savoy, across Mont Cenis to Milan, and then joined Byron in Venice. The poem "Julian and Maddolo" offers a graceful picture of the united life of the two poets in the ancient town of St. Mark. But that did not last long : Shelley was doomed to new misfortunes. He lost quickly one after the other, first his daughter, then his son, and sick and restless he now roamed about Italy. In Rome he wrote his " Prometheus Unbound," a hymn to the liberating power of love over mankind, and the tragedy "The Cenci," the historical subject of which is one of the most fearful that can be imagined. A man, grown old in murders and unnatural vices, ill-treats his family in the most revolting manner, tries to kill his sons, rejoices at their death, insults his daughter, and after he has wickedly broken all the ties of nature, he is killed at the instigation of those he ill-treated and brings perdition upon his family from his very grave. One would have thought the visionary tendency of Shelley's mind would have recoiled from such a subject ; but he took a powerful grasp of it, and mastered it fully. This tragedy is one of the few really great ones which have been written in England since Shakespeare, and the central point of the poem, the beautiful and unhappy Beatrice Cenci, calls forth our deepest sympathy. At the time he wrote "The Cenci" he also composed the two bitter political satires, " Swellfoot the Tyrant " and " The Mask of Anarchy ;" the former occasioned

by the scandalous suit of divorce which George
IV. instituted against his wife, Queen Caroline, and
the latter by the infamous butchery of Manchester. During his stay at Pisa, in the year 1821,
Shelley, deeply touched, like Byron, by the cause
of Greece, composed his drama "Hellas," overflowing with enthusiastic love of liberty. In this
and the preceding year he also produced his three
most perfect lyrical poems, the two beautiful elegies
"Adonaïs,"[7] and "Epipsychidion," and the ethereally delicate song of "The Sensitive Plant."

   [7] Composed on the early death of the poet, John Keats.
In the procession of shadowy figures which mournfully pass
by the grave, Shelley has also introduced his own; and in
some beautiful stanzas, showing the peculiarity of his style,
he describes his fate and his aspirations :—
"Midst others of less note came one frail Form,
  A phantom among men; companionless
  As the last cloud of an expiring storm
  Whose thunder is its knell. He, as I guess,
  Has gazed on Nature's naked loveliness,
  Actæon-like, and now he fled astray
  With feeble steps o'er the world's wilderness;
  And his own thoughts, along that rugged way,
Pursued, like raging hounds, their father and their prey.

  A guard-like spirit beautiful and swift—
  A Love in desolation masked;—a Power
  Girt round with weakness, it can scarce uplift
  The weight of the superincumbent hour;
  Is it a dying lamp, a falling shower,
  A breaking billow;—even whilst we speak
  It is not broken? On the withering flower
  The killing sun smiles brightly: on a cheek
The life can burn in blood, even while the heart may break.
  His head was bound with pansies over-blown,
  And faded violets, white, and pied, and blue;

In April 1822 Shelley and his wife left Pisa and went to live at Villa Magni, situated on the bay of Spezia, not far from Lerici. Here, in quiet seclusion, he spent most of his time on the sea. He and his intimate friend, Captain Williams, had had a boat built at Genoa which they could navigate by themselves without assistance. In this vessel they went to Leghorn on the 1st of July to meet a third friend. They spent a week there and at Pisa and then started to return home. A friend watched the bark by telescope from the Leghorn lighthouse. It had arrived at Via Reggio when a sudden thunderstorm broke out. When that was over, their friend looked anxiously for the boat: it had disappeared. The sea which Shelley had loved so much had engulfed him. A few days later his corpse was thrown on the strand. Byron came from Pisa with a few friends to pay the last honours to the dead. A funeral pile, adorned according to the fashion of the ancients, consumed Shelley's remains. The ashes were collected and buried at Rome near the pyramid of Cestius where a year and a half ago Keats had also found a resting-place.[8]

> And a light spear topped with a cypress cone,
> Round whose rude shaft dark ivy-tresses grew
> Yet dripping with the forest's noonday dew,
> Vibrated, as the ever-beating heart
> Shook the weak hand that grasp'd it. Of that crew
> He came the last, neglected and apart ;
> A herd-abandon'd deer, struck by the hunter's dart."

[8] In August 1822 Byron wrote to Moore: "We have been burning the bodies of Shelley and Williams on the sea-shore,

to render them fit for removal and regular interment. You can have no idea what an extraordinary effect such a funeral pile has, on a desolate shore, with mountains in the background and the sea before, and the singular appearance the salt and frankincense gave to the flame."

In another letter to the same he says : "There is thus another man gone, about whom the world was ill-naturedly, and ignorantly, and brutally mistaken. It will, perhaps, do him justice *now*, when he can be no better for it."—In a letter to his publisher Murray, he says on the same subject : "You were all mistaken about Shelley, who was, without exception, the *best* and least selfish man I ever knew."—A beautiful monument, equally honourable to the dead and to her whom he left behind, is the book of his widow mentioned in note 1 :—" The comparative solitude in which Shelley lived was the occasion that he was personally known to few; and his fearless enthusiasm in the cause which he considered the most sacred upon earth, the improvement of the moral and physical state of mankind, was the chief reason why he, like other illustrious reformers, was pursued by hatred and calumny. No man was ever more devoted than he to the endeavours of making those around him happy ; no man ever possessed friends more unfeignedly attached to him. The ungrateful world did not feel his loss, and the gap it made seemed to close as quickly over his memory as the murderous sea above his living frame. Hereafter men will lament that his transcendent powers of intellect were extinguished before they had bestowed on them their choicest treasures. To his friends his loss is irremediable. The wise, the brave, the gentle, is gone for ever ! He is to them as a bright vision, whose radiant track, left behind in the memory, is worth all the realities that society can afford. Before the critics contradict me, let them appeal to any one who had ever known him. To see him was to love him ; and his presence, like Ithuriel's spear, was alone sufficient to disclose the falsehood of the tale which his enemies whispered in the ear of the ignorant world."

CHAPTER XV.

MODERN AND CONTEMPORARY POETS AND AUTHORS,
POETESSES AND AUTHORESSES.

Leyden, White, Keats, Elliott, Hunt, Landor, Wolfe, Procter, Barton, Hood, Milnes, Aird, Aytoun, Mackay, Tennyson, Swinburne, Rossetti; Felicia Hemans, Letitia Landon, Caroline Norton, Elizabeth B. Browning. The Drama: Maturin, Milman, Sheil, Talfourd, Knowles, Taylor, Browning, Mary Mitford. Novel writers: Hannah More, Jane Austen, Hope, Morier, Trelawney, Rowcroft, Lover, Lever, Croker, Carleton, Griffin, Mrs. S. C. Hall, Wilson, Marryat, Chamier, Glascock; Hook, Warren, D'Israeli, Harriet Martineau, Bulwer, Dickens, Thackeray, Trollope, Ruffini, Kingsley, Chas. Reade, Collins, Currer Bell (Charlotte Brontë), Miss Craik, Miss Kavanagh, Miss Yonge, Miss Braddon, George Eliot (M. A. Evans). Writers on history: Malcolm, Napier, Alison, Tytler, Turner, Lingard, Hallam, Mackintosh, Miss Martineau, Macaulay, Froude, Kemble, Wright, Grote, Buckle. Parliamentary oratory: Canning, O'Connell, Peel, Brougham. Reviews and Reviewers, history of literature, and essays: Jeffrey, Gifford, Hazlitt, Lamb, Mrs. Jameson, John Payne Collier, Isaac D'Israeli, Shaw, Dunlop, Carlyle, Dixon, Grant.

HITHERTO we have been able to present to the reader the historical development of English literature, but the subject of our present consideration obliges us to give up that method; for the present phase of English literature is still developing, and therefore does not offer a finished picture to historical contemplation. The English literature of our own time and that immediately preceding it may be compared to an unfinished piece of mosaic work.

Many compartments within the slightly sketched outline are still perfectly empty, others contain fragmentary forms; others again present finished figures and groups of excellent drawing and fine colouring, but their relation to the whole is undecided. We must look upon all this as it is, and refrain from forcing an organization into what is not naturally organized. We wish the following pages to be looked upon as a mere sketch.

Since Byron's death no poet of equal greatness has appeared in England. Shelley appears like a herald, of the future, and is more or less a stranger in his country, though it may easily be shown that some poets have drawn their inspirations from his social-philosophical poetry. Byron found imitators, but no successors. The historical novel, founded by Scott, has produced compositions not unworthy of the master himself.[1] Moore's influence on poetry was not slight, but it is to be questioned whether it was altogether beneficial. What the "Ettrick Shepherd" said of the exaggerated sweetness of Moore's poetry, may be said in greater measure of its imitators.

Poetesses especially cultivated the "delicate" and the "lovely," and met with so much applause

---

[1] E.g. the novels "Cesar Borgia," "Whitefriars," "Jeanne d'Arc," by an anonymous author.

applause, that the vigour and manliness of poetry were much endangered. Wordsworth's poetry of nature and of sound opinion formed a wholesome counterpoise to this affectation, while on the other hand its reflective character contains a danger for true poetry, which must always be inspired by strong and passionate feeling.

But we have done with generalizing, and must limit ourselves to the introduction of prominent figures in the different departments of English literature. We shall be obliged to rank the contemporaries of Scott and Moore, of the Lake poets and of Byron, with the younger generation of authors, for essential differences are not apparent in many of them.

In the region of poetry, to the exclusion of the drama and the novel, the ballad-writer John Leyden (+1811) and the lyric poet Henry Kirke White (+1806) deserve to be mentioned first. Both died before their talent had attained maturity. Such was also the case with John Keats (1795—1820), who in 1818 published his first work, the romance "Endymion." An unfavourable critique of the poem in the "Quarterly Review" increased the hectic irritability of the poet and is said to have hastened him to an early grave. His second and larger poem, "Hyperion," was published as a fragment. Keats has been called a mythological poet; we should prefer to call him a mystical writer. He has a strong resemblance to Shelley; nature revealed herself to him in unveiled magni-

S

ficence, and inspired him with descriptions of extreme delicacy and with lofty visions.[2] The greatest possible contrast to Keats is "Ebenezer Elliott" (1781—1849). The former is all extravagant imagination and fantasy; the latter, sound and stern principled. Elliott was self-taught, a blacksmith in the village of Masborough, near Sheffield. He is called the "Corn Law Poet," because his collection of poems which created a sensation in 1832 is entitled "Corn Law Rhymes." They are chiefly directed against the Corn Law of 1815, which, contributing to the advantage of the landed proprietors, increased the price of bread for the poor. Elliott is altogether a poetical advocate of the people and unites a deep understanding of nature with a powerful and pregnant style. The epitaph which he composed on himself furnishes an excellent example of the spirit and form of his poetry.[3] Leigh Hunt (1784—1859) has been

[2] "Works," 1844. "Life, Letters, and Literary Remains of John Keats," ed. by R. Monckton Milnes, 1848, 2 vols.
[3] "Stop, mortal! Here thy brother lies,
   The poet of the poor;
His books were rivers, woods, and skies,
   The meadow, and the moor;
His teachers were the torn heart's wail,
   The tyrant and the slave,
The street, the factory, the gaol,
   The palace—and the grave!
Sin met thy brother everywhere!
   And is thy brother blamed?
From passion, danger, doubt, and care
   He no exemption claim'd.

called the "delightful" poet, and proves his right to the name by his poetical tales, "The Story of Rimini" (1816), the subject of which is Dante's famous episode of Paolo and Francesca ("Inferno," v. 75—142), and "The Palfrey" (1842). He also attempted to write a tragedy, "A Legend of Florence" (1840). But he is most delightful as an essayist and memoir writer.[4] Walter Savage Landor (1775—1864) is also a better prose writer than poet. His epic poem "Gebir," and his dramatical "Acts and Scenes," do not and cannot pretend to much merit; but his "Imaginary Conversations" are of great excellence; they consist of 125 dialogues between authors, statesmen, and artists, and exhibit an extraordinary amount of knowledge and ideas presented in a very attractive form. Charles Wolfe (1791—1823) is a poet little

> The meanest thing, earth's feeblest worm
>   He fear'd to scorn or hate,
> But honouring in a peasant's form
>   The equal of the great.
> He blessed the Steward, whose wealth makes
>   The poor man's little more ;
> Yet loathed the haughty wretch that takes
>   From plunder'd labour's store.
> A hand to do, a head to plan,
>   A heart to feel and dare—
> Tell man's worst foes, here lies the man
>   Who drew them as they are."

[4] "Men, Women, and Books," 1847, 2 vols. "The Town," 1848, 2 vols. "The Autobiography of Leigh Hunt, with reminiscences of friends and contemporaries," 1850, 3 vols.

known except by one poem, "The Burial of Sir John Moore;" it was attributed to Byron for a long time, and is so masterly a composition that its author will never be forgotten.[5] Bryan Waller

> "Not a drum was heard, not a funeral note,
>   As his corse to the rampart we hurried;
> Not a soldier discharged his farewell shot
>   O'er the grave where our hero we buried.
> We buried him darkly at dead of night,
>   The sods with our bayonets turning,—
> By the struggling moonbeam's misty light,
>   And the lantern dimly burning.
> No useless coffin enclosed his breast,
>   Not in sheet or in shroud we wound him;
> But he lay like a warrior taking his rest,
>   With his martial cloak around him.
> Few and short were the prayers we said,
>   And we spoke not a word of sorrow;
> But we steadfastly gazed on the face that was dead,
>   And we bitterly thought of the morrow.
> We thought, as we hollow'd his narrow bed
>   And smooth'd down his lonely pillow,
> That the foe and the stranger would tread o'er his head,
>   And we far away on the billow;
> Lightly they'll talk of the spirit that's gone,
>   And o'er his cold ashes upbraid him;—
> But little he'll reck, if they let him sleep on
>   In the grave where a Briton has laid him.
> But half our heavy task was done
>   When the clock struck the hour for retiring;
> And we heard the distant and random gun,
>   That the foe was sullenly firing.
> Slowly and sadly we laid him down,
>   From the field of his fame fresh and gory:
> We carved not a line, and we raised not a stone,—
>   But left him alone with his glory."

Procter (born 1790), better known as Barry Cornwall, was a schoolfellow of Byron's. The beautiful poetic tale "Marcian Colonna," his best epic composition,[6] is written in Byron's style. His "Miscellaneous Poems" contain good lyrical compositions, and his "Dramatic Scenes" and the tragedy "Mirandola" are also rich in poetical beauties. The Quaker Bernard Barton (1784—1849) mingled many a delicate lyrical thought and many successful images with the outpourings of his religious feelings. Thomas Hood, on the other hand (1798—1845) distinguished himself by his humorous lyrical sallies. Take, for instance, his facetious poem, "A Parental Ode to my Son," where the expression of fatherly tenderness forms a charming contrast to the behaviour of the unmannerly boy. But he is not wanting in pathos either, proofs of which are found in "The Dream of Eugene Aram," and in the famous "Song of the Shirt" and "The Bridge of Sighs," which produced an extraordinary sensation and touched many hardened hearts. There are not many poets who have found so powerful an expression for social misery as Hood has done in these two splendid poems. Richard Monckton Milnes (born 1809), now Lord Houghton, has written many successful lyrical poems. More original and more powerful is the talent of three Scotchmen: Thomas Aird (born 1802), William

[6] With the exception of his short but most powerful poem, "The Last Day of Tippoo Saib."

Edmondstone Aytoun (born 1813), and Charles Mackay (born 1812). Aird tried to combine Moore's eastern fantasy with Southey's Christianity, as may be seen specially from his poem "The Devil's Dream on Mount Aksbeck," which appeared with his other poems in 1848. Aytoun is a spirited imitator of Scott's patriotic epics in his "Lays of the Scottish Cavaliers" (1849) and in his romance "Bothwell" (1856). Mackay's first work, "The Hope of the World" (1840), reminds us of the didactic and reflective poetry of Pope's age; but with his beautiful poetical tale "The Salamandrine" (1842) he entered the ranks of the romantic poets of Tennyson's school, which tries to combine the passionate feelings and fantastic opinions of the middle ages with the modern principle of liberty, by means of a poetical style which is to unite antique plastic drawing with the glowing colours of the Renaissance. The best of Mackay's later poems are: "Voices from the Mountains," "Egeria," "The Lump of Gold."

If the characteristic which has just been given of Tennyson's poetical efforts justifies the claim to have touched a new chord in the human heart, to have founded a new school of poetry, Alfred Tennyson (born 1810 at Somersby) may raise this claim, and Alison may say of him in truth "he has opened a new vein in English poetry." It is a proof of utter ignorance of Tennyson's works to judge him, as has been done, merely as a specimen of the smooth academical style. He has a style of his own, and one of the first rank; the six volumes of his works prove it beyond doubt, but they also prove that he is a real and true poet. His romances and rhapsodies, as "Mariana" and "Mariana in the South," "The Miller's Daughter," "Lady Clara Vere de Vere," "Dora," "Œnone," "The Lotos-Eaters," "Simeon Stylites," are original conceptions of deep feeling and masterly composition. A pearl of psychological delineation is the legend "Godiva," and a full tone of passion rings through the magnificent elegy "Locksley Hall," which recommends itself at the same time by the fulness and loftiness of its thoughts. The first mark of talent, productiveness, is also found in Tennyson, and has been improving and progressing since the publication of his first "Poems" (1830). We do not, however, mean to pretend that all his longer poems are perfect successes. "In Memoriam," a lament for the dead, dedicated to the memory of a departed friend, is full of melancholy tenderness, but rather monotonous. The so-called romance of "The Idylls of the King" has little to recommend it, and "The Princess, A Medley," is positively tiresome. But "Maud" draws the reader irresistibly along in the passionate flow of its diction. "Aylmer's Field" handles a subject that has been treated over and over again, but in a new and deeply touching form; and the glory of the poet's genius is the pastoral epic "Enoch Arden," because Tennyson's characteristics, both in the choice of the subject and of the form, are there shown most decisively and brilliantly. The chief members of Tennyson's school, if we may speak of such a thing, are: John Brent, Aubrey de Vere, Alexander Smith, T. Ashe, Dante Gabriel Rossetti, and Algernon Charles Swinburne. The "Poems" of the Anglicised Italian painter Rossetti are successful instances of the characteristic features of most modern English poetry, whose tendency has been happily characterized by an English critic as "the renaissance of mediæval feeling." Swinburne's poetry has the same character, but he is also gifted with the luxuriant imagination and freshness of style of an original poet. His glowing delineation of the life of the soul in his "Poems and Ballads," the tragedy "Atalanta," and the romantic drama "Chastelard," are pervaded by a breath of mysticism which recalls Shelley, whose influence, as well as that of Carlyle, is powerfully felt in all these latest utterances of the English muse.

Among poetesses, Felicia Hemans (1798—1835) still occupies the first rank by her songs and romances. No other literature can boast of a more beautiful expression of womanhood than may be found in her poems. Tender melancholy, tempered by a deeply religious faith, is the key-note of her songs. She is very productive, but the warmth of her colouring, the music of her rhythm, are always the same; it is a language full of elegiac sweetness, but her melancholy is perfectly free from sickly sentimentality. Her songs : " The Song of Night," " The Better Land," " I dream of all things free," " The Hour of Prayer," " The Homes of England," and many others, are pearls among English lyrics. She is not wanting either in epic power ; her " Songs of the Cid " are masterpieces of ballad writing. Her imagination also enabled her to produce works of greater length, such as the two romances " The Indian Town " and " The Forest Sanctuary." The latter she rightly considers her best work. It is written in the Spenserian stanza and describes in two cantos the solitary life of a Spaniard in the forests of South America, whither he has fled on account of religious persecution at home, and who recalls in succession before his mind the scenes of his former life.[7] Only Letitia Elizabeth Landon (1804—1838), whose tragical death by poison has not yet been fully explained,[8] rivalled the popularity of Mrs. Hemans. She produced many fine poems, her " Improvisatrice," " Troubadour," " Golden Bracelet," " Golden Violet," for instance, are graceful romances, breath-

---

[7] " Memoirs of Mrs. F. Hemans," by H. F. Chorley, 1836, 2 vols.

[8] She married in June 1838 George Maclean, Governor of Cape Coast Castle, and followed him to South Africa. In the following October she was found one morning dead in her room, a phial with prussic acid in her hand. Her husband had formerly lived with a black woman, who was still in the house when the poetess entered it as a bride.

" The Life and Correspondence of Letitia Elizabeth Landon," by Blanchard, 1839, 3 vols.

ing the sunny air of Italy and of Provence, which countries were the favourite scenes of her poems. Among her novels " Ethel Churchill " is the most remarkable. Caroline Elizabeth Sarah Norton (born 1808), a granddaughter of Sheridan's, has been called the female Byron, because her fate[9] and style have some similarity with those of the author of "Childe Harold." Her first production was the idyll "The Sorrows of Rosalie," and she afterwards attempted one of the grandest subjects, the legend of the wandering Jew, " The Undying One " (1837). She was more successful in her Poem " The Dream " (1840), in which the phases of a woman's life are represented with the fidelity to nature of Wordsworth and the power of Byron. Still greater admiration was aroused by her " Child of the Islands " (1845), which puts the bright and dark side of English life in poetical contrast to each other. The young Prince of Wales is to be understood by the " child of the islands." Among her later publications the " Tales and Sketches " (1850) and a novel, " Stuart of Dunleath " (1851) are the most remarkable. Other poetesses of note, are: Mary Howitt, Flora Hastings, Emmeline Stuart Wortley, Eliza Cook, Anna Twamley, Geraldine Jewsbury, Jean Ingelow, Dora Greenwell, and Elizabeth Browning (1809—1861), the wife of the poet of the same name. Her first work was the

---

[9] In 1840 she was divorced from her husband after a painful lawsuit, the scandal of which, however, fell on her husband.

fruit of learning very estimable in a young lady, a translation of the "Prometheus" of Æschylus. Her own poems move almost exclusively in the higher regions, to which she is transported by unflagging enthusiasm. Her chief work, "A Drama of Exile," is a vision in lyrical dramatic form, a mystery, in which man's loss of the ideals of his youth is beautifully typified by Adam and Eve's expulsion from paradise. Eve is a figure of truly ethereal loveliness.

The dramatic poetry of England in modern times and in the present is much more tentative than creative. With very few exceptions the modern English drama has not gone beyond vague and sometimes promising attempts, but supported by dramatic artists of the first rank: Kean, Macready, Miss O'Neil. The dramatists themselves do not seem to have faith in their own art, and therefore some, and those the more able among them, write plays to be read rather than to be acted. Joanna Baillie's tragedies have been mentioned before, but they have had no success on the stage. The forced emotions which Robert Maturin presented in his "Bertram" and "Manuel" disappeared from the stage after a short career; nor could the lyric notes of Henry Milman's Biblical plays gain a footing there. Richard Sheil's writings are merely passionately sketched outlines of dramas, and offend the poetical sense of probability on all sides. Thomas Noon Talfourd experimented in his pieces in the style of ancient Greece. His "Ion" (1834) was much praised by connoisseurs of the Greek drama; but though it was acted with applause under Macready's management, a lasting influence could not be expected from an attempt which stood in opposition to all the traditions of the English stage.

James Sheridan Knowles (born 1794) wrote some dramas suitable for the stage and not at all wanting in poetic conception. In his historical pieces, "Virginius," "Gracchus," "Alfred," the talent of the poet does not quite come up to his subject; but his comedies "The Love-Chase" and "The Hunchback" are altogether satisfactory. There is a loftier impulse in the tragedies of Henry Taylor, to whom the first rank among modern dramatists has been assigned. He began with his "Isaac Comnenus," a character satiated with the world: the five acts close with a horrible scene. In "Philip van Artevelde" the characters and motives are of firmer mould, but this firmness impresses us as proceeding rather from the reflection of the poet than from the characters themselves. In a third drama, "Edwin the Fair," whose hero is St. Dunstan, Taylor has made a successful attempt to delineate the character of a priest made up of hypocrisy, conceit, and fanaticism. A fourth piece, "The Virgin Widow," is of an imperfect melodramatic character. Robert Browning is a poet who does not understand that the drama is a poetical form which does not suit his genius. He possesses a great mind and much imagination, but he has no idea of dramatic technicalities. He is a philosophical poet; but on the stage philosophy must be translated into action, and that is what Browning has not been able to do. His poetry much resembles Shelley's, but he has never succeeded, as the latter has in the "Cenci," in replacing his visionary ideas by plastic forms. His "Paracelsus" (1836) is a sort of English Faust, but more religious than the German prototype. A second lyrical drama, "Sordello," represents the struggle of genius with the misery of life and with the idle indifference of the multitude. Browning has also treated some historical subjects, but he moves by preference in metaphysical regions, as we see in his two poems "Christmas-Eve" and "Easter-day."[1] Among the tragedies of Mary Russell Mitford the prize must be awarded to "Rienzi," for it is appropriate for the stage, its effect is produced by proper motives, and its characters are worked out with consistency; the language is flowery, but not to an extreme. The merit of this lady is still greater in the descriptions she has given of English country life. Her rural sketches are an ornament to English literature; their truth and cheerfulness are almost unequalled by anything that has been written of the kind.[2]

In England, as elsewhere, the novel has con-

[1] "Poems by Robert Browning," 1849, 2 vols.
[2] "Our Village, sketches of rural character and scenery," 1824—1832, 5 vols. Illustrated edition. Sampson Low, Marston, & Co.

tinued to be the most popular branch of literature since the days of Defoe and Richardson. The novel is to modern society what the epic rhapsody was to the ancients, what the songs of the troubadours, minstrels, and minne-singers were to the mediæval world. For numbers of people the novel has to take the place of theatre, opera, and concert; it is the medium by which the masses are brought into contact with the ideal side of life. After the taste for the novels of the eighteenth century began to decline in England, the novel writing of the nineteenth received a new and powerful impulse in Walter Scott. As long as his activity endured the historical romance reigned supreme; even Hannah More's religious, and Jane Austen's quietly social novels, were eclipsed by the Waverley series. But Scott's imitators were less able to please the public; a change became desirable, and authors were not wanting to satisfy the demand. Geography and ethnography now opened a large field to novel writers, by affording them the assistance of excellent works on travel:—the most distinguished of these are by Basil Hall and Reginald Heber, the famous Bishop of Calcutta. All countries furnished materials as well to English novelists as to English merchants. Thomas Hope by his masterly novel "Anastasius" (1819) opened the path to the East, and many followed in his track. James Morier, in his novels "Hajji Baba," "Zohrab," "Ayesha," describes the public and domestic life of Persia and Kurdistan. Trelawney in his unequalled biographical novel "Adventures of a Younger Son," gives us a glowing picture of the highly romantic career of an adventurer on the seas and islands of East India; Charles Rowcroft in his "Tales of the Colonies," presents pictures of a society still in course of formation. Nearer home too, Ireland offered a field for novelistic research, and the peculiarities of the Emerald Isle are brought to our view in the novels and sketches of Samuel Lover, Charles Lever, Crofton Croker, William Carleton, Gerald Griffin, and Mrs. S. C. Hall. The nautical novel, which had been revived by the American author Cooper, was looked upon by the English as their special field, and Marryat, Chamier, Glascock, and others gained distinction in it. "Tom Cringle's Log," written by Michael Scott, contains more of the poetry of the sea than any of the works of these novelists. Captain Marryat's faithful delineations of life at sea are very popular. Novels of "high life" have been written by Lady Blessington, Mrs. Frances Trollope, Mrs. Gore, and Mrs. Marsh; but authors of the other sex also, such as Lister, the author of "Arlington" and "Granby," Ward, the author of "Tremaine" and "Cecil," and Lord Mulgrave, author of "Miserrimus," &c., have been more or less successful as writers of fashionable novels. The narrator *par excellence* of town stories was Theodore Hook; he powerfully portrayed the hollowness and emptiness of fashionable life. There is more psychological depth in Samuel Warren's "Passages from the Diary of a late Physician," but the effect of his longer novel, "Ten Thousand a Year," is spoiled by unchecked diffuseness and by extreme political views. The tendency of the novels of Benjamin Disraeli (Lord Beaconsfield), the well-known Conservative statesman, is still more evident. His novel of travel "Vivian Gray," and his formless "Revolutionary Epic" did not attract much notice; but his novel "Coningsby" (1844) created a great sensation. It contains statements, in the form of a novel, of the principles of the so-called "Young England." Disraeli's other novels, "Sybil," "Lothair," and "Tancred," also advocate social reforms. Miss Harriet Martineau's novels are what she calls them—"illustrations of political economy."

At the time when the historical novel was still flourishing, the novel of manners and morals was revived, and taken up where Fielding, Smollett, and Goldsmith had left it. At first a rival of the historical novel, men like Bulwer, Dickens, and Thackeray soon caused it to triumph over every other kind of composition in the favour of the public. Edward George Lytton Bulwer (1803—1873) is almost more popular in Germany than in his own country. The metrical attempts—"O'Neil the Rebel" (1826) and others—with which he made his first appearance, met with little success; but his novel " Pelham " (1828) directed the attention of the public to him, and he proved himself capable of retaining and deserving it by a long series of novels. His compositions are ably planned and executed with the pen of a poet. A comprehensive knowledge of men, refined psychology, an extraordinary power of grouping, and a clear spirited dialogue, combine to give to his works a lasting value. In the rich variety of his characters he is second only to Walter Scott, but in fascinating narrative he is second to none. He is never tedious, at least never in those works which were written in the fulness of his talent; he is weak where he leaves the soil of English realism to rise to the spheres of German idealism, as he has done in the "Pilgrims of the Rhine." Nor are his historical novels, "The Last Days of Pompeii," "Rienzi," "The Last of the Barons," "Harold," the best proofs of his ability. But where English society of past or of modern times is the subject of his novels the peculiarity and excellency of his genius shows to the best advantage. " Pelham," "The Disowned," "Paul Clifford," "Eugene Aram," "Ernest Maltravers," "Alice," "Night and Morning," are creations which would do honour to the literature of any nation.[3] Two of Bulwer's later

---

[3] Bulwer has also written for the stage and has treated some historical subjects in the manner of the French conversational pieces. He gave us besides an excellent sketch of character in "England and the English," and in the historical

T

novels, "The Caxtons," and "My Novel," are equal to his best; others show that his powers were on the wane. His love of production was so great that he looked for subjects in every direction, and mistakes were not always avoided. Such a mistake was the Rosicrucian novel "Zanoni," with its mystic confusion. His novel "Lucretia" was the signal for so-called sensational-novelistic writing in England. His posthumous work, "The Parisians," describes the state and temper of Paris at and after the time of the war of 1870 had been declared; parts of it reveal the full talent of the famous author, so that the close of Bulwer's life was illumined by a fine sunset.

Charles Dickens (1812—1870) first became famous as "Boz," under which name he wrote his "Sketches of London" (1831—1837), and gave to the world a series of those poetical types that impress themselves indelibly on the memory, producing pleasure and merriment wherever they appear.[4] Mr. Pickwick, before all others is one of these types. He is the hero of the "Pickwick Papers" (1837), round whom is assembled a company of original characters from the middle and lower classes of society. In his two succeeding novels "Nicholas Nickleby" and "Oliver Twist" Dickens pleads for the poor and

---

essay "Athens, its Rise and Fall." Bulwer's brother Henry wrote: "France, Social, Literary, Political," which may be considered a very successful pendant to "England and the English."

[4] "The Life of Charles Dickens," by Forster, 1871.

neglected against the rich and privileged ; he does this as a poet, and while portraying the dark shadow which the life of the "enjoying" classes throws on that of the working and needy ones, he also points out the possibility of reconciliation. Another novel, "Master Humphrey's Clock," is somewhat diffuse and its characters are exaggerated. Dickens is fond of drawing figures which the French would call "chargés ;" their grotesqueness often exceeds the limits of good taste. Another of his favourite inclinations is the representation of characters made up of deficiency of intellect and half unconscious humour. In his "Barnaby Rudge" one of these characters is even made the hero of an historical novel. Three later novels, "Dombey," "David Copperfield," and "Bleak House," are again written in his best style. In "David Copperfield" especially, Dickens's humour shows itself in the richest colours, recalling Smollett's power and Sterne's lightheartedness. The novel "Martin Chuzzlewit" is a bitter but just satire on Yankeeism. From Christmas 1843 to 1847 he presented the public every year, and at the time appointed, with a charming fairy-tale novel; and in 1850 he established the periodical "Household Words," in which social problems were discussed in a popular form. Here as everywhere Dickens has practical aims in view, and he knows how to attain them. The bolts of his humour have gone home to many a prejudice that was deemed invulnerable, and many a carefully-hidden abuse, and his influence belongs to the most beneficial which ever author has exercised. The later novels, "Little Dorrit," "Hard Times," "A Tale of Two Cities," show a slight decay of the author's power.

Next to Bulwer and Dickens, William Makepeace Thackeray (1811—1863) ranks as the third master of the novel of modern manners and morals. He began his literary career, under the names of Michael Angelo Titmarsh and George FitzBoodle, in "Fraser's Magazine." His "Paris Sketch Book" (1840), "Chronicle of the Drum" (1841), and "Irish Sketch Book" (1843), were his first publications. His "Snob Papers," which clearly announced the future development of his caustic wit, appeared in "Punch." His tale "Vanity Fair," a novel without a hero (1847), makes him rank with the first authors of his country. The heroine of the book, Becky Sharp, is one of those original types which are rarely produced in such perfection. The book sparkles with wit, humour, and noble indignation. In this as in his two other great novels, "The History of Arthur Pendennis," and "The Newcomes," Thackeray satirizes with unheard-of boldness all the hypocrisy and false respectability, in fact the "cant" of modern society. He was made to be a satirist; his gaze penetrated to the very hearts of men, and the caustic acuteness of his description cut into and laid open the most secret blemishes with the inexorable accuracy of a dissecting-knife. Scarcely ever has a great satirist proved so great a narrator as Thackeray. His characters, taken from the reality of life, live before us so entirely that we say involuntarily, "Yes, such alas! are men," for we never receive from him a cheering impression; Thackeray is a decided pessimist. But that Thackeray's sense of the folly and wickedness of mankind did not destroy his love of the race is proved by the figure of Esmond in his "History of Henry Esmond" (1852), written in the form of an autobiography. The "Virginians" is the most carefully planned of his novels, and the most mature as regards his ideas, but the work has not been carried out so perfectly as some others. Thackeray also delivered "Lectures on the English Humourists of the Eighteenth Century," and on the age of the "Four Georges," and these ingenious and important investigations have also appeared in print.

We could not attempt to mention all the English novel writers who have made their appearance during the last twenty years, for their name is legion; we shall content ourselves with the following. Among those who cultivate the novel of manners and morals Anthony Trollope is distinguished by his versatility and great productiveness: "The Bertrams," "Doctor Thorne," "The Warden," "Barchester Towers," and others. The tales of Signor Ruffini: "Doctor Antonio," "Lorenzo Benoni," "Lavinia," "A Quiet Nook," are very attractive. Deep feeling pervades them all. Charles Kingsley is the author of several interesting tales, "Westward Ho!" "Two Years Ago," &c.;

his "Hypatia" is an historic theological novel, which does great credit to its author. Charles Reade's novels, "It is Never Too Late to Mend," "A Terrible Temptation," and others, illustrate the "social conflicts" of our time, and may almost be called sensational. But the acknowledged master of the sensational novel is Wilkie Collins, who introduced himself into the literature of his country by the biography of his father (1848), the well-known painter William Collins. After some hesitation he recognized the fact that "the dark deed," the mysterious crime, perversity, and wickedness, were the field for his novelistic activity, and he wrote accordingly a whole series of sensational novels—" Hide and Seek," " After Dark," "The Dead Secret," "Armadale," "Man and Wife" —which give undoubted proofs of great talent for narrative writing, and an extraordinary power of complicating and surprising. He attained the height of his reputation by his novel "The Woman in White," in which the talent of making probable the most improbable things reaches its utmost limit. His later novels, "The Moonstone," "Poor Miss Finch," "Miss or Mrs.?" "The New Magdalen," are also very well told. But Collins appears to have made the most conscientious use of his talents in his novel "No Name." Charlotte Brontë (Currer Bell) gave her best in her first work, "Jane Eyre." A large number of authoresses have produced domestic and sensational novels, among them Georgina

Craik ("Lost and Won," "Leslie Tyrrell," "Esther Hill's Secret," and others), Miss Kavanagh ("Daisy Burns," "Grace Lee," and others), and Miss Yonge ("The Heir of Redclyffe," "Dynevor Terrace," and others). The most sensational female writer is Miss M. E. Braddon, whose stories about robbery, arson, and murder fill a catalogue by themselves. Of a very different order from the above-mentioned writers was the late Marian Evans, who wrote under the name of George Eliot. She was a poet, for she creates characters and shows us forms and developments of psychological facts; her characters are true to life, and their development is strictly logical; and it is this truth and correctness which constitute the charm of her writings. The acuteness and decision of her poetical realism are admirable; her motives and expositions are proofs of a deep and full knowledge of human nature; and she never wrote merely for effect. "George Eliot" first became known in 1857-58 by her "Scenes of Clerical Life." Then appeared her novel "Adam Bede," which we feel inclined to call her best work; for though the succeeding ones, "The Mill on the Floss," "Silas Marner," "Romola," and "Felix Holt," denote an improvement as to the details, the conception of the whole is less perfect, and "Middlemarch," with its undeniable excellencies, is a somewhat disjointed composition, and disperses the interest of the reader *ad infinitum*.

The novelistic prose writing of the nineteenth century occupies an honourable place by the side of that of the eighteenth, and the same may be said of historical prose. Excellent historical and biographical works have been mentioned in former paragraphs; we will now add the most distinguished of modern date. Among these must be reckoned the "History of Persia" (1815), by John Malcolm, the "History of the War in the Peninsula" (1834—1836), by Sir Wm. Napier, and Sir Archibald Alison's "History of Europe of 1789—1815," a work whose historical value and powerfully descriptive style make one overlook the extreme political views of the author. Writers of great ability devoted themselves to national history. Chalmers, Pinkerton, and others, took upon themselves the difficulties of antiquarian research, the results of which alone are the solid foundation of true historiography. Tytler wrote a comprehensive "History of Scotland;" Turner and Lingard were as comprehensive in their "History of England;" the former, however, is somewhat encumbered by his great learning, and the other is more versatile and elegant as an advocate for Roman Catholicism than is becoming to an historian, of whatever creed. Sir James Mackintosh first became famous by his "Defence of the French Revolution" (1791), directed against Burke, and was one of the most distinguished political writers and parliamentary orators of his time. He also intended to write a History of England, and the sketch which appeared on the subject in Lardner's "Cyclopædia" was only to be a preparatory exercise. The plan was not carried out, and Mackintosh's "History of the Revolution in 1688" had also to be finished by another hand, after his death in 1832. Henry Hallam has enriched the history of Europe, that of his country, and that of literature equally; the former by his book, "The State of Europe during the Middle Ages" (1818), the second by his "Constitutional History of England" (1828), and the third by his "Introduction to the Literature of Europe in the Fifteenth, Sixteenth, and Seventeenth Centuries" (1837). Thomas Keightley has narrated the history of England from its commencement to the accession of Victoria. "A History of England during the Thirty Years' Peace," was written by Miss Martineau, in which she purposed to prove that the liberal political reforms of 1816—1846 have done nothing towards the material and ideal improvement of the people. Her chief attention is directed to the economical circumstances of the country, and her statements are such as may be expected from an authoress who has made political economy the task of her life's study. But her style, which is rather abstract and colourless, weakens the effect of her arguments. Very rarely does a breath of poetry enliven her narrative, and yet the great historians of antiquity show how effective such a combination may be made; and in our own time Thomas Babington Macaulay has proved this (1800—1859). He occupied high offices of state in England and India, and was a distinguished speaker in Parliament. We cannot highly appreciate his "Lays of Ancient Rome," but we consider him peerless as an Essayist. His critical, historical, and biographical treatises, which from 1825 were an ornament of the "Edinburgh Review," were collected into six volumes in 1843. Macaulay has a method of criticism which is peculiarly his own; he takes a good or a bad book on some important man or subject, and his discourse develops into an independent historical or biographical work of art. Such historical masterpieces of finished beauty are his essays on the "Roman Popes," on "Milton," "Addison," "Macchiavelli," "Robert Walpole," "Pitt," "Warren Hastings." His celebrated description of the trial of the latter, is indisputably unique in its graphic grandeur. In 1848, the two first volumes of Macaulay's "History of England from the accession of James II.," prefaced by a summary account of the development of English nationality and constitution, appeared. This work has made Macaulay's name popular in the whole civilized world. The course of English history seems to pass under our very eyes; English society in its different grades and in its historic development talks and acts, suffers and fights, intrigues and prays—aye, eats and drinks before us. Everything is alive; historical motives are clearly revealed to our understanding; historical characters are made known to us down to the most secret recesses of their hearts and minds. The grouping of the historic materials, the harmony of light and shade in the representation, the ever-bright diction of the author, all this produces a vivid and pleasurable sense of satisfaction, increased by the fact that no heartless diplomatist but a patriotic and experienced statesman is talking to us. Macaulay is a Whig, and it is true that his ideas do not go beyond the traditions of his party; but their great and ever fertile thoughts are presented by him from so many different points of view, that the reflections and maxims which are woven into his work never fail to produce an impression.

Not only Macaulay, but all modern English historians, pay to the history of manners and morals the attention due to such an important factor in the development of our race. James Anthony Froude, in his "History of England from the Fall of Wolsey to the Death of Elizabeth" (1861), has also successfully attempted to represent the whole time of which he treats in all its different aspects—except one, namely, the dark side of the character and actions of Queen Elizabeth. Very good works on the history of civilization are also, " The Saxons in England," by J. M. Kemble, and a " History of English Culture from the Earliest known Period to Modern Times" (new edition 1874), by Thomas Wright. In the last-mentioned book especially the middle ages are treated in a masterly manner. Political history also profits by the regard paid to the history of culture, as the famous " History of Greece" by George Grote (1794—1871) sufficiently proves.

Grote was a man of extraordinary attainments, and an earnest lover of truth. His style is excellent, and his work on Greece ranks with Gibbon's classical work on Rome. Another name in the science of history is Henry Thomas Buckle; his premature death (in 1862) prevented him from writing anything but his "Introduction to the History of Civilization in England." Even in its unfinished state the book is undoubtedly of great significance. Buckle set himself the task of giving quite a new basis to history, and of making a new use of it, namely, to discover by it the laws which govern the intellectual world, just as natural science has discovered and fixed the laws of the physical world. The idea was indeed only a dazzling illusion; for history has to do with man, who is made up of contradictions, wavering between good and evil, between folly and passion, who will ever remain inconsistent, and whose mode of action can never be foretold. Buckle's scheme therefore could not prove a success, and the history of the most modern times is in flagrant contradiction to some of his prognostications. Compare, for instance, what he says of the Spaniards, with the recent events which have taken place in their country; and yet some paragraphs of his book, such as those on the courses of the French Revolution, or the history of Protestant fanaticism in Scotland, oblige us to look upon him as a master in the history of civilization. In this same field W. E. H. Lecky (born 1838) produced two works of note: "The History of Rationalism in Europe," and "The History of

European Morals from Augustus to Charlemagne." But the author's ignorance of German works on similar subjects may often be distinctly observed; and the same failing appears in his "History of England in the Eighteenth Century." In English and European historiography the following works are of lasting value: "History of the Norman Conquest," by E. A. Freeman (born 1823); "The History of the Holy Roman Empire," by J. Bryce (born 1838); "The History of the Invasion of the Crimea," by A. W. Kinglake (born 1802); "The Constitutional History of England," by W. Stubbs (born 1825); and finally the important "Life of the Prince Consort," by Sir Theodore Martin (born 1816). Nor should an earlier publication, "The History of England from 1713 to 1788," by Lord Mahon (later Earl Stanhope), be forgotten here.

We have said above that Macaulay belonged to the best parliamentary orators that England has produced in modern times. There were not a few, but we must limit ourselves to mentioning the most famous. They are: Charles Grey, the "father of reform;" George Canning (1770—1827), the enlightened antagonist of the policy of the Holy Alliance, during whose ministry English politics returned to the principles of liberty;[5] Daniel

---

[5] Harriet Martineau, in her "History of England," gives the following eloquent estimate of the spirit and the form of Canning's eloquence: "Never did the fires of western forests run through the wilderness more gloriously than the speeches of Canning through the political wilds of Europe under the deep night of the Holy Alliance. In those

O'Connell (1774—1847), "the great agitator" of Ireland, the chief mover in the emancipation of Roman Catholics; Robert Peel (1788—1850), who, though a leader of the Tories, was obliged to yield to public opinion by annulling the tax on corn made by the Tories; Francis Burdett, whose character and eloquence were somewhat like a chameleon; Henry Brougham (1779—1868), who at all times advocated the cause of justice and of the people with the eloquence of a Demosthenes and with an almost southern enthusiasm.⁶ These have been succeeded

Western wildernesses the unaccustomed and the timid tremble and shriek, and hang together as they see the spreading flame, and hear the rush and roar, and think of the waste of ashes that will be seen to-morrow: but the hardy fireman enjoys the sight—enjoys the sprinkling and scattering blazes, which seize upon decay and rottenness to turn them into freshness and fruitfulness. And so it was when the utterance of Canning in the British Parliament ran over Europe, kindling as it went. It was hateful and terrific to despots, because it leapt upon their abuses and scorched their vanities, and made of their antiquated dogmas ashes or a new growth of opinion."

⁶ Brougham's manner as an orator has often something of the theatrical action of the French, of whom he was very fond. When he closed his famous speech on Parliamentary Reform with the solemn adjuration: "By all you hold most dear, by all the ties that bind every one of us to our common order and our common country, I solemnly adjure you, warn you—I implore you, yea *on my bended knees* I supplicate you —reject not this bill!" he actually bent his knee on the woolsack. Brougham was also an excellent political writer, as is proved especially by his "Political Philosophy" (1842—1844), and his "Historical Sketches of Statesmen in the Reign of George III." (1842-43).

in our times by Lord John Russell and Lord Palmerston on the Liberal side, and Disraeli (Lord Beaconsfield) and Lord Derby on that of the Conservatives.

Criticism plays a great part in the modern literature of all nations; it is no longer confined to judgment on matters of taste or learning, but has become a mediator between literature and social and political life. In England the various "Reviews" and "Magazines" have become its organs, and the conductors of those periodicals occupy an important place in literature. There is scarcely a distinguished English author of modern times, Byron and Shelley excepted, who have not furnished articles for one or other of the Reviews. The "Edinburgh Review" is of longest standing; it was founded in 1802, and during its most brilliant period—that is to say, down to 1830—it was edited by Francis Jeffrey, whose sarcasms were much dreaded by poetasters. In opposition to the "Edinburgh Review," as an organ of the Liberals, the Conservative "Quarterly Review," was founded, in 1809, by William Gifford, and edited by him with great ability till 1824. In 1825 the "Westminster Review" appeared, chiefly to disseminate the Benthamist principles of Political Economy; and before that, in 1817, "Blackwood's Magazine" became one of the influential literary periodicals, whose number has much increased of late years. One of the first positions, if not the first among reviewers, is occupied by William

Hazlitt,[7] a versatile and refined critic, rather paradoxical at times, but who always hits the mark. Hazlitt's intimate friend was Charles Lamb (1775—1834), the most amiable of essayists, whose conversation, prose, and verses brim over with geniality and humour. His sketches of English life, which he has collected under the title " Essays of Elia," (1823 — 1833) are written with a quiet peculiar heartiness. His wit in this attractive book seems to proceed from the heart and not from the head. In the departments of æsthetic criticism a woman, Mrs. Jameson, also distinguished herself, especially by her " Female Characters of Shakespeare," in which she analyzes the poetry of the master with fine feeling and great tact. The chief among those who have written on Shakespeare is Payne Collier, whose " History of Dramatic Poetry " is still one of the most important productions of literary history. Other books on this subject, by Warton, D'Israeli, Cunningham, Chambers, and Craik, have been mentioned before. Isaac D'Israeli is a facetious narrator of anecdotes in his "Curiosities of Literature " and in his " Calamities and Quarrels of authors." Thomas Shaw's " Outlines of English Literature" (1849) possess the merit of a clear and orderly arrangement of his materials, but the critical views of the author are often faulty ; and we

---

[7] Hazlitt's Essays are collected under the titles : " Table-Talk," " The Spirit of the Age," " The Plain Speaker." His chief work is " Characters of Shakespeare's Plays."

must repeat what we have said in another place, that the English do not yet possess a satisfactory historic representation of their national literature. W. Spalding's "History of English Literature" in nowise contradicts our statement. Mr. Spalding (a Scotchman) treats the earliest period of English literature with great fairness, but in an unpleasing form. The literature of the nineteenth century, on the other hand, is discussed in a disconnected, defective, and superficial way, and of phenomena—such as Byron—he has no understanding whatever. John Dunlop, also a Scotchman, has written a learned history of the Novel, which contains an excellent analysis of the prose works of antiquity and of the middle ages; but the author seems to have had no idea that his interesting subject is an important factor in the history of civilization.

Thomas Carlyle, born 1795, in the village of Ecclefechan, in Scotland, occupies a peculiar position in the most modern development of English literature. He is a connecting-link between English and German literature, and his admiration of everything German is so great that he has even given a German tone to his style—by no means to its advantage. If Carlyle wanted to Germanize his style he would have done better to have copied Lessing, Goethe, and Schiller, for good thoughts are everywhere valued the more for being simply and clearly expressed. But Carlyle's style is dark, symbolical, restless, and full of imagery. He began his career as an author with his "Life of Schiller" (1825), which excited the greatest attention. Possessing great critical acumen, cultivated by profound study, he made known to his countrymen the most thoughtful poet of a nation similar in race to their own. In the same year Carlyle published his translation of Goethe's "Wilhelm Meister," and in 1827 appeared his "German Romances," containing translations from the works of Goethe, Schiller, Tieck, Jean Paul, Fouqué, and Hoffmann, with biographical and critical notes. The chief result of his literary criticisms are his "Critical and Miscellaneous Essays," in 4 volumes (1839), collected from various reviews. In the oddly entitled book "Sartor Resartus, or the Life and Opinions of Herr Teufelsdröckh" (1836), Carlyle tried to give a more systematic form to his philosophical ideas, gathered chiefly from the study of German philosophy. Carlyle's philosophy, as it appears in this book, is a pantheistic feeling and believing, which might be aptly characterized by Wordsworth's beautiful lines on the child with the shell.[8] But he does not dream of advocating an

"I have seen
A curious child, who dwelt upon a tract
Of inland ground, applying to his ear
The convolutions of a smooth-lipped shell :
To which, in silence hushed, his very soul
Listened intensely : and his countenance soon
Brightened with joy : for murmurings from within
Were heard, sonorous cadences ! whereby,

inactive sentiment of union with the soul of the world, as is the way of mystics of ancient and modern times. On the contrary, he deifies action, and assigns to work the chief place in history. This worship of work, expressed in ideal and material creations, stamps Carlyle as a socialist, that is to say, makes him an apostle of the great truth that man is a worthy member of society only when he is an active and productive worker; and that society is furthered by such members alone, and not by political phrases and systems. In this sense Carlyle is a socialist in his three writings: " Chartism " (1839), " Past and Present " (1843), " Latter-Day Pamphlets " (1850). He is everywhere against cant and false appearances, and demands action as a proof of worth; his enthusiasm for men of action rises to hero-worship. This gives a peculiar charm to his work on " The French Revolution " (1837), which is rather a revolutionary epic than a history. His original philosophy of history is presented still more clearly and comprehensively in his " Lectures on Heroes, Hero-Worship, and the Heroic in History." In his rhapsody on the French Revolution he celebrates as its truly heroic characters, Mirabeau, Danton, Charlotte Corday, and Madame Roland. In the lectures he places Mohammed as a prophet; Dante,

> To his belief, the monster expressed
> Mysterious union with its native sea.
> Even such a shell the universe itself
> Is to the ear of faith."

Shakespeare, and Goethe as poets; Luther and Knox as priests; Johnson, Rousseau, and Burns as authors; Cromwell and Napoleon as kings—in the temple of hero-worship. Two other important works, founded on loving and comprehensive study, are offerings to this worship: "Oliver Cromwell's Letters and Speeches," and the "History of Frederick the Great." The former is a monument worthy of the great Lord Protector; the second is considered the best work that has been written on the subject, its perfection being only impaired by the author's excessive peculiarities of style. Looking upon Carlyle's productions as a whole, we must acknowledge him fully competent to enrich the realism of his country by German idealism, and the English literature of the future will ever owe him a truly grateful regard.

Among the later and latest essayists may be mentioned W. Hepworth Dixon, whose earlier publications, "Her Majesty's Tower" and "Spiritual Wives," excited hopes which his later works did not realize; and J. Grant, whose "History of the English Newspaper Press" is a work of much merit.[9] On consideration, we should call the cleverest essay that has been published during the last ten years at which the poet Swinburne has written as an introduction to the "Selections from the Works of Lord Byron" (1871). In it the genius of the great poet meets with full appreciation.

[9] Mr. Hepworth Dixon's "Life of Penn," was earlier than these, and gained him a considerable reputation. He was also Editor of the *Athenæum* for several years.

CHAPTER XVI.

SKETCH OF THE ANGLO-AMERICAN LITERATURE. ITS RISE AND CHARACTER.

Poets and Poetesses : Hopkinson, Barlow, Dwight, Pierpoint, Sprague, Brainard, Street, Percival, Dana, Whittier, Halleck, Holmes, Bryant, Poe, Longfellow, Mary Brooks, Lydia Sigourney. Novelists : Irving, Cooper, Brown, Paulding, Fay, and others ; Catherine Sedgwick, Harriet Beecher-Stowe. Orators, Political Writers, Essayists, and Historiographers : Henry, Adams, Clay, Webster, Calhoun, and others ; Franklin, Jefferson, Audubon, Catlin, Channing, Everett, Hudson, Tuckermann, Emerson, Prescott, Sparks, Bancroft.

ON the evening of the 11th of November 1620 the good ship "Mayflower" cast its anchor in the bay of Cape Cod, on the coast of New England. It brought the first band of those Puritan emigrants who, fleeing from the Act of Conformity, looked for a place of refuge for their religious convictions beyond the Atlantic. Within view of the lonely, forest-covered shore, they thanked God on their knees for having brought them to the goal of their pilgrimage, and then assembled in the cabin to plan their Constitution, the first in history which afforded perfect equality of privilege and law to all. Another month passed before the pilgrims, founders of the colony of Plymouth, could gain a footing on the American coast. The day on which this happened, the 11th of December, old style (the 22nd according to our reckoning), is still celebrated by the name of "Forefathers' Day" throughout the great republican union of North America.

One hundred and fifty-six years later, on the 4th of July 1776, the representatives of the colonies of North America were assembled in Congress at Philadelphia; and there, on the motion of Richard Henry Lee, they made the famous Declaration which dissolved the tie between the mother country and the colonies, and constituted them free and independent states. The day on which this happened is the greatest festival of the year in the great Republic.

Between these two dates lies a short but significant history, full of troubles and dangers, of privation and heroic endurance; the history of the foundation of a new state of society, which began from the first with the citizenship of equal rights, with religious and political freedom, privileges which even to this day European nations have not wholly acquired. The development of this society bears a very sober character, unpleasing to the romantic taste, for reason, free from all illusion, was its chief element. It was altogether directed to practical aims; and it could not be otherwise. Life was not wanting in idealism, but this idealism consisted in a religion whose Puritanically dismal character condemns as sinful whatever beautifies life. The Puritanism of the mother-country was intensified into an iron harshness; but it must be acknowledged that only by being such as it was could it achieve its great work. It has given to the earlier history of the Union a certain stamp of dismal monotony, yet it was not altogether wanting in romance. The sea breaking against an unmeasured length of coast, the charm of the solitude of forest and prairie, magnificent lakes, endless streams, a varied virgin vegetation—all these were elements of nature which could not fail to impress the human soul. Added to these was the poetry of danger which is inseparable from a settler's life in the primitive forest; the life of the hunter with its privations and toils and simple joys; the bold wanderings on discovery in the mysterious Far West; the buffalo and panther-hunt, the struggle with the fearful grizzly bear, and those heroic fights with the cunning natives, not easily irritated, but pitiless in the outburst of their rage. The wars with the Indians, continued through several generations, rich in adventures, in tragical or deeply touching episodes, form the heroic age of the history of North America, and have naturally become a chief subject for its own poetry.

It is not difficult to explain why this poetry, so far as it deserves the name, awoke only in the nineteenth century. North American society for a long time had plenty to do to satisfy the prose of life before it could attend to its poetical side. Puritanical theology also, so long as it was the first power in the growing New World, confined the spiritual activity of the people to its narrow views of the world. The example of tolerance set by Roger Williams, the famous founder of the State of Rhode Island, was not imitated for a long time. The North Americans, who inherited the language of their English ancestors[1] were also accustomed to draw their spiritual nutriment from the mother country. This literary dependence on England long prevented the rise of poetry and learning at home. It was thought and said : How can poets and learned men thrive in the wilderness, or be able to compete with those of the mother country? Such boldness could not be expected from the Americans of the eighteenth century, especially when the beauty of poetry was believed to consist in the most elaborate correctness. Even in our days, when the promising beginnings of an Anglo-American literature have been made, the literary protectorate of England is still silently acknowledged. England's criticism in its turn looked with distrust upon every literary production that came across the Atlantic. At the same time it is but just to say that the English were also the first

[1] Compare on the subject of the American English, Herrig's introduction to his anthology, which is a work of great merit, "The American Classical Authors," 1854. On Anglo-American poetry and poets : Broth. Duyckink, "Cyclopædia of American Literature," 1856; R. W. Griswold, "The Poets and Poetry of America;" and "Female Poets of America," by the same.

in later times who so readily recognized the merit of the first American authors of consequence that the reputation which they gained at home only seemed to be the echo of the applause they had received in England.

The victorious War of Independence gave to North American life a powerful impetus. The nation was not satisfied with its wonderful material progress, but began to pay serious attention to the furtherance of mental cultivation. With a quickness and energy unheard of and impossible in the Old World, the new society cultivated commerce and industry, applied Fulton's great invention on a colossal scale, spread across the solitudes of the Rocky Mountains to the Pacific, brought wildernesses of enormous extent under cultivation, caused numberless cities to rise from the virgin forests, and the starry flag to wave on every sea. At the same time colleges and universities and schools of all kinds were founded. The printing-press was introduced into the log-huts of the West; political meetings were held where a short time before the wandering Indian was hunting the bison; newspapers were published in numbers, and literary life began to awake.

If by the word "literature" anything printed is to be understood, the North-American colonies had no lack of it from the beginning of their existence. When the Puritan of olden times came home in the evening from his field-work, from hunting and fishing, or from an inroad against the "red heathen," he took up a quarto volume and meditated by his fireside on its contents—polemical theology. His clergy took care that he should never be in want of such reading. The most famous of these theological writers, Cotton Mather, is said to have written nearly 400 books. The divines also wrote verses, of course mostly on sacred subjects, and the first book ever printed in New England was a metrical translation of the Psalms (1640). Gradually the fabrication of verses —for the poetical attempts of the Americans do not deserve another name down to the close of the eighteenth century—was extended to subjects not strictly religious; and about the time of the War of Independence poetry emancipated herself more and more from theology. At that time the two famous national songs were composed: "Yankee Doodle," which is nothing less than poetical, and Hopkinson's "Hail, Columbia!" written with a feeling of patriotic pride which has since continued to be the key-note of American literature.

If we inquire into its general character, we must recognize that the Germanic spirit which breathes in English literature, is also the foundation of Anglo-American culture and literature. The pilgrims had taken the traditions of the poetry of their home across the sea; and though these voices had long been silent before the urgencies of life and before the authority of Puritanical theology, they broke forth when material well-being and political independence produced more liberal views of existence, and the desire for an ideal adornment of life. It cannot be denied that an element of Yankeeism has been added to the Germanic-English element in America, but it is certain that the latter forms the real essence of North-American culture and literature. Independent of the specifically patriotic expressions of the Anglo-American poets, and of their minute local descriptions, it must be admitted that their poems might have been written by Englishmen. Their poetry is chiefly of the lyric-epic kind; the dramatic is but poorly developed. The reason for this is undoubtedly to be sought in the influence of the Puritanical spirit which was more lasting in New than in Old England, and whose inimical relation to the stage has been mentioned in its proper place. The dramatic productions of the American poets are insignificant, and the theatre of the United States is almost entirely a spiritless, noisy show, deriving its materials from the offal of the French melodrama. The pilgrim fathers would be not a little horrified if they could witness the operatic display and the ballet-dancing which amuse their descendants. The Americans have not yet attained that degree of æsthetic cultivation which is necessary for the enjoyment of a dramatic work of art.[2]

[2] The first representation of a theatrical piece in North America—Shakespeare's "Merchant of Venice,"—took place September 5th 1752, at Williamsburg, in Virginia. The history of the American stage has been written by Dunlop, "History of the American Theatre," 1832.

The American poetry of the eighteenth century is only a faint echo of the contemporary English. This dependence on the latter prevented it from producing anything that might claim to be original. The heroic poems, "The Columbiad" and "The Conquest of Canaan," which were composed by Joel Barlow (1755—1812), and Timothy Dwight (born 1752), appeared tough and indigestible even to their countrymen who were most lenient to home-bred attempts of the kind. A breath of poetry began to be felt in the pious songs of John Pierpont (born 1785), which grew more powerful in the lyrics of Charles Sprague (born 1791), John Brainard (born 1796), Alfred Street (born 1811), and James Percival (born 1795); and still more so in the poems of Richard Henry Dana (born 1787), and John Whittier (born 1808). Dana was really the first poet who possessed power enough to delineate the natural peculiarities of his country and to discover the romantic treasures lying hid in its history. His most original creations are the two poems "The Dying Raven" and "The Buccaneer," the former a melancholy picture from nature, the latter a poetical tale whose hero is the pirate Matthew Lee—a night-scene of blood and horrors, painted with a vivid imagination, and producing characters of most powerful delineation. Whittier's narrative poems, especially "Magg Megone," describing the life of the pilgrim fathers as settlers in Massachusetts, are distinguished by their faithful rendering of the ancient Puritanical spirit. FitzGreene Halleck (born 1795) became popular by his humorous poem "Fanny," which is a clever copy of Byron's style in "Don Juan;" and he became a still greater favourite by his battle-scene "Marco Bazzaris." Next to Oliver Wendell Holmes (born 1809), the master of irony, Halleck is considered the wittiest poet of America. Bryant, Poe, and Longfellow enjoy universal admiration and favour. William Cullen Bryant (born 1794) is able to hear the great harmony of nature in her gentlest and in her most powerful tones. But he paints by preference the quiet life of nature and of man, and the depth of his feeling enables him to find the most precious pearls of song in the simplest scenes. Such are the "Indian's Complaint at the Graves of his Fathers" and the "Song of the Pitcairn Islander." His poetry much resembles that of Cowper and Gray, but there is such a specifically American tone in it that he has been rightly called the first original poet of his country. A certain didactic seriousness is a graceful element of his lyrics, as may be seen in his famous poem "Thanatopsis." His longer poem "The Ages," written in the Spenserian stanza, points out the development of mankind from age to age, thus proving its capability of development and preaching a truly poetical optimism. Edgar Allan Poe (1811—1849) is the romantic poet *par excellence* among the Anglo-Americans; the fantastic splendour of his romances "Annabel Lee," "Ulaline," and "The Raven," has not been equalled by any other. "The Raven" is indeed the most original production of American poetry, a strange and original form of the idea that the dark side of nature enters into the existence of man. Unfortunately Poe led a very irregular life; he was an incorrigible drunkard, and died prematurely in an Infirmary. His novelistic attempts also—" Arthur Gordon Pym," " M. Valdemar," " The Descent into the Maelstrom "—despite their fantastic extravagancies prove him to have been a true poet. Henry Wadsworth Longfellow (born 1808) was deeply impregnated with German culture. He travelled through Germany and carried a thorough knowledge of the German tongue and literature into his home beyond the sea. His novel " Hyperion " (1839) hardly belongs to that kind of composition; it is an account of travels, lyric rather than epic, adorned with pictures of German landscapes, and interwoven with very successful translations of German poems. In this book as well as in his lyrics, in his narratives, and in his poetical activity in general, gracefulness is the distinguishing characteristic. Longfellow does not portray great passions, he is an essentially elegiac poet in the best sense of the word. His poetry may be compared to a peaceful landscape, traversed by a calmly-gliding river and by a chain of hills from whose woody summit romantic ruins are looking forth here and there, while soft sunset-clouds shed a gentle glory over the whole. Such also is the character of " Evangeline, a tale of Acadia," a pastoral novel, written in hexameters, founded on the sad history of the inhabitants of the French colony Acadia (Nova Scotia) who were driven from their homes by the English in 1755. The chief beauties of the charming poem are its magnificent descriptions of nature, for which a motive is given by Evangeline's pilgrimage in search of her lost lover; the description of her journey down the Mississippi is surpassingly beautiful. The poet developed the greatest activity and tried to introduce dramatic poetry into the literature of his country. His attempts—" The Spanish Student," "The Golden Legend," "The Divine Tragedy," "The New England Tragedies"—are neither planned nor executed in such a manner as to create an American drama. On the other hand Longfellow has enriched universal literature by a truly indigenous American epic, the " Song of Hiawatha." This " Indian Edda," as the poem has been rightly called, is undoubtedly the most important poetical work that has been accomplished by an American. Longfellow's lyric productions culminate in the highly and deservedly famous poem " Excelsior." One of the poet's latest compositions, " The Courtship of Miles Standish," ranks with his best; it is a novel in verse, founded on an event in the time of the Pilgrim Fathers.

A younger generation of poets has given proof of marked talent. Foremost among them are: J. R. Lowell (born 1819), an excellent painter of nature in verse, and a hard-hitting satirist; R. H.

Stoddard (b. 1825), a lyric poet of much sentiment; Bayard Taylor (born 1825), talented and fertile, not only as a lyric, didactic, and idyllic poet, but also as a novelist and essayist, and chiefly distinguished as the masterly translator of Goethe's "Faust" into English; T. B. Aldrich (born 1836), a lyric poet and novel writer; G. H. Boker (born 1842), who has composed political lyrics, tales in verse, and tragedies, in which he has unquestionably been more successful than any other American before him. There is besides, W. D. Howells (born 1837), a lyric poet in Heine's style, and a novel writer of much refinement both of feeling and diction; Nathaniel Hawthorne (born 1804), whose remarkable tales fill eighteen volumes; Mark Twain (S. L. Clemens, born 1835), the humorist *par excellence* in the American sense of the word, i.e. caricaturist and jester; finally, Joaquin Miller (born 1841), whose wildly original tales in verse, "Songs of the Sierras" (1871), belong to the most individual poetical productions which have come to us from beyond the ocean.

But the greatest sensation among their own countrymen was created by Walt Whitman (born 1819) and Francis Bret Harte (born 1838). We are not able to join in the praise which the works of these two writers received in America, and also for a time in Europe. Whitman's formless verses, and the oracular expressions of his thoughts (collected under the titles "Leaves of Grass" and "Drum-Taps") astonish us at first by their wild originality. But we soon perceive that a very poor store of ideas is hidden by this curtain of assumed haziness. Bret Harte's poems and sketches, prose and poetry, present to us the squatters and gold-diggers of California with the most vivid realism ; but when he speaks of the tender feelings and of the sublime self-devotion of his Californian drunkards, gamblers, and murderers, we wonder how he has the audacity to ask us to believe such impossibilities.

The United States boast a number of poetesses, and amongst them are ladies of undoubted talent. As the earliest, may be mentioned Anne Bradstreet (1613—1672). She was succeeded by Mary Brooks and Lydia Sigourney. Then came Emma Embury, Caroline Sawyer, Grace Greenwood, Frances Sargent Osgood (1816—1850), and Mary Stuart-Sterne, whose real name is Gertrud Blöde, a German, born 1848. The two last-mentioned have carried off the prize among the competitors. Frances Sargent Osgood's lyrics may be placed by the side of those of Felicia Hemans and Letitia Elizabeth Landon.

Transatlantic novel writing first convinced Europe of the existence of an American literature, and the names of Washington Irving and Cooper especially strengthened this conviction. Washington Irving (1783—1859) has much of the manner of the English novelists of the last century. His style must be acknowledged to possess Addison's grace, but his narratives have a property which is characteristic of all American novels, with rare exceptions ; the intention of offering rather a poetical description of real life and history than the bold creations of pure fiction. Irving's humorous work, which he called "Knickerbocker's History of New York," delighted his countrymen, his three novels, "Sketch Book" (1819), "Bracebridge Hall" (1822), and "Tales of a Traveller" (1824), make him a favourite of the whole civilized world. Equally charming are his three later sketch-books, "The Alhambra," "A Tour of the Prairies," and "Abbotsford and Newstead Abbey." Grace, humour, and brightness also distinguish him as an historian, as is proved by his "History of the Life and Voyages of Columbus," and still more by the work with which he has crowned his life and his activity as an author—his "Life of Washington."

The novels of James Fennimore Cooper (1789—1851) paint sea-life and life in the American forests and prairies with the rich colours of a master. His naval captains and boatmen, his sachems and trappers, are among the most popular figures of the works of fiction of our century. The romantic elements in the history of his country became as effective under his treatment as Scottish romance under that of Walter Scott. Scott indeed was Cooper's avowed model, but Cooper is much more realistic than Scott. He has an extraordinary power of description. With objective quietness he places before us the grand character of the wilderness or of the sea, the strange and wild scenes that are enacted in these places, and we see and understand it all with the greatest distinctness. This talent is already evident in his first novel "The Spy" (1821), to which "Lionel Lincoln" forms a patriotic but weaker pendant. The famous "Leather-Stocking Tales" constitute a drama of five acts: "The Deer-Slayer," "The Path-Finder," "The Last of the Mohicans," "The Pioneers," "The Prairie," in which a simple woodman, Cooper's favourite character, acts the chief part. All these five novels are full of thrilling scenes. But we believe that among Cooper's Indian novels the prize must be awarded to his "Wept of the Wish-ton-Wish," just as among his sea-novels to "The Pilot." Cooper's later novels are not in any way equal to his earlier works; a great prosiness almost stifles the narrative, whose poor conception makes us feel all the more Cooper's want of psychological depth. The art of delineating the psychological development of character, in which Cooper is wanting, is possessed in a high degree by Charles Brockden Brown (1771—1810), whose most important work "Wieland, or the Transformation," appeared as early as 1798. This novel is the history of a fanatic, whose religious mania incited him to murder his wife and children, and at last to commit suicide, and is one of the most masterly stories that has ever been told of the human soul. Brown's other novels, "Ormond," "Arthur

Mervyn," and "Edgar Huntley," are grand conceptions.

The novels of Theodore Sedgwick Fay (born 1807) are also distinguished by a fine psychological drawing of the inner workings of human passions; while the novels of James Kirk Paulding (born 1779) describe the outward exhibitions of human folly with a certain home-bred humour. Other novel writers of note are Nathaniel Hawthorne, Joseph Neal, John Kennedy, N. P. Willis, and Robert Bird. Among the female novelists Catherine Sedgwick was the most popular, until this distinction had to be awarded to Mrs. Harriet Beecher-Stowe (born 1812), the authoress of "Uncle Tom's Cabin" (1852). This book had a world-wide circulation and was read everywhere with the greatest eagerness, as its humane tendency well deserves, but it has obvious deficiencies as a novel.

One of the best expressions of the intellectual life of North America is its political eloquence; this took rise in the old provincial assemblies, and has been much cultivated during and since the War of Independence, which necessarily excited all rhetorical talents. There is a peculiar brightness and originality in this eloquence, which here and there shows somewhat rudely, but which in the mouths of the better orators is moderated and ennobled by cultivation of mind. In the time of the War of Independence, Patrick Henry was so incomparable an orator that the power of his words became, and still is, proverbial. In the succeeding period John de Quincy Adams was considered the first speaker ; after him, and down to our times, Henry Clay, Daniel Webster, John Calhoun, William Preston, Thomas Corwin, and George Duffie have obtained the greatest reputation. Political eloquence is closely allied to political activity. The greatest name on this field is Benjamin Franklin (1706 —1790), the great citizen who, together with Washington, occupies a position unlike any hitherto known in the world's history. It is superfluous to praise the merits of the man who has "robbed heaven of its lightning and tyranny of its sceptre," and who was politically and morally one of the most enlightened public men that ever lived. Thomas Jefferson (1743—1826), the author of the Declaration of Independence, became by his political writings the real framer of the American democracy, and therefore of the democratic principle in general.

American literature boasts of some excellent *Essayists:* Washington Irving may be considered one, as well as John James Audubon, who has described the American world of birds, from the most faithful study of nature and with the most impressive forest poetry, in his "Ornithological Biography." Henry Rowe Schoolcraft's accounts of his travels as a naturalist are as valuable. An exceedingly attractive and interesting book is the one in which George Catlin has published the results of his researches on the "Indians of North America" and his adventures among their different tribes. The famous preacher and apostle of temperance William Ellery Channing is also one of the distinguished founders of æsthetic criticism in America: " Essay on National Literature " (1832); and A. H. Everett, H. N. Hudson, and H. T. Tuckermann (" Thoughts on the Poets"), have successfully trodden in his footsteps. A most excellent performance in literary history is George Ticknor's " History of Spanish Literature." The busy activity which reigns in all the departments of American literature is well shown in the essays of Ralph Waldo Emerson (born 1803), who is a zealous interpreter and proclaimer of German philosophy, and excels equally in his characteristic description of nationalities as of poets : " English Poets," " Representative Men," " Shakespeare and Goethe," " Essays." How well historiography in its stricter forms has been cultivated in America is proved by her historians, whose great excellence will be acknowledged by the severest critic. William Henry Prescott (1796—1859) must be mentioned before all others ; his " History of Ferdinand and Isabella," and " History of Philip the Second," treat the most important periods of Spanish history in a masterly manner ; and his works on the two great romantic episodes of American history— " History of the Conquest of Mexico " and " History of the Conquest of Peru"—are of equal excellence and beauty. Jared Sparks (born 1794) is another name worthy of mention. His collection of documents on the American Revolution, and comprehensive biographical work on Washington—"Life and Writings of Washington" (1833—1840) have thrown light upon the history of that great epoch in every direction. Lastly we must name George Bancroft (born 1800), who, formed in the school of German historical research, produced in 1834 the first volume of his " History of the United States." This work, in eight volumes, comprises the history of the great Transatlantic Republic from the first beginnings of colonization to the complete obtaining and ensuring of its independence. Bancroft writes the history of his country with the spirit of a statesman and with the love of a patriot, and there is no other book existing which gives Europeans such a clear view of the marvellous development of the United States as his work on the subject. In the preface to his last book, Prescott pointed out a young historian who would have capacity to pursue the path traced out by him. This was John Lothrop Motley (born 1814). Prescott's favourite subject of investigation and description was Spain and the Spaniards in the Old and New World ; the predilection of his successor was for the history of the Netherlands ; and he enriched the historical literature of his country, and that of Europe, by his three works : " The Rise of the Dutch Republic," " A History of the United Netherlands, from the death of William the Silent to the Twelve Years' Truce," in four volumes, and "The Life and Death of John of Barneveld," in two volumes. Some years earlier John William Draper had undertaken to write and to publish a History of the Intellectual Development of Europe, on the so-called inductive method recommended by Buckle. But the author has made the great mistake of utterly disregarding and ignoring art in her various forms. How is an intellectual development possible without the element of the Beautiful? And what would the world and the existence of man be without Beauty?

America needs, perhaps more than any other nation, the cultivation and the worship of the Beautiful. Her future will depend in a large measure on this cultivation or non-cultivation. The development of the United States has been gigantic until now, but materialism alone will not be sufficient in the long-run. A frank recognition of this truth is to be felt in their recent literature, which is a decided protest against the all-powerful worship of Mammon. May it grow and flourish, and become strong enough to send the light of the Ideal like a stream through the veins of the nation!

THE END.

www.ingramcontent.com/pod-product-compliance
Lightning Source LLC
Chambersburg PA
CBHW022019240426

43667CB00042B/941